D1611431

Marriage Secrets

MARRIAGE SECRETS

How to Have a Lifetime Love Affair

by Rosanne Rosen

A Birch Lane Press Book
Published by Carol Publishing Group

A Birch Lane Press Book
Published by Carol Publishing Group
Birch Lane Press is a registered trademark of Carol Communications, Inc.
Editorial Offices: 600 Madison Avenue, New York, N.Y. 10022
Sales & Distribution Offices: 120 Enterprise Avenue, Secaucus, N.J. 07094
In Canada: Canadian Manda Group, P.O. Box 920, Station U, Toronto,
    Ontario M8Z 5P9
Queries regarding rights and permissions should be addressed to
Carol Publishing Group, 600 Madison Avenue, New York, N.Y. 10022

Carol Publishing Group books are available at special discounts for bulk
purchases, for sales promotions, fund-raising, or educational purposes.
Special editions can be created to specifications. For details contact:
Special Sales Department, Carol Publishing Group, 120 Enterprise Avenue,
Secaucus, N.J. 07094

Manufactured in the United States of America
10 9 8 7 6 5 4 3 2 1

Library of Congress Cataloging-in-Publication Data

Rosen, Rosanne.
        Marriage secrets : how to have a lifetime love affair / by
    Rosanne Rosen.
                    p. cm.
        "A Birch Lane Press book."
        ISBN 1-55972-166-9 (cloth)
        1. Marriage. 2. Man-woman relationships. I. Title.
    HQ734.R7566 1993
    306.81—dc20   3-9442
                                              CIP

To Mark

With love and appreciation for
being my partner

Contents

Acknowledgments

Marriage Secrets does not represent one writer's work. *Marriage Secrets* represents the hard work that hundreds of husbands and wives have invested in over years. It is to them that I owe the most thanks. I am greatly indebted to each man and woman who filled out a questionnaire or agreed to speak with me; and to the friends or business associates who introduced me to these couples. I appreciate their efforts, and the time, honesty, and secrets of the couples who participated.

Without my friends and family, particularly Nancy Meyer and author Robert Shook, *Marriage Secrets* would probably still be a very private affair. I am grateful for Bob's invaluable guidance, as I am for the professional assistance of my Columbus, Ohio, colleagues, Frieda Douthitt and Terri Stone-Conrath; my agent, Jeff Herman; and my editor, Gail Kinn.

I would like to say a very personal thank you to my two daughters, Halley and Sara Jane Rosen, for their help with and interest in *Marriage Secrets,* and for the love they give me every day.

It is only fitting that I thank my own husband, Mark, who has worked with me to make our marriage a special lifetime love affair. Neither one of us could have done it without trying to master the prudent art of developing our own brand of Marriage Secrets.

ix

Introducing the Secret Concept

When my husband and I sat down to eat dinner at home one evening, the atmosphere was relaxed and quiet. It was conducive, I thought, to springing the news of my latest project—a book. I feared the subject might initially cause him a twinge of discomfort. Although Mark is used to having a certain amount of our family life exposed in my newspaper and magazine articles, I suspected marriage secrets sounded a bit too personal for his taste. Early in our marriage, I vowed never to reveal my secrets. But twenty-five years later, I feel confident that the partnership we have built will survive the exposure of some of the surprises that I have kept tucked away.

The need to dig deeply into the lives of happily married couples and tap the best secrets used in successful marriages became apparent to me a few years ago when I received an anniversary card from a friend that read, "Congratulations to a Dying Breed." Until this message arrived in the mail, I was not aware that happily married couples were considered an endangered species.

Marriage is probably one of the most complicated relationships we enter into in our lives. Granted, there is no easy formula to help one breeze through the complexities. But it is foolhardy to drift through marriage without a plan, a strategy, or a few tricks. Marriage takes a lot of hard work, endless patience, ample love, a sincere commitment, a dash of humor, a bit of luck, some painful self-control, and lots of secret formulas.

The *practical* tools I refer to as "secrets" may be construed negatively by some as sneaky ways to manipulate your spouse into submission, conjuring up an image of victim and victor. This is not what is intended.

Rather, secrets provide the self-confident, goal-oriented, smart wife or husband with a masterful means to nurture a healthy, *realistic* partnership.

Secrets frequently serve as tools to use in avoiding unnecessary and damaging conflicts. Secrets promote careful, thoughtful behavior. True, secrets can even be used with the intention of securing luxurious gifts and giving or receiving pleasure. But most importantly, marriage secrets help keep love on track, multiplying the odds for achieving a lifetime love relationship.

Marriage Secrets come in two styles, artful and prudent; employing them takes skill and knowledge. Using them wisely requires *love, respect,* and *commitment.* It is out of love and respect for your spouse, and commitment to your marriage, that you want your relationship to work. Secrets should be used only if they provide satisfying results to both partners. With this in mind, it is possible to handle all kinds of situations with secret strategies.

Some of you may have difficulty with what I am saying. But trust me! I have used many of these tools in my marriage and enjoy a reputation of being half of one of the most successful duos around. Good marriages need tending. It takes skill and technique to put up with the stresses, strains, and irritations that arise out of living day in day out, year in year out with the same person. You must have a keen awareness of the needs and desires of your partner, as well as of the strengths and weaknesses, in order to make a marriage work.

Sounds time-consuming and demanding? There is no denying that it is. Consequently, you may want to make certain before you embark on this journey that your spouse has the potential to appreciate and return the affection, attention, and understanding you will be bestowing upon him or her. These are not freebies. Make no mistake about that. You ought to be rewarded for your efforts in the form of a more devoted spouse and a happier, more fulfilling lifetime partnership.

I recently asked my husband if he is aware that I use marriage secrets and even resort to manipulation in *managing* our relationship. His response was comforting: "Yes, I know that you manipulate me, but I don't care, because it works. I'm happy, and I love you. I don't think what you do makes me henpecked. I think it serves a purpose."

Of the hundreds of married men and women I encountered in doing my marriage survey, the most contented of them, through trial and error, mastered the secrets of creating an ongoing love affair with each other. I found these couples through the help of a large network of friends and business acquaintances across the country. The candor and honesty with which they responded, and our direct and open conversations, became a vital and integral part of the book. Because of the intimacy of their tales, their names have been changed. Their stories, however, are truthfully recounted.

Marriage Secrets: How to Have a Lifetime Love Affair presents secrets in a very particular sequence. Consequently, I strongly suggest it be read from front to back. In Chapter 1 you will be immediately introduced to the two basic categories of secrets: *Artful Means of Persuasion* and *Prudent Guidelines for Action*. In Chapter 2, "Steering the Ship Takes a Worthy Captain," you will be alerted to the number one prerequisite for using secrets.

In order to maximize the potential of secrets, you must meet your spouse's most basic needs. The first secret you should grasp is knowing the value of this. Satisfying needs encourages your spouse to be more pliable, flexible, and receptive to your wishes. *It will engender support in building the most important areas of your relationship.* Therefore, chapters on great sex, love talk, and the ego connection are designed to pave the way toward reaching your ultimate goal of the best possible marriage partnership. Enjoying each other is perhaps the best secret of all.

Once these considerations are well taken care of, you will have greater success with later techniques that promote meaningful communication and an intimate friendship with your spouse. Without these latter two qualities you can't have a really good, solid marriage. They not only add substantial satisfaction and fulfillment to your relationship, but they fortify your marriage against the certain wear and tear it will incur over the years. Later, we'll look at "Doing It Right the Second Time Around" for those who failed to incorporate secrets in their first marriages.

Finally, in Chapter 13 you'll find couples who boast of having achieved a fulfilling and long-term marital relationship and who reveal the rewards of being one another's special Babe. They will help you chart a destination for your love match by setting the standards and defining appropriate expectations for the best that marriage has to offer.

Because marriage is a dynamic institution with an ever-changing climate, you can never learn too many secrets. Be smart as you read the chapters and select those secrets that work for you. Do not feel overwhelmed by the abundant information. It is not necessary to use each and every secret to achieve a lifetime love affair.

By the time you turn the last page of *Marriage Secrets,* you should be motivated to protect, manage, and strengthen your marriage relationship as never before.

Marriage Secrets

1

Marriage Secrets, You Can't Get Along Without Them

I get tired of my friends asking me, "Do you know how lucky you are to have a husband like Mark?" My question back to them is, "How do you think he got to be that way?"

There is no doubt that my secrets have helped to make this man the fabulous husband he appears to be. In the name of love, I have learned to turn down the heat when his temper flares, ignore his childish outbursts, rev up his romantic motors, compromise when necessary, and nourish his ego.

Inadvertently over the years, he has learned to work the same magic on me. Together, we have uncovered one of the most important secrets to a happy marriage: *The Golden Rule is to please and appease.*

Let's take an example: Our wedding anniversary and his annual fishing trip to Canada always coincide. The first time Mark proposed the getaway I thought it was good strategy to reward his year-round behavior and let him go without the slightest fuss. During his lengthy layover in Minneapolis on the way home, he and the boys hit a shopping mall where

Mark bought me an elegant nightgown. I was pleased with the sentiment.

When he proposed the trip the next year, I was more reluctant to let him go. Before his departure that year, however, we celebrated our anniversary, and I was presented with an elaborate gift. After four or five years of surprise packages and praise for being so understanding, I began to like the material peace offerings. I especially enjoyed feeling I was a model wife, unselfishly excusing my husband from being with me on our anniversary. It became a joke that never spending an anniversary together was the secret of our happy marriage.

In a way, it's true. Our anniversary demonstrated a growing mastery over how to please and appease one another, although Mark's effort to manipulate my opinion of his annual trip was not the result of strategic planning. Men tend to pull these tricks off unconsciously. Women, on the other hand . . . well, that's another story.

SECRETS ARE A CONTROVERSIAL BLEND OF TRIED, TRUE, AND NEW TECHNIQUES THAT ENABLE CRAFTY, WILLING SPOUSES TO ELEVATE MARRIAGE TO ITS RIGHTFUL PLACE AS A GRATIFYING, SATISFYING, AND EVEN ENVIABLE UNION.

Here's how to use them effectively.

ARTFUL MEANS OF PERSUASION

The conscious practice of what I call "artful means of persuasion" is used more frequently by women. According to my research, married women both traditionally and today tend to create elaborate schemes to cajole or wheedle their spouses into specific behaviors. Prior to the women's movement and the entrance of massive numbers of women into the labor force, it was assumed that wives used manipulative measures to gain power in an unequal relationship. *However, women who contribute equally to the money pot can still benefit from artful strategies.*

How Diane Secretly Got What She Wanted

Diane, an attorney who practiced law in an office with her ex, reflects on her marriage: "I was raised to think I was a liberated woman and would find an enlightened man to marry. What I found was typical—a 'traditional' male. I had little knowledge of how to handle him." Unequipped to defuse the constant tension created by a very intrusive mother-in-law and the head-on collisions with her husband, who battled for the upper hand, Diane left him while pregnant with their first child.

Armed with determination, Diane resolved to improve upon her mistakes when she married a second "traditional" man. "After the rug was pulled out from underneath me, I wasn't afraid to learn all I could to help my new husband understand that I wanted and needed attention and affection. I realized this required some retraining." One of Diane's first goals was to make this rugged, athletic man more romantic. It took a little experimenting before she found out what approach would work best in getting the little and not-so-little things she wanted out of this relationship.

She quickly learned that complaining to him about forgetting her birthday provoked only a grumble and a guilty retreat. "Expressing my feelings in an accusatory manner was entirely wrong for him. I have now made a practice of leaving notes and flirtatiously joking that there are only fourteen more shopping days to my birthday. It's fun, and it works. One year I received a necklace that was the envy of my friends. I have learned to be subtle in my hints," Diane explains, noting that some men have difficulty getting the point. Consequently she is quite careful to get her message

across, no matter who is the messenger. "I even got one of
Sam's coworkers to tell him explicitly that women like to get
flowers," she says.

**NOT EVERYTHING IN LOVE COMES NATURALLY—DEVELOP
POSITIVE STRATEGIES.**

Diane is only one of the hundreds of happily married
women who already use secret strategies. When I asked a
young professional working mom if her twelve-year marriage was a good one, she responded, "Very." I then asked
her if she had any marriage secrets that helped make her
relationship so satisfying. It was apparent immediately that I
had struck the right chord. She smiled, giggled a little,
hesitated, and said, "Yes. Mike needs a little help in doing
the things I want him to do. For now, I accept his bathing the
kids haphazardly and putting the dishes away semi-clean as
the first step to creating the kind of helping hand I need. I
always reinforce this by demonstrating my appreciation of
his pitching in. Once I get him into the habit of doing these
things routinely, then I'll guide him into doing a better job.
Why create a fuss now? It wouldn't get me what I want in
the long run."

A woman who works full-time as a head nurse is more
overt in her attempt to manipulate her mate; she has a
specific goal in mind. She likens her conscious effort to
develop a new behavior to Pavlovian conditioning. Exhausted from a long shift at the hospital, she prefers to eat
out. Her husband prefers to eat at home. To resolve this
difference in a way that is satisfying to both, the nurse
decided to initiate an evening of sexual intimacy following
each dinner out. By attaching a significant level of pleasure
to something her husband normally found distasteful, she
was able to change their eating patterns radically.

I can already hear some groans and see some heads

shaking. But the solutions these women propose are no different from that of the husband who told me, "My work takes me away from home frequently. One night I was several hours late getting back. My wife told me over the phone that she was preparing a candlelight meal for my return. I knew she would be upset, so I bought her flowers. When I walked into the apartment, I found her in the shower adding her own steam to the hot water. I stepped in fully clothed and handed her the bouquet. She laughed. I knew she would."

In each of these examples, spouses engineered sound management of a marriage relationship. *They kept their partners and themselves happy, reduced stress and strain, solved problems, avoided unnecessary conflicts, achieved their objectives, and added a measure of spice by working the magic of marriage secrets.*

Now, all of us hate to admit that love and love alone is *not* the only secret to a happy marriage. Love does not, will not, cannot conquer all. It may make your partner more tolerant of your idiosyncrasies. It may calm the waters after an unsatisfying evening of sex. It may force you to make up after a ridiculous fight. It may help you hold your tongue when dangerous words are trying to escape. It may help you to cherish, honor, and obey...momentarily. And love may certainly be the motivation for wanting to please and appease your spouse. But to keep all the embers red hot, love needs the assistance of these little conscious and unconscious twists and tricks.

Achieving a maximum level of marital bliss requires you to go after what you want unabashedly and use every ounce of ingenuity in creating your own brand of secrets.

Linda, the forty-five-year-old president of a major company, and married a quarter of a century now, is not the least bit embarrassed about her winning tactics. "On our honeymoon I wore a certain perfume for ten days. I wanted my husband to learn to associate a specific scent with pleasure,"

says Linda with a mixture of teasing giggles and serious
sentiment. "It was important that this be a unique scent. I
had to make sure no one else could accidentally arouse his
passion." To this day, twenty-five years later, she wears that
perfume when she wants something, whether it is to have a
good time at a party he prefers not to attend, to heighten his
sexual expectations and desires, to melt his objections to a
special purchase, or to put him into a receptive mood when
she wants to talk.

Although this sounds much too calculating—even out-
rageous—who can argue with the success this happy
woman reports? She knew she had married a difficult
cookie, one who was reluctant to compromise, hard to
budge, not easy to talk to, a little tight with their change.
Her intuition and willingness to pull out a secret saved them
both a lot of trouble. And most important, her motives were
pure: "I wanted our marriage to work," she explains in
defense of her behavior.

Robin's Secret: Vigilance

Robin, outspoken and confident after forty years of marital ups and downs notched on her belt, would give the
perfume lady a nod of approval. "You have to be able to feel
what is going on and be able to do something about it. Keep
your eyes open," she advises. A general rule of thumb from
Robin and a vocal majority: **You have to be a smart woman
to have a happy marriage.**

Robin would most likely shake her finger at the number of
young women I encountered who say they would not dream
of demeaning themselves with such behavior. "Persuade?
Manipulate? Who me? Never!" they assert, without the
benefit of time and experience in their corner. Straightforward, they want all the cards on the table, out in the open.
Like Robin, I see the wisdom in a change of heart.

I wish these young women could have sat in on some of
my interviews with spouses who emphatically stated, "I

don't play games." In my estimation they sure should have. It took an inordinate amount of self-control to contain myself and not make such a suggestion after sitting for more than an hour and a half listening to a woman married thirty years talk about a relationship she rated only a three or four on a scale of one to ten—even though she felt she loved her husband. She tried therapy, she tried slamming doors, she tried reading books, she tried leaving, she tried expressing her feelings—but she never tried secrets—to get him to listen, to get him to therapy, to get him to pay attention. She just begrudgingly plodded along. After all these years, she said, "I think that we could have had a better marriage if he wouldn't have been such a fathead and would have been brave enough to go in and get help."

Complaining about his "rigid German personality," she seemed to ignore the implications of her own self-description and a number of missed opportunities: "I am very straight on with Bill. He knows I am not a game player. What you see is what you get. His mother is a big game player. She plays the game great. In fact, there was a period she told me I should play the game. I said if he doesn't like the way I am, that's tough rocks. I said I have never been a game player and never will be. It might have made it nicer for Bill, but it would have made me miserable."

I wanted to say *au contraire*, but instead sincerely thanked her for her time, wished her good luck, and got in my car feeling more than a little sad.

Stacey's Intuitive Secret: Warmth

Stacey, a typical young wife, denied the use of artful persuasion. To her this was a terribly negative notion. Further conversation revealed, however, that she already practiced her own special brand of secrets. "Oh, I guess I do it," she said with surprise. Here is one of her examples:

When Stacey and her husband have a fight, she says his behavior is entirely predictable. He turns off completely, usually sulks on the couch, and turns on the TV. If she wants to call a truce, recognizing that the source of contention is not worth the strain or for that matter a verbal apology on either side, all she must do is cuddle up next to him and whisper she loves him. No one loses. They both win in the long run.

Apparently, her husband never tires of the routine. Men are flattered by secrets, no matter how obvious or repetitive. Interpreted correctly, they mean, "I care. I know what you like. I enjoy pleasing you."

Yes, Stacey was more intuitive about her marriage and more aggressive than she realized about keeping love on track. Secrets came naturally to this loving, caring wife who understood her man. She would have gotten points from Robin for using the tactics of a smart woman: **Know your husband and know him well!** This is the most effective way to ensure that secrets work and to reap their rewards.

How Roberta Makes Love Instead of War

Well-versed in her husband's likes and dislikes, Roberta, married twenty-five years, learned long ago what it meant to please and appease her husband. She drew from her bag of secrets when she coaxed him into taking trips with her to big cities when he would rather have been playing golf.

"Sex is very important to Ralph. I don't mean to imply that I don't enjoy it too, but it's even more important to him. I realized I would have to, and of course wanted to, make these trips good for him, too. I always plan plenty of time for sex to say 'thank you' for indulging my whims. I show that I love him and enjoy this opportunity for intimacy away from the intrusion of the kids. I am also just as careful not to overdo the things he hates about these trips. I have it down to a science. No more than two hours of shopping, two hours in a museum, one play, and a sporting goods store for him to browse in to his heart's content."

How Men Use Secrets Naturally

The benefit of this lesson applies equally to men who wisely adopt and implement the philosophy behind marriage secrets. Well aware of his wife's soft spots, a husband of fifteen years reveals that he plays records or recites poetry to evoke a special memory when he wants to put his lady in a romantic mood or win his way on the summer vacation plans.

A super-salesman I spoke with created a strategy based upon his wife's strengths when it came to getting her to participate graciously in those dinners with clients and coworkers she disliked and frequently did not attend. "It took time to change her mind," he said. "I needed her to be an asset, not a liability at these functions. I managed to do just that by repeatedly telling her how proud I was of her on these occasions. I knew that she would have a lot to contribute once her attitude changed. It worked like a charm. After a while she enjoyed many of these evenings, determined to add her own lively, intelligent touch to the conversations."

Now, Joe knows that his Katherine is not a good listener. She usually picks up on the last thing he says. So each Saturday night he proposes several things to do. The last on the list is his personal preference. When Katherine inevitably chooses his final recommendation, he suffers no grief if the evening doesn't work out to her satisfaction. Joe can never be accused of being bossy, selfish, or overpowering. He gives Katherine all the choices.

Using artful means of persuasion is fundamental to the successful marital strategist.

PRUDENT GUIDELINES FOR ACTION

Not all of the marriage secrets you will read about are so playful. More fundamental but just as important are marriage secrets that offer prudent guidelines for action: sensible, cautious, practical, and discreet practices. You won't have difficulty accepting the challenge and enthusiastically jumping into the trenches ready for the hard work it takes if you keep an open mind and a clear vision.

Why Millie Insures That She Spends Time With Her Husband

Millie's story, for instance, not only illustrates how prudent guidelines color the way she chooses to act and react to her spouse of forty-three years, it demonstrates the rewards that naturally accrue to one whose plan of action includes secrets. Early in her marriage (which she calls an "endless love affair"), Millie accidentally became aware of how much simple routines pleased Rob. His work schedule often resulted in late night arrivals home. As a young mother, she preferred to feed the kids and put them to bed, savoring time alone with Rob. No matter what hour he walked through the door, she was ready to share his day over a drink and a warm supper. Today, Millie says, "Sure, there were and still are times I would like to be out of the kitchen earlier, but since Rob has told me so many times how much he appreciates and looks forward to coming home to this typical evening, I would never stop doing it."

Why should she?

Millie's evenings may require a certain amount of self-sacrifice, but her mornings at breakfast with Rob, fresh and loving, are a mighty reward. "There is never a morning that goes by that Rob doesn't give me an extravagant, even ridiculous compliment, like I have the body of a thirty-five-year-old woman," reports this attractive, trim, sixty-year-old, gray-haired wife.

Years of mutual satisfaction and contentment have given Millie confidence in her prudent and loving judgment. "I have made plenty of mistakes in my life, particularly in the child-rearing department, but one thing I'm really good at is marriage." Before you get the impression that Millie's story is becoming a fairy tale, don't fret. It isn't perfect. *The word "perfect" has no place in the marriage dictionary.* "Things go wrong cyclically," admits Millie. "There are times we don't like each other very much."

Experience and commitment see Millie through the thick and thin of things, as they do many other couples who have learned to survive the cracks in their marriage and their love.

Why Fran Kept Knowledge of Her Husband's Betrayal Secret

"I have never told anyone this story," Fran began. "I think Alan had an affair." Alan is her husband of over forty years. The alleged affair took place at least fifteen years ago. Fran thinks it lasted no more than several months.

"It was a really bad time. It was just by a number of coincidences that I even began to suspect anything was happening. A long-distance operator verifying his call home revealed that he wasn't exactly where he was supposed to be. Several other factors—an address he tried to flush down the toilet, a Valentine gift that was charged but never given to me, and calls at night with silence on the other end— convinced me there was something going on. I hired a detective, but he found out nothing. I'm sure, though, that Alan was having an affair. I just don't know who it was. I was very upset.

"I am also a very curious person," Fran added. "I could have gotten in the car and driven in an hour to the hotel where the operator said the call originated from. Or I could have gone to the bar where I thought he was meeting her. I just didn't. I couldn't. If I had, things would probably have been a whole lot worse, and I'm not sure what would have happened. It was easier not knowing who she was."

But Fran did not hesitate for a moment to put an end to these escapades. Her husband denied the indiscretion and had an excuse for every accusation. In return, he accused Fran of having her own affair. "I wasn't at that time," she told me, unwilling to confirm or deny her own indiscretions.

Healed and looking back, Fran feels she handled the situation well. "I have no qualms about it now. Alan is basically not a wanderer. I didn't try to punish him." This is perhaps more generous than most of us could be. In her case, however, perhaps it was as wise as we would all hope to be.

"I did ask him to stop going to that particular bar," she continued. "I really do think it was more of a mid-life crisis thing. Maybe I wasn't fulfilling all of his needs at the time. It just took time for things to bottom out. The toughest part was in the bedroom. With the idea that he was having an affair in my mind, I couldn't get near him. We had some arguments over this. I just let it go after a while. I wanted my marriage to continue. We had a good foundation and a good marriage before this. That's probably why we both got over it."

It appears that Fran was prudent to recognize the limits of her tolerance and the fact that she would never get her husband to admit the affair. By keeping it from being fully disclosed, Fran and Alan were evidently able to put it to rest and get on with their lives together, rather than impose a permanent toll on their relationship. Practically speaking, Fran is even more convinced today that she made some very sound choices. She is fully aware of the loneliness she might have incurred had she left Alan, not to mention forfeiting the last fifteen years of marriage, which have been loving and rewarding. Forgiving and forgetting enabled her to concentrate once again on the qualities she loves in her husband.

After forty-three years, Fran has no trouble sincerely describing her man as "gentle, wonderful, exciting, and funny." Even if he is "stubborn," which she emphasizes he most certainly is, she respects and admires him and is satisfied with the years they have had together: "I have a sense of accomplishment that my children, my husband, and I have all benefited from a happy marriage. It has given me a feeling of well-being and, I believe, a happier life," she concludes practically enough.

What Rita's Support of Her Husband's Ego Gave Her

Rita also has a lesson to share. She decided more than thirty years ago, after a visit from her husband's doctor, that her marriage would require some real thought, soul searching, and prudent consideration. The doctor dropped the bomb that her partner, aged twenty-nine, had severely high blood pressure brought on by stress. She was told to expect this serious and potentially dangerous condition to be a lifetime problem. With the responsibility of four children under the age of ten, the thought of his poor health sent her into a panic and prompted a plan of action.

Resourceful and realistic, she decided that she would need to secure her future in case she was left alone. Loving and protective, she kept this to herself. Cunning and respectful, she vowed always to make her partner feel as if he was the head of the roost. She knew all three conditions would have to be in place if she wanted her marriage to work with this new revelation. She knew life would be different. She knew she could not bewail his shortcomings or let resentment fester in her heart. She hoped his sense of humor, which always got them through tough times, would continue to function. Luckily, she has been laughing with him for well over forty years now.

It wasn't long until Rita wriggled her way into his busi-

ness and suggested she help out when commitments necessitated he be in two places at one time. Once in, there was no
turning back. She was a natural in the world of business and
quickly got hooked on the challenge. Her husband quickly
felt assured by her presence, and she felt more secure about
her family's future. There were trepidations, she admits,
working full-time and often being out of town on business
with four children at home. Her schedule was exhausting
and trying. "This might not have been the kind of marriage
my friends wanted, or even that my parents wanted for me.
But I wanted it, and I was going to make sure it stayed intact
no matter what I was required to do," Rita proclaims.

Her independence created a measure of husbandly dependence that she accepts. To Rita, her husband will remain that
young college man she fell in love with, frailties and all.
Prudently, she never demanded credit for being the glue that
held this family of six together or needed praise for providing a significant portion of the family income. Not only Rita,
but a significant number of long-term married wives, confide that the success of their marriages is due in part to a
constant monitoring of their spouse's feelings and ego.

Sound old-fashioned? Maybe, but have you checked your
partner's ego recently?

How Debra Benefits From Her Flexibility

Debra, a doctor in her mid-thirties married to another
doctor, practices flexibility on a regular basis. "We are fairly
well matched and are equal partners. But when it comes to
his masculinity, I don't challenge that! I give him the
courtesy to voice his opinion first if it relates to medicine.
Then I will state my own opinion in a nice way if it differs. I
am not uncomfortable doing this. I am not any less of a
feminist or a person," she explains.

Debra's motivation is clear-cut. "If I had a choice between

being married or single, I would rather be married. Marriage is the most important thing to me. I like having a family. I like the security of being married and knowing that a person is there to depend on. I don't think life would have much meaning without it. I don't want to go it alone in life, and I'm willing to go the extra mile for my husband."

Consequently, Debra has chosen to be practical. She concentrates on what she calls "the big picture," instead of dwelling on individual situations. She accepts and uses two important axioms she has discovered through her own observations. One: "Women are the people who are more conscious of the workings of a relationship and do the extra things to make it work." Two: "Long-lasting marriages seem to follow the traditional family pattern."

Debra has a lot more to say on both issues. "There are basic differences between men and women," she explains over a sandwich during her lunch hour. "You have to take those differences into account. I'm not threatened by doing that." A new body of research seems to bear out her theory. *Study after study indicates that men communicate, relate, and feel differently than women.* In Debra's opinion men are less flexible than women, not as good listeners, and have more immediate sexual needs. So she takes up the slack. She doesn't buy into the formula that some of her medical classmates did when they married. "They thought everything had to be split fifty-fifty right down the line," she says. "It didn't work, and many of them are divorced."

That is an unrealistic equation for most of the women and men I spoke with. *Blissfully happy spouses gave equations of sixty/forty and eighty-twenty. Equity in tasks and effort is a fluctuating proposition, with one party tilting the scale.*

Patterning her work and family life in as traditional a fashion as possible, Debra describes the workings of her household. Daytime: "I prepare the meals. I'm the one that packs our daughter's lunch for school. I'm the one who takes the kids to the doctor, does the laundry , and maintains the house. My husband handles the business aspect of our lives because he is better at it. Professionally, I spend three-quarters of a regular work week in the office. That was my choice. I don't fault him for that. I'm sure my husband would think our household responsibilities are more equal, but I only remember him preparing three or four meals and changing a half dozen diapers at the most."

"Sometimes you are tired from working all day and are not ready for a romantic evening. I think you gave to get past that. Several hours of tenderness would help, but it is not realistic in the hectic lives we lead. Sometimes you have to step past that and not worry about the preliminaries and do whatever it takes to make men feel loved. So when it comes to energy, I feel a woman may have to give more. I can't say I never refuse my husband sex, but most of the time I don't. I read somewhere that men have sex and then feel loved, and women need to feel loved then have sex." There are those differences she started with again.

"If you realize this about men," Debra says, "you do what you have to, and you're both going to be happier. I know that sounds like a cop-out, but it really works. There are less hurt feelings, less arguments, and we are both able to overlook a lot of things because he is satisfied. That is the way it is. I don't consider it being *manipulative*. I consider it being *smart*. The way men think and function, when they are satisfied it is so much different. I don't think they even realize it. People talk about PMS and mood swings, well men are much *worse!* I'm thankful I had the foresight to see these things."

Debra and women like her are not subservient and certainly are not pampering their husbands at their own expense. No. Debra has accurately assessed her man and her marriage, devising the best possible formula for their relationship. No one is taking advantage of her willingness to be the flexible, giving partner. Every six months she says she whips her family back into shape with her "Queen Speech," outlining for her husband and their two children a list of responsibilities they cyclically seem to forget.

THE BASIC INGREDIENTS OF A LIFETIME LOVE AFFAIR

No one can get along without Marriage Secrets if they want to achieve a lifetime love affair with their spouse. There are three things to remember when using them.

1. Secrets should form the foundation of your basic value system.

2. Secrets should become Standard Operating Procedure.

3. Secrets should periodically be approached with renewed vigor.

Valuing the Hard Work of Marriage

Secrets comprise a value system that emphasizes the joy of a good marriage and blends the best of conventional wisdom and contemporary insights. Those who accept this value system are encouraged to work hard at marriage. There is little time off for good behavior. The odds against a lifelong love match are frighteningly high. Once you acknowledge the importance of your marriage and your mate, you will be ready to begin using secrets.

Making More Carefully Planned Reactions Your Standard Operating Procedure

I can't imagine not using secrets in my sometimes explosive marriage. Without careful analysis, how would I ever have realized that the best way to handle my husband's childish temper tantrums is either to ignore them or humor him? My previous loud, exasperated response made no impact. Instead, I employed carefully planned reactions: a playful rub on the back of his head; a soft, nurturing "Calm down. It's bad for your health"; or, when I am feeling less generous, a fast exit from the scene. All took years to cultivate.

Now these are Standard Operating Procedures. Fortunately, they have prevented any number of secondary eruptions and curbed some of the outbursts that once irritated me to the very core of my being.

I don't mean to pass myself off as the perfect little playmate in this partnership. I can also drive this man up and down a few walls. My constant worrying over the children, my demand for immediate answers, my ridiculous behavior on the golf course and, I will admit, my nagging can be grounds for some major dissatisfaction. On more than one occasion I have sent my husband storming out of the house and back to the office until I have gone and gently retrieved him. Therefore, fully aware of Mark's level of tolerance, I had to devise some secret guidelines for the limits of my own childish behavior. Just enough, that is, to keep him from reaching wits' end and denying me the sympathy and comfort I obviously seek.

Renewing Your Vigor to Work at Love

No matter how many anniversaries you have, stockpiled secrets need to be used periodically with renewed vigor.

After spending several hours getting to know each woman I interviewed—many of whom ranked their long-term marriages near perfect—rarely did I depart before they made the declaration that the discussion reminded them of something they were neglecting and needed to work on in one area or another. When a Mrs. couldn't respond with a romantic anecdote or an example of a thoughtful gesture, they knew they were taking their Mr. for granted.

If you find yourself in the same predicament, it is time to get motivated and start. Don't cheat yourself or your spouse out of the pleasures and rewards derived from Marriage Secrets.

THE POWER OF SECRET STRATEGIES

As you become more familiar with the concept of using secret strategies, you will also become more adept at discovering how and when to use them. Be aware of all that secrets can do for you.

- **Secrets help communicate ideas, feelings, and needs in a nonthreatening manner.**
- **Secrets have the potential to quiet troubled waters.**
- **Secrets express love, concern, and respect.**
- **Secrets add immeasurable pleasure, fun, and intimacy to a marriage relationship.**
- **Secrets encourage personal growth.**
- **Secrets balance individual needs and healthy interdependence.**
- **Secrets offer handy tools that ward off potential dangers.**
- **Secrets heal the wounds from inevitable hidden pitfalls.**
- **Secrets empower you to create a mutually satisfying marriage partnership and achieve a gratifying union with your love mate.**
- **Secrets make it possible for you to have it all.**

Digest this important material and get ready to indulge, enhance, nourish, and protect your marriage. It is time to take the great secrets out of the bag and keep your love match going. Unleash your creativity, reaffirm your commitment, and acknowledge that the stakes are high. There is no doubt that these secrets will produce some admirable, loving couples whose happiness may add a new luster to the tarnished image marriage has suffered of late!

2

Steering the Ship Takes
A Worthy Captain

"I just love her," responded an unsuspecting husband married for more than two decades. He couldn't come up with any secret reasons how or why his marriage works. His wife, on the other hand, was definitely more creative in her three-page summary.

This husband's notion that love is the only elixir needed for a successful marriage is not surprising. Some sociologists suggest that men take a more romantic view of marriage than women do. The reason is simple: They base their choice of partner on attraction and love. While women use these important criteria, they also consider serious practical issues: Will he make a good husband? Will he make a good father? Will he make a good living? Will he be a supporting, loyal partner? Will I be able to mold him into all of the above?

WHO IS IN CHARGE?

Women are plainly more in tune with the state of their marriage. Women see themselves as ready, willing, and eager to analyze the relationship that men frequently don't even want to discuss. Out of the hundreds of surveys I circulated from coast to coast, women not only answered the questions in more detail but filled out 20 percent more of them than men. Wives were easier to corral into interviews than their husbands. None of the men I interviewed spent three hours divulging marriage secrets, as did many of the women, *the majority of whom believe they take a more active role in making love and marriage work.*

According to a number of contemporary researchers, these women are not exaggerating their importance in making a marriage relationship successful. Better communication skills, the ability to detect problems, the determination to confront issues squarely and honestly, and the know-how to maintain calm waters are the qualities that more often than not put them at the helm of the ship.

What the researchers don't know is that these skills are contagious when they are backed up by Marriage Secrets and complemented by a husband's willingness to help guide the ship. Who cares if the wife is the first to begin using them as long as both partners get the knack of it?

THE SECRET POWER OF BEING AT THE HELM

No matter how idealistic or how much in love one or both partners may be, it should be no secret that a good marriage requires someone to steer the ship to port. Through default or choice, most of the officers taking the responsibility for the state of their marriage are women. A woman, however, does not always have to be the full-time captain. But even as an ensign, she must have the stuff captains are made of when called to duty!

A point of clarification. I am not talking bosses, breadwinners, or henpecked mates here. Be patient and this important concept will unravel itself with a thorough explanation.

But be sure to grasp it. Being a good and worthy captain is a precondition that empowers you to use Marriage Secrets. Often, it is a precondition to getting a partner!

Taking a Chance on Taking Charge

I happened across a female captain purely by chance while buying an expensive piece of exercise equipment. As I was getting my charge card out to pay for the stair climber, I casually remarked to the owner of the store that perhaps I should call and tell my husband I was making this purchase today, even though we had discussed it previously. I thought his comment was rather peculiar. "Yes, we like to hear those things."

Thinking he meant that a phone call to my husband would assure payment, I readied myself for battle. I was about to attack him verbally for his insinuation that I did not have my own income when, fortunately, he finished his statement: "We husbands like to be a part of these things, even though your minds are made up. I appreciate it when my wife does that." I called my husband and winked at the store owner.

I had an inkling that this man must have had some good training at home. I asked him how long he had been married. "I am married twelve years now and am happier than I ever thought I could be," he volunteered. With very little prompting he told me it was his second marriage and that he had been running around having a great time as a single man with absolutely no intention of getting married when he met his wife, the first woman to give him an ultimatum. Basically, the message was, "If you want me, get rid of all the others."

All the while I am thinking, "This is one smart wife. I need to meet her."

"I bet your wife knew exactly what you would do," I said.

"I'm sure she did," he replied with a laugh.

When I did visit this pretty, soft-spoken woman at her home, I asked how she had managed to get this confirmed bachelor to the altar. "He certainly was a ladies' man and definitely not looking to get married. Everyone thought he had it made. He had a different girl every night of the week. I was Friday. After I went out with him twice, I knew I didn't want to see anyone else. I also knew that the worst thing I could do was to tell him I felt that way. So I never let on. I just enjoyed myself when I could be with him. We had a ball together, and I graduated to Friday *and* Saturday."

In her final plan, intuition took over where experience was lacking.

"I knew I was going to have to play this smart. I had only had one serious relationship before, but I just felt that the best way to lose him was to let him know how much I liked him. After seeing him seven months, I decided to make my move. I knew I wanted to marry this man. Everyone was telling me he would never get married again. He had women falling all over him. When he was leaving for California to spend a week with another woman, I told him that while he was away he should think about our relationship. If he wanted to continue his current life-style, I wanted out. I knew I was taking a chance, but it was either all or nothing in my own mind and heart."

At first he asked himself, "Who does she think she is?" Unaware of his own intense feelings, he got on the plane, stepped off in L.A., took one look at the other gal, and realized he only wanted to be with this *woman* at home.

He didn't return and ask her to live with him. "Absolutely not," says his wife. "He knew I wouldn't go for that. He asked me to marry him."

Here's where I saw the real potential of this woman as a captain. "He calls me his princess, but I don't like that. It has a negative connotation. I like to be called the queen or the Prime Minister, something that infers more equality."

How Susan Took Charge and Changed Her In-Laws' Bad Example

Susan, another smart captain, made some valuable observations which helped guide her action. Assuming that her in-laws' relationship served as a model for her husband's behavior, she studied their interaction carefully and then set out to change her husband's perception of how things should work in a number of areas.

"Paul's father and mother did not have a very close relationship," she tells me. "I could see right away that they spent little time together and spoke to each other even less. I wanted a husband who was my companion, not a housemate. While I was dating Paul, there were times I worried he might follow in his father's footsteps. After we were married, I planned weekend activities that we could both enjoy. If we went to a baseball game one day, the next day I would plan for a long drive to give us the opportunity to talk. Of course, we don't spend all of our time together. But I can tell we are moving toward a more communicative relationship than his parents'."

Penny Takes Charge by Keeping Things in the Open With Little Reminders

Penny knew that she would have to keep a different kind of eye on her marriage. Stuart was flirtatious. It was a quality that attracted her to him. But she worried that it could create a problem in the future. Besides doing all the wifely things that might keep him faithful, she decided to give him regular doses of guilt before he had anything to feel guilty about.

Penny describes her technique: "Stuart told me one day that he went to a TV station to deliver some press releases and pick up advertising material. A secretary led him into a darkened studio under the pretext of hunting down some

posters. She got a little touchy and I guess pretty close.
Stuart said that by the time she ended up in a corner near a
couch, her intentions had become quite obvious. He turned
and walked out without saying a word. Rather than ease his
conscience, even though he did the right thing, I asked him
why he went in with her in the first place and why he didn't
run!"

Thus far we have determined that captains take charge,
set a direction, and assume responsibility for meeting their
goals. In nautical terms, *a captain charts the course, navigates
the vessel through calm and turbulent seas, and is not afraid to take
charge of the ship in an emergency.*

Don't Miss the Boat—Use All Your Resources

Joyce certainly knows what I am talking about. Pam
doesn't. Joyce and Pam are two women in similar circumstances who would have much to say to one another if they
ever met. Both Joyce and Pam's husbands, Pete and Randy
respectively, were superb jocks and college stars who'd
received some minor offers to play professional sports. Pete
and Randy each found it difficult to pass up their dreams of
glory as pro athletes. Naturally, they devoted all their after-
work hours to sports and tournaments, neglecting their
wives by leaving them either at home or sitting on the
benches.

"Shortly after we were married, Pete, an accountant,
would go from tax season to basketball season to golf
season," Joyce explains. "On Saturday mornings he would
get up early and travel out of town for tournaments. He
returned late at night and repeated the scenario on Sunday.
If I ever met the man who set up all these games, I think I
would have killed him. I finally had enough and told Pete, 'I
am a high-maintenance person. I need attention and so do
our children. You're not spending enough time with them or
me.'

"I would never have let things get out of hand and break up our marriage," she says authoritatively. Well aware of the value of setting limits, she adds, "I may have given him an ultimatum at the time, but since he is very logical and realistic, he knew he needed to put things in perspective."

Did Joyce's demands hurt their marriage? Absolutely not. Her message was well accepted and eventually strengthened their relationship. Pete says he has always loved his wife, thinks they have a great marriage, and appreciates the fact that he feels loved. Today he explains, without prompting, "Joyce is a high-maintenance person who needs a lot of attention."

Joyce didn't really change Pete, but she did modify his behavior. Propelled by her own needs, she did not hesitate to take the helm and act decisively. *Joyce not only knew she wanted more of Pete's time, but felt she deserved it. This is an essential trait in a well-conditioned captain.* Valuing the family more than the fairways, Pete was willing to acquiesce once Joyce made her move.

Pam, on the other hand, failed to score Joyce's success. Over the past fifteen years she had lost her leverage by becoming a nonparticipant, by withdrawing from the struggle to draw Randy's attention to the problem. Having allowed Randy to fail her without putting up a fight when he dropped her off to get a premarital abortion as he went to play a tennis match, Pam set the pattern for their future relationship. Since then she has quietly stored up resentment and given up on her marriage. Unhappy but still with Randy, Pam is not totally convinced that she took advantage of all her resources.

Can we fault her? No. For one, she had no concept that she needed to take charge. Secondly, there are those men and women out there who will never listen, even to a seasoned captain. Randy may be one of them, but Pam will never know for sure unless she uses her authority and some of the secrets in the rule book.

NONCAPTAINS FREQUENTLY OVERLOOK OPPORTUNITIES
TO KEEP LOVE ON TRACK

"The second wife will get it all—his money, his love, his time, his attention." Some women think this way. Many accept failure before they have even tried to get what they want. Instead of relishing defeat, you should be asking yourself: **"Why don't I have it all? And what should I do to get it?"**

For some women this is simple, while for others it becomes a monumental task. Without basic acceptance of yourself, without the assumption of your right to expect attention, respect, and love, your relationship cannot work as it should.

A CAPTAIN WITHOUT A SENSE OF SELF-WORTH NEVER GETS COMMISSIONED

More often than not, noncaptains avoid taking an aggressive stand because they lack self-esteem. Captains, on the other hand, function from a position of strength, not weakness.

A BELIEF IN HER INDIVIDUAL SELF-WORTH EMPOWERS A WOMAN TO MOVE FORWARD WITH THE NECESSARY CONFIDENCE AND CONVICTION TO PROTECT HER INTERESTS AS WELL AS FULFILL THE NEEDS OF HER PARTNER AND THEIR MARRIAGE RELATIONSHIP.

Curiously, some women come by this attitude naturally. Many are brought up with a positive self-image that is reflected in their lives. Some develop it from success. And still other women look for it on a therapist's couch. *Whatever it takes, get it!*

Only You Can Be Your Own Best Ambassador

At a reunion luncheon, nearly ten years ago, I overheard two women friends talking. Their conversation has stayed in my mind all these years. Right then and there, sitting at the table, I silently predicted that Martha's marriage would not last. Unfortunately for Martha I was right. Her situation was a powerful illustration of the weak position noncaptains, with their low level of self-esteem, find themselves relegated to. She was a classic noncaptain.

Martha was a schoolteacher who married a lawyer. She tied the knot several years later than most of her female friends. She described to her friend Sharon her sense of relief and gratitude when she married. Her husband had rescued her from the prospect of lonely years as a single woman. With her focus placed entirely on Ted's wishes and his future, Martha thought her own needs should be secondary to her husband's.

Paralyzed by feelings of insecurity and inferiority in her relationship with Ted, she was unable or unwilling to attach significance to her personal needs. She could not demand her own rewards, nor did she want to. Without ever putting herself first, she didn't give him the opportunity to be a better husband. So there was no way of knowing if he could be.

I doubt Sharon would find herself in this predicament. She gets right to the heart of the matter and seems fully versed in the philosophy of being a captain. She says that one of her secrets to a good marriage is to keep her husband aware of the fact that she is a "prize package."

"I remind my husband how fortunate he should feel being married to me," she explains for openers. "I don't have any problem listing my good qualities. And I would never complain to my husband, like so many women do, that as I am aging my breasts are starting to sag or that my thighs are getting flabby. That's crazy when you think of it. Isn't it?"

If You Don't Think You're Special
Why Should Anyone Else?

Madge knew that she had a case of low self-esteem. What she didn't understand was how that would get her into trouble when dealing with the opposite sex. Though she spent seven years of her life as the mistress of a married man, she struggled and finally won the family she deserved. It took three sessions of interviews to get to the bottom of her story.

As can be expected, Madge's problems all started out innocently enough. Just after college, when she was waiting to begin her job as a high-school math teacher, Madge met Nelson at the hospital where they both worked the night shift. At the time Nelson was working a total of one hundred and five hours a week to fulfill some hefty financial obligations. He owed child support, the result of a college love affair, and he was struggling to pay his second wife's bills— a prolific spender who came with her own small group of youngsters.

Feeling unhappy, trapped, and sexually dissatisfied at home, he worked round the clock. Then Nelson met Madge, tall, dark, sexy, but deeply insecure. Friendly coffee breaks, confidential talks, and a mutual attraction swept Madge off her feet and into bed.

"Honey," she began, "I wouldn't have had an affair and gotten into a relationship like that if I had had a better self-image. One of my college professors told me he had never seen anyone who had so little self-confidence. I attribute that to the unending criticisms of my father. Nelson was my first experience. I was already twenty-two. My guilt trips were heavy, and my religion was weighing on my mind. But there was a magnetism between us that you only find once in a while. I really tried to get out of this, but he was so great in the bedroom. Once you have that, it's difficult to find a substitute for it. I hate to say it, but most men aren't that good."

The sex must have been fabulous and Nelson pretty lovable for this woman with a logical, mathematical mind to put up with what appeared to be a no-win situation. Madge stayed by Nelson's side through two pregnancies and deliveries—his *wife's*, not hers. When she started teaching, she went without sleep to meet him at the hospital and bring him warm dinners in the hopes of grabbing some intimate moments. Madge was about as far from being a captain as one can imagine.

"His marriage was on the rocks. He said he really loved me and told me he was only staying with his wife because of the children, which was okay by me until Christmas and all the holidays normal people have together came around. I began to realize that it would have gone on forever. I told him I didn't want to see him anymore, but that I wanted to have his baby. I figured I wasn't going to marry, and I wanted a child," she explains. "I told him that was all I wanted from him. After seven years I wanted something out of the relationship. He didn't have to see me afterwards. I was looking at reality. I knew it wouldn't be easy, but I hadn't found anyone I wanted as much as Nelson, and I knew I couldn't have him.

"I spent the pregnancy by myself. He never helped me financially. He had been seeing me all along during the pregnancy. He kept saying he was going to marry me, and I didn't believe him. He filed for divorce while I was in the hospital. The baby and I moved into an apartment with him the day I came home, and we lived together for a year before we got married," Madge told me, amused by my surprise and the details of her own life.

"The kids meant more to me than my wife," said Nelson, explaining what *he* was thinking in those days. "I had lost my first child. The mother wanted me to marry her in name only and left just after the baby was born. I didn't want to lose these kids too. I had to get to the point, though, and say, 'This is foolishness. I'm not happy.'" Nelson was able to strike a deal with his second wife to get custody of the kids by paying off her debts and handing over a significant lump sum of money.

Madge finally got her man, but she was still far from a real take-charge position. "When we first got married, I thought I was worthless because I hadn't been able to find a husband and have children the normal way. It took years before I felt good about myself, not until I was about thirty-two. I catered to Nelson hand and foot. For years I was the doting wife, even serving him breakfast in bed."

It took more than three years before Madge started using her rational mind outside of the classroom to relieve her of the drudgery of caring for her two babies, two stepchildren (one a terror), and an absentee husband. Nelson, in his climb up the corporate ladder, was absent Monday through Friday and returned on the weekends to question and criticize Madge's handling of his problem child and household.

WE HAVE MORE POWER THAN WE ADMIT

Love took a dive until Madge made an important discovery and began voicing her opinions loud and clear. "That was my novice period. My position had been weak. I didn't have the confidence to know what I had as a woman and what I could give to the marriage. *We have power! It is incredible!* I finally told him not to judge me, not to criticize me, and not to ridicule me. Just be there for me as a friend."

The ultimatum—that Nelson begin to offer a little help and support and curb his demeaning and inconsiderate outbursts—revealed to her that he was easier to influence than she had presumed. She dragged him to sessions of Marriage Encounter Groups, where Madge became particularly adept in the art of communicating and learning to employ artful secrets. She shaped her marriage up quickly.

This was not a temporary change. Madge and Nelson have

been at it for sixteen years. "He is now willing to listen and to talk. He takes responsibility in the house and caters to me. He has turned around three hundred and sixty-five degrees." What's her secret?

"What does a man want?" she asks. "He wants to have his family love him. He wants to work hard, and he wants to feel he is important. He wants to know he is the best he can be. I give him all of that," Madge says. **"But it wasn't until I knew what *I* wanted that I could be so generous to him without sacrificing myself."**

Madge is in the captain's seat now. But if she or any woman wants to stay there, she'd better make sure that as a captain she doesn't abuse her power.

QUALITIES OF A WORTHY CAPTAIN

1. A worthy captain is not a prima donna who invites mutiny. She does not make the mistake of thinking she is so special, so wonderful, that she flaunts her authority. In fact, more often, her power is confined to below decks and kept out of sight. She uses her *love, intuition,* and *sensitivity* to set the course, calling on her spouse to help run the ship smoothly.

Karen is a good example of a woman who handles this maneuver really well. After a lengthy conversation over coffee in the back room of her boutique, I was surprised to find this feisty and aggressive businesswoman sounding rather docile and passive when it came to her relationship with her husband. It took quite a while for the real scene to surface.

In the first half of the interview she described how she waits patiently for her husband to make up his mind about household furnishings, cars, and trips even when he is ridiculously slow and indecisive. Even though she makes more money, he controls the checkbook and would be intimidated if she took over this responsibility. She spoke of how she enjoys catering to him by buying his underwear, outerwear, and even his shoes, which she selects by trying on and estimating the size!

She continued to describe her husband as a man she dearly loves, despite the fact that he's quite spaced-out. "If he won the lottery," she concludes, "he is so indecisive he wouldn't know what to do with it." Assessing her own situation, she says, "You have to have love to hold this together." No doubt that is what she thinks about when she rechecks the checkbook.

"I accept his financial capabilities and my ability to earn more than he does. I never say anything. I give him all of the money and never compare incomes. I allow him to make decisions. As far as he is concerned, he is the man of the house. I don't think he realizes he isn't capable of making these decisions and I don't want to undermine him by making an issue out of it. I don't want to be without him. I never stop loving him, and I want to grow old with him. I've learned to accept this. He has a lot of other good qualities, or I would never have stayed with him. You can't get a better father for our children or a better friend."

2. A worthy captain must be acutely aware of constructive ways to use her authority. Many of the women I encountered *failed* to sense the need to use their own power and strength constructively to improve their marriage relationship.

Don't fool yourself for one moment. Men like and respect women who demonstrate their decisiveness and independence. Many husbands I spoke with expressed their preference for strong women, women who won't allow anyone to walk over them, even lightly.

Stephanie is a noncaptain who, after an unsuccessful sixteen-year marriage that ended in divorce, says she too was unaware of how often she could have taken a more powerful stance in dealing with her difficult husband,

Martin. "I realize now that Martin wanted me to make decisions and take charge. I was thoroughly intimidated by him, and he was probably thoroughly aggravated by my inability to act."

3. A worthy captain is willing to explore and develop the potential of Marriage Secrets to enrich and expand her influence in creating a lifelong love relationship. Stephanie failed to realize the power inherent in secrets. Opposed at the time to using any "tactics," she now admits they might have worked since normal verbal communication always seemed to end in heated confrontations.

Every one of you must develop your own style of influence and become savvy enough to determine the lengths you must go to to create the best possible relationship. Sounds like hard, concentrated labor? It is. Make no mistake about that. But it is a work ethic with more than ample rewards.

4. A worthy captain accepts the commission. She is energized by her sense of self-worth and her commitment to that worthy spouse she was lucky enough to discover. It takes courage to explore your own strength and ability to build a better relationship. *Don't be timid!* At first it may seem like you are being manipulative, but later you will realize that what you are doing is learning skills that other people have naturally.

Once you understand and accept the secret that it is necessary to be strategic and deliberate for the well-being of your marital relationship, you will not hesitate to take power and even enjoy it.

I admit that in my own marriage, when I slack off, become really disagreeable, and fail to keep my irritability in check, Mark becomes a less-than-perfect mate. We bite and snap at each other like two pit bulls. Inevitably, because of all we've worked through together, he will eventually say, "We're not getting along. What's wrong?"

At those times, I repeatedly try to explain that the level of my effort has sunk, that I've become distracted from my goal of a well-run relationship, and that I have chosen not be so accommodating or loving. He does not understand this at all. Instead of becoming angry at him as I might have in the past, especially when the kids were young and my responsibilities more pressing, I am committed to accepting the challenge because the results are satisfying to both of us. This is a fair price to pay when you think of the rewards, the consideration, and the pampering I receive, and the calm, serene atmosphere we live in.

Passing the Test

Make sure you have the concept of a worthy captain down pat. Take the following test. Be honest and open with yourself in writing your answers.

BE GUIDED BY YOUR SELF-WORTH, YOUR LOVE FOR YOUR SPOUSE, AND YOUR ACCEPTANCE OF THE PRINCIPLE THAT MARRIAGE IS A RELATIONSHIP MADE FOR THE MUTUAL SATISFACTION OF TWO PEOPLE.

Rank your answers 1 through 5. On a scale of frequency, "1" signifies the minimum and "5" the maximum amount of time you assume the attitude in question. Add up your points and check the score against the analysis that follows.

How Much of the Time:

- I like myself.
- I work on making myself the person I want to be.
- I expect and receive respect.
- I have no problem making my feelings and demands known at work or at home.

- I am aware of what makes my spouse tick.
- I am aware of what makes me feel happy and satisfied.
- I am able to use the art of compromise to settle conflicts.
- I am accepting of other people's viewpoints.
- My top priority is my own self-interest.
- I am cognizant of the wind shifts in my marital relationship and take them seriously.
- I am able to identify the factors that cause tension in my marriage.
- I will not keep silent in order to maintain the peace.
- I want my marriage to work.
- I put my partner's needs ahead of my own.
- I respect my spouse as much as I respect myself.
- I am willing to try anything to create a lasting marriage relationship.
- I like and love my mate.
- I am ready to be a captain.

Total
Points

Where do you stand? If you tally up between 75 and 85 points, you are right on. Anything less than 70 means you might need a little assistance in thinking about yourself, your spouse, and your marriage. Over 85? **Watch out!** You may need to adopt a little more humility and a little less self-confidence.

SET SAIL

Now you are ready to proceed. *Armed with a valuable new perspective emphasizing your self-worth, you are well-equipped to set sail and begin to steer your marriage toward a port which ensures your own satisfaction as well as your mate's.* Read carefully, test the waters, and confidently use Marriage Secrets to keep this relationship on an even keel. Don't be overwhelmed by the magnitude of your task or all of the secrets that await you. If you use them correctly, there will be many a day to experience and enjoy them one by one.

3

Great Sex, a Matter of Consensus

Do you identify closely with the couple in *Annie Hall,* who, when asked individually by their respective therapists how often they engage in sex, give vastly different interpretations to the same answer? "Hardly ever," says Woody Allen. "Maybe three times a week." "Constantly. I'd say three times a week," says Diane Keaton.

You don't have to look too far to find confirmation that couples often don't share the same perspective when it comes to their sexual relationship. Ann Landers received a note from a disgruntled wife who happened across her partner's response to Landers's question on marital sex. She wrote, "I just saw my husband's postcard. He says our sex life is terrific. The big ox doesn't even realize I haven't had an orgasm in fifteen years."

Studies reveal that more than one half of the happily married population express some problem with their sex lives. **Although a less-than-satisfying sex life with your marriage partner rarely constitutes the number one reason for divorce, it doesn't mean it shouldn't be high on the list of repairs and improvements.**

SEX, A MEGA-ISSUE

Sex, good sex, is of mega-major importance to your husband, and it ought to be to you too! There is no room for a lack of consensus on this point! Satisfying each other's sexual needs is rewarding and of paramount importance. According to the *Kinsey Institute New Report on Sex*, sex among committed partners nurtures "a sense of emotional security that is valuable to a person's sense of well-being, happiness, and perhaps even physical health." And, sex is certainly a matter of marital safety.

Sex for Him

Sex is a way of communicating to your husband that you love him, accept him, and enjoy being intimate with him. Refusing sex is flirting with the possibility of communicating rejection and bruising his delicate ego. Without a satisfying level of sex, there might not be anyone around to communicate with.

DON'T FOR A MOMENT MAKE THE MISTAKE OF UNDERESTIMATING THE POWER OF SEXUAL PLEASURE. DON'T SHORTCHANGE *YOURSELF*!

If you doubt what I am saying, listen to the opinions of some happily married men. "It might have been two weeks since we had sex and she gives me the headache excuse. I get mad," admits this husband, who is on his second marriage. "A lot of guys would contemplate and have affairs, guys like me go for a walk. Our relationship would be better if we had a better sex life. Instead of getting mad all the time, we'd be having fun."

Another man, married twenty-nine years, is not so patient with his wife's refusal to participate in sex for several years.

"If you can't enjoy sex at home, you enjoy it somewhere else. I love her spiritually, but I haven't given up on sex." Surprisingly, this gent rates his marriage a hearty seven and the need for a good marital sex life a nine plus. It is a lucky wife who can survive such a narrow margin.

More than ninety percent of the men who rated their level of marital satisfaction eight or higher said they had a good sexual relationship with their wives. Men suffering through a less-than-happy union gave a unanimous show of hands when it came to ranking their sexual relations at the same dismal low level.

But what do the women have to say?

"I don't think I have ever turned Ralph down." (A record few women, including myself, could boast of this.) Said one woman, married more than thirty years: "In my opinion, if you don't have a good sex life, you can't have a good marriage. You can cook, you can scrub, and you can work, but if you're not loving and warm, you're not giving happiness to anyone else and you won't bring happiness to yourself."

Go for a test close to home. See what sex means to your man. Try systematically charting your husband's moods as they correspond to your level of sexual activity. If he is anything like most of his peers, it won't take long for a clear-cut picture to develop. If he is satisfied sexually, chances are he will be more pleasant, more flexible, more receptive, more agreeable, and more willing to overlook things that generally get his dander up. If he is not sexually satisfied, he may growl, snap, and bite.

HARMONY BARELY STRIKES A CHORD IN MARITAL RELATIONSHIPS WITHOUT THE ORCHESTRATION OF SEX.

A simple chart will help to prove this point.

Day of the Week	Sex Yes No	24-Hour Attitude Check Excellent Good Average Below Average Poor
Monday		
Tuesday		
Wednesday		
Thursday		
Friday		
Saturday		
Sunday		

If you want to get spicy and complex, create your own chart to monitor the effects of specific sex acts on his responsiveness to you and his overall attitude around the house. Witness firsthand the power of great sex. This movement will end up in a vibrant crescendo.

Sex for Her

It is just as important for women to hear the music! But if you aren't turned on and tuned in, your lack of sexual responsiveness will deprive you of one of the most pleasurable aspects of a loving relationship. If this shoe fits, you'd best ask yourself some pretty serious questions:

- **Why don't I get as aroused as my husband?**
- **Do I see myself as a sexual person?**
- **Am I too inhibited to express my sexual desires?**
- **Have I explored my sexual needs?**
- **Is my response important to my husband?**
- **Am I really concerned with meeting my husband's sexual needs?**
- **Am I having fewer orgasms and faking more?**
- **Why am I willing to settle for so little in our sexual relationship?**

A number of factors might be contributing to your sub-
dued enthusiasm for sex.

YOUR BODY IMAGE

For starters, you have to feel good about your own body.
"When I am thin, I'm always more eager to have sex. I want
to flaunt my body, and I'm not concerned about turning off
the lights. I just feel sexy and desirable when I am thin," is
one woman's answer.

Feeling good about your body is not a matter of size and
dimension. It is a matter of an awareness of the pleasures of
the body. The ideal body is the one that makes you feel good
about yourself and that your husband finds appealing and
sexy.

Feeling desirable and knowing that you attract men can be
a big turn-on. "I overheard two guys who were redoing my
kitchen tell each other how they'd love to have me just one
time," begins a woman in her forties over the telephone. "I
guess they thought I was pretty neat. It was all I could do not
to smile and thank them. When my husband came home that
night I was more than excited. I think that marked one of my
most passionate times with my husband. I felt so fabulous."

You can't always count on overhearing a sexy compliment
to get you aroused. A more reliable source, according to one
adventuresome/lover wife, is to learn enough about your
own body to know what makes you tick. "If you find out,
your husband will find out," she advises. How do you do
this? Through books and self-exploration with masturba-
tion, vibrators, feathers, or whatever stimulus you choose.
Sounds kinky? Good. It works, is the word from a sixty-year-
old woman who never understood her sexual needs until she
had been married close to two decades! There is so much
room for experimentation. Researchers have concluded that
there are undiscovered erogenous zones all over the female

body which, when stimulated, can produce near orgasmic feelings. One interviewee said that she experiences a sensation akin to oral sex when her husband licks between her fingers.

YOUR SATISFACTION

Still having problems getting excited over the topic? Check with your doctor. Maybe you are suffering from a physiological problem. Are you holding out to punish him? Maybe you have a case of unexpressed anger and resentment caused by conflicts in other areas of your relationship. Or are you waiting for him to guess what turns you on?

Search for the answer, find a solution, and be honest with yourself and your spouse when it comes to your sexual needs. That is the only way you can achieve the satisfaction and pleasure that is rightfully yours.

For some women, young and old alike, this has been and still is a tall order. For encouragement, just think of what one happy husband told me when talking about his wife. She was raised with a sexually restrictive attitude and then broke out of the barnyard in a gallop to become an extremely aggressive and creative sex partner: "Once she realized that there was no sexual aberration that would bother me, she was able to be herself and feel that anything she wanted was fine. If it floats her boat, it doesn't bother me."

Women who take their lovemaking seriously want complete satisfaction and are open to achieving all kinds of orgasms, whether from intercourse or oral and manual manipulation. They are intent upon reaching an orgasm and adamant that their gratification be no less/no more important than their mate's climax. Who wants to be the lady in the Ann Landers column? Not me!

WOMEN WHO ENJOY SEX AND ARE OVERTLY RESPONSIVE, SPUR THEIR MEN ON TO BECOME BETTER AND MORE PROFICIENT LOVERS.

"What pleases me is pleasing her," explains Nick. "It's not what my wife does to me, it's what we do together to bring out her sexuality. She is the red dragon here. She is the one who blossoms. This is what makes her such a good sex partner. She *really* likes to be pleased," he says with emphasis. "I mean, that's the big turn-on for me. That's what really plugs me in. It's not what she wears or how she smells. That's all window dressing, although I would notice those things too."

Psyching oneself up for sex is a secret used by women who are conscientious about meeting their spouses' needs and their own. If imagery, anticipation of an orgasm, or the pleasure inherent in being intimate with their spouse doesn't work, they take a stab at fantasizing. They might pull a sexy scene from a movie or book out of the hat. If you close your eyes and pretend to be making love to the attractive man you spied in a restaurant, you certainly won't be the only woman on the block doing this!

Developing an enthusiasm for sex puts you in the right frame of mind to begin working it out in bed with your husband—the man who should be your best lover ever, just as you should be his!

SPECIAL ALERT

• **Too many men and women have alarmingly bad attitudes toward sex.** They are nonchalant and unconcerned about the lack of sexual activity in their marital relationship.

I was tempted to offer some sisterly advice to a young woman who told me, *"Sex isn't that important to Dan and me."*

I maintained my interviewer's composure and inquired, "How often do you have sex?"

"Once a month, maybe," was her answer.

Something is wrong here. *Someone should be asking and answering some questions about who is getting it and where or why not!*

• **Husbands and wives have an obligation to maintain**

their sex appeal. Why risk turning off your partner, when the object is to turn each other on? Be honest with your spouse if you are disappointed in the lack of care he takes of his body, and don't be mad when he returns the favor. It is a favor. You both need to know how important it is to retain your physical appeal. If he compliments you and can't keep his hands off, things are probably just right!

But if you sound like the sister in this story told to me by an older sibling, then change your ways: "My sister was a natural beauty. She looked gorgeous walking down the aisle. When she settled down she looked terrible. Her husband never looked at her again and has been having all kinds of affairs for years."

Some women will do this on purpose, even gain huge amounts of weight to keep their husbands away! But for those of you who are careful to maintain sex appeal, check out this list, from *Secrets About Men Every Woman Should Know* by Dr. Barbara DeAngelis.

THINGS THAT MAKE MEN LOOK THE OTHER WAY

- *UNSHAVED UNDERARMS AND LEGS*
- *BAD BREATH*
- *MUSTACHES*
- *UNSTYLISH CLOTHING*
- *UNHEALTHY DIETS*
- *OVERPROCESSED HAIR*
- *MUUMUUS AND TENT DRESSES*
- *UNPLEASANT VAGINAL ODOR*
- *FLAB*
- *BAD SKIN, COVERED WITH TONS OF MAKEUP*
- *BODY ODOR*
- *CHIPPED AND PEELING FINGERNAIL POLISH*

Sounds superficial? Not any more than drooling over some hunk.

FORMING A CONSENSUS

Now that you know where you and your husband might be coming from, it is time to work for a sexual relationship that keeps love on track, everyone in their proper beds, and a gleam in your heart. Take a good, honest look at your sex life with your spouse. Examine your differences and purge your sex life of harmful discrepancies. Get to the root of even the smallest amount of dissatisfaction.

If you achieve a real consensus, a satisfying level of *giving* and *receiving* the pleasures of sex, the rewards will permeate many other aspects of your marriage.

Varying Appetites

A major-league secret for a fulfilling sexual relationship is: **Pay close attention to the size of your partner's sexual appetite and be sensitive to it.**

Beth, a young classical performance artist who shared the same profession as her husband, understood his needs in this department. Once schedules separated them for several weeks. When he was traveling and only passing through their home town for three hours, he walked off the plane and right into an airport hotel room she had booked.

At forty Cathy knows that her husband's sexual appetite is more active than hers. "I have to be careful just getting undressed in front of him at night," reveals this attractive, curvy blonde. "He gets excited with the slightest provocation. There is nothing like sexual rejection to put him in a sour mood. But do I have to be on call all the time? No, but I do have to remind myself when I'm not really in the mood to undress out of sight. When I am ready, you can bet I make a real production out of getting that sweater off." Cathy has things well under control and remembers to *please,* to *appease,* and *never to tease,* when dealing with her partner's sexual appetite.

Being *ready* with the same degree of frequency is one of the big marital issues relating to sex. According to my personal interviews and the questionnaires answered by married men, husbands are more often ready than their partners. One might have thought there was a conspiracy, judging from the consensus on this one. A thirty-three-year-old husband tried to be generous in exploring his wife's lack of enthusiasm. "There is nothing we disagree on sexually other than the frequency. It upsets me at times that my wife cannot get into sex as often as I would like, but I understand her side and try to refrain when I know she has had a hard day." The problem is particularly acute for another wife, whose husband wants it every night and feels hurt if she doesn't climax a dozen times.

In most instances, this complaint was not significant enough to lower the level of marital satisfaction below an eight. *But who is going for mediocrity here?* According to a survey of 1,400 households, married couples have sex an average of 67 times a year. Don't be so easy to dismiss this disparity. "He just has a more active libido," responded one woman.

A LIBIDO STEWING IN A PORRIDGE OF DISCONTENT AND UNMET NEEDS MIGHT BE SERVED UP TO SOMEONE ELSE.

Granted, women do have the right to be tired, to be uninterested, and to say, "Not tonight." So do men for that matter. And I will concede life is more than challenging for those playing the game of wife, mother, and career person. A new mom wrote me, "We're not concerned with how to make our sex life more interesting; we're more worried about keeping a sex life period!"

Keith, happily married to his childhood sweetheart, is candid about how he feels when he is turned down. "Sometimes I get irritated. It makes me worry about my physical appearance, and at times I wonder if there is someone else.

Usually I don't get an excuse. I hear nothing at all, she just rolls over and says, 'No.' An excuse would be reassuring." One important piece of advice: **When turning down your wife or husband's sexual advances, it is always better to offer some excuse than to remain silent.**

GO FOR A COMPROMISE

With all the above in operation, enjoying the intimacy of sex is still preferable. Didn't the results on your chart bear this out? So don't be stubborn like the woman who complained of an unsatisfactory sex life: "He likes it in the morning and I like it at night." *Compromise!* Go for it one day in the morning, and one day in the night. If the kids are in the way, rent a motel room or meet at home during your lunch break. There is always time if you make sex a priority. I am sympathetic to the working mom trying to do it all, but this is just so darn important!

If you don't totally buy this, maybe Libby's approach to her eager husband is more up your alley. She negotiated a settlement with her husband on the sexual front. Libby, in her mid-thirties, prefers emotional intimacy after a long day as a form of support. "It is necessary for me to connect in that way," she explains. Her husband prefers sexual intimacy. Exhausted from work to the point where sexual excitement seems impossible, Libby often asks her husband, "Wait a minute. Are you sure you could have sex every day?" His standard reply is, "Well, maybe I could skip one day."

"I enjoy doing it," Libby tells me in the privacy of her office, "but it's not something that I need and look forward to every day. It has been our strongest area of disagreement over the years. It took a while before I realized it was okay for me not to want to have sex as often as my husband, that there wasn't something terribly wrong with me. Basically, we came to a compromise after much talking and arguing. He was pushing for more times a week. I was pushing for less. This was going on for a long time, but we didn't address it until after a few years. What we decided was to make Saturday night date night and then add one other time a week. It is also easier for me to have sex on the weekend when there is time to really enjoy it rather than just go through the motions. The way we worked it out is really fun for both of us."

If you opt for this solution, make sure that "date night" is *very* special. **Quality,** to an extent, can make up for **quantity.**

What happened to the thrill of a spontaneous night of passion? It just doesn't seem to figure in Libby's life-style at the moment. But even though she and her husband agree their arrangement has eased tensions, I can't help but think how overjoyed he might feel with sex every night—even if it is only temporary.

SEX EVERY NIGHT?

I became so curious about the prospect of sex every night that I decided to try it out on my own husband, who had made similar complaints in the past. I hate those accusatory remarks: "Do you know that it has been five nights since we had sex?"

"Who's counting?" I ask, listing in defense the nights he fell asleep before me on the couch or in bed. I suppose he thought I should have awakened him and initiated something.

So that's what I did, night after night after night. I went for overkill. I did worry that Mark might have a heart attack, what with racquetball and jogging, but he seemed healthy enough to take it. Let me tell you, he hasn't ever been so happy, so content, so ready to please. Incidentally, this playfulness seemed to put me in a pretty good frame of mind, too.

Mark knew exactly what I was doing. We both laughed over it plenty, but I was still determined to keep this up until he hollered, "Let me go." After two weeks, I told him if he complained of fatigue, I would sentence him to another full month. I think this helped to reduce his unhappiness over the temporary slight decline in our bedroom activity. What finally happened is that the kids came home for summer vacation, and all remnants of privacy were temporarily lost.

A MATTER OF PREFERENCE

The second-biggest gripe that came across loud and clear is men's desire for oral sex and their partner's unwilling-ness. These women, however, might be surprised to find themselves in the minority. One study I found reported that **over four-fifths of the married women surveyed regularly engaged in some form of oral sex!**

One can feel the sad resignation in a remark made by a twenty-eight-year-old husband whose wife isn't part of that majority: "My wife does not engage in oral sex. I have to live with it." I am sure he would rather be in the pants of the man who wrote, "The most romantic thing my wife did for me was give me oral sex. It was great!"

"I do it in a heartbeat," I was told by a woman in her fifties. "I overhear men my age talking, and I know they aren't getting it, but they would die for it. There is no way I wouldn't do it." For her and a whole gang of betting couples, oral sex is better than currency when paying off a wager.

Remember: Anything goes if you both like it, feel comfort-able doing it, and derive satisfaction from it.

KINKY IS OKAY

Here's one of my favorite stories about the peculiarities of one's sexual preferences. I heard it on the radio. Police were called to a home after neighbors heard cries for help coming from a nearby house. After forcing entry, officers found a woman tied to a bed and her husband in a Superman outfit on the floor moaning in pain. Evidently, he fell jumping to her rescue.

Often what is good for Susie and Bill, however, is not good for Joanie and Tom. Sex is a matter of personal taste. For example, Susie cited Bill's desire for her to "dress up" as one of the reasons for their divorce. Garters, scanty adornments, and seductive disrobing—a signal in many households that the night will hold delights—are distasteful to her. But Joanie, who says "dressing" is not her most favorite activity, but who also rates her sex life a ten, says this is something she occasionally performs for Tom because he loves it. In return, to make this a good sex life on both sides of the mattress, he is patient in engaging in lots of foreplay, which is extremely satisfying to her. Feminine nightgowns and dainty underwear—also sexy but more conventional—are preferences husbands and wifes easily live with.

X-RATED MOVIES

Another popular turn-on, X-rated movies, may not work wonders for both partners, even though many couples report that this is a popular way to spice up sex and learn a few new twists. Women in general are not as enthusiastic about this turn-on as men are. More often, the women prefer the quiet voice of a lover, sexy dialogue, music, or wine.

Rebecca found X-rated flicks to be a major turn-*off*, but she was willing to try them repeatedly because her husband, Mike, loved them. He would run out and rent a few as soon as the kids left the house for an overnight, get home quickly, light a fire, and pour two glasses of wine. But Rebecca wanted to scratch the flicks and keep the rest of it. She tried things Mike's way, but eventually she told him she didn't much care for the movie buildup.

"It was no use," Mike adds, "they had no effect on her."

"I could tell he was disappointed so I found some less-than-X-rated films that were steamy and acceptable. They turned us both on in a way that was less offensive to me," Rebecca reports happily.

Speak Out

There is no way to compromise or find the formula that works best for you and your husband unless you are willing to be honest and discuss it.

**COMMUNICATING YOUR SEXUAL DESIRES CAN BE STIMULAT-
ING AND WORTHWHILE.**

This isn't meant just for men. Sexual communication can be touchy, but if you are willing to be explicit about what you like and dislike, sex will be more gratifying for both of you.

Too bad the man and woman who wrote the following answers and who, I have a sneaking suspicion, come from the same household, didn't talk directly. *His:* "She was taught that it was her job to satisfy the man, but she will not be explicit about her needs and fantasies. She expects me to read her mind." *Hers:* "I'd like him to talk to me more during sex. I think it would help me express my needs and feel more involved."

Men can be shy about expressing their sexual preferences as well. A middle-aged man married almost thirty years wrote on his survey that he is uncomfortable telling his wife that he enjoys anal stimulation.

But one happy-go-lucky lady has no problems telling her man how she feels and uses these discussions to stimulate him. "On our way home from an evening out, or even on the phone, I explain in detail to David what kind of sex I want that night and what I have planned for him. It gets us both aroused, and we both know the sexual agenda. No, we don't seem to have a problem satisfying each other. There are no disappointments this way."

Once you have established some agreement on taste and

time, you still need to work together to keep your sex life exciting and out of the doldrums. Make sure there are ample menus and fancy new desserts you *both* find tasty.

Sometimes a change of menu is required before serving up sexual satisfaction. I'm sure you are not surprised that many married people complain that sex is routine, boring, and less exciting after marriage. "She used to be the aggressor before we got married and couldn't get enough right after we got married. She acted like I was the greatest lover she ever met. Now that she caught me, the magic is gone." Admittedly, you can't be Houdini all the time, but you can have fun proving the magic still exists. Take that famed family recipe and change the spices now and then. Perhaps routine is one of the reasons sex drops off by approximately one third after the first year of marriage, and why an attractive gray-haired lady over sixty said, "After thirty years, you need some toys and games to arouse your partner."

ADD SURPRISE

I love the story I heard about a somewhat reserved wife and her husband on a long train journey through Canada. After a week of the train's motion and the confinement of their compartment, she came out of the small private bathroom cubicle naked with a hat on her head, a flashlight in her hand, and said, "Stick 'em up." Her husband was startled, to say the least, but after the initial shock he knew what could shake the monotony of the ride.

You don't have to travel to enjoy this one. Appearing without a stitch on at the door, wearing a long, open shirt with nothing under it, or wrapping yourself with a great big red ribbon and a bow may not sound new, but *they are new unless you already did a version of them last night.* And I can almost guarantee you a response in your mate you haven't seen in a while!

Into nudity? If so, consider surprising your spouse by cooking in the buff. If you're like Eileen and Phil, you'll inevitably be eating a cold dinner.

She boasts, "I seduced Phil while someone was waiting in the driveway for him to go play tennis. I got him to come back into the house and into our room. I got him excited and made him have sex. After sex, he quickly put on his shorts and left." She follows with another surprise moment for the books. "It was Christmas morning. The girls were downstairs playing. We went upstairs for our showers, and it ended up with me getting Phil onto the closet floor. It was fun. The next day he called from work and said, 'I'm thinking of the closet.'"

Another appealing surprise came to me by way of one of my friends. Tell your husband you need to meet him at home during lunch because there is a flood in the basement (or pick any excuse that seems valid), but enjoy a matinee instead with lunch on the bed. Be sure you both have time for this one. It takes more than an hour!

Be on the alert for spontaneous surprises and take advantage of situations as they arise. A man with a grin from ear to ear told me that his wife insisted they make love in the backseat of the car while out in a snowstorm one night. Parked on the street, the foggy windows provided a degree of privacy.

BREAKING ROUTINES MAKES FOR MEMORABLE MOMENTS

In addition to the element of surprise, it is worth your while to seek inventive techniques for *breaking the routine pattern of sex* that you and your spouse generally fall back on.

If he is always on top, do a flip-flop and more. Need ideas? There are numerous graphic books out there with more

positions than you could dream of. Make a point of trying
them all. In fact don't try them all in that cozy bedroom with
the door locked. Whether you are escaping kids for privacy
or just opting for new spaces, go to the office on a Sunday,
visit a hotel on Friday, and try every room in the house when
you can. Jody was brave and tried a deserted green on the
golf course she and her spouse were playing one weekday
eve. What a sport!

**BREAKING PATTERNS PROVIDES THE POSSIBILITY FOR MEM-
ORABLE INTIMATE MOMENTS OF LOVE AND SEX THAT WILL
LAST LONG AFTER THE CLIMAX.**

Sally attests to that: "Bob always wanted to make love in
our boat in the bay. I'm not talking cabin cruiser here! One
afternoon there weren't too many other boaters out, so I told
him to lie down on the floor. I will try anything, but I don't
want others to witness it. Anyway, we had intercourse
quickly, and I looked up to find several sailboats well within
view. My first instinct was to start fabricating a loud story
for any possible onlookers and shouted, 'Where is my
contact,' as I crawled around naked on the floor," laughs this
woman with twenty-twenty vision. "I'm waiting for the
cabin cruiser to try this again, but we laugh about this every
now and then. It's a good story we don't tell too many
people."

**Bodies of water, of all shapes and sizes, are a reliable
resource for breaking the routine.** I met one other boater
who rented a glassbottom job for her husband to look at
more than the fish, and spoke to couples who take joy rides
on water beds. I no longer have to wonder why a home I saw
on a house tour several years ago had a bath tub in the
middle of the bedroom. I can now envision the antics of the
woman who said, "I treat my husband to candlelight bubble
baths with champagne and me." If you opt for this one, be

sure not to get so sidetracked you forget to blow out the candles. One brave husband wrote about a technique he couldn't tell me face to face. It seems he and his wife climb into the tub, and he positions her in such a way that the pressure from the water faucet acts as a stimulant on her clitoris.

From those lucky stiffs with swimming pools who look forward to summer, we hear of sex on new rafts under the stars. With the advent of so many in-house hot tubs, water offers many new tricky opportunities. Don't feel you have to spend thousands to experience this one. There are hotels that have suites with private hot tubs.

Hotels are really a great place for changing the pace of sex. Room service means you never have to get out of bed. If you want to add a few surprises to this one, put a package on top of his pillow. "Jay thought it was something from the hotel until he unwrapped it," says Cynthia who had gone shopping for some unbelievable nighties and sex toys.

Food and sex seem to be a natural mix. Several times a year when the opportunity arises for an evening of prolonged privacy, Stan and Elizabeth carry in a gourmet dinner with a number of courses. Spacing sex in between the appetizer, main course, and dessert gives them plenty of the energy needed for this marathon. I doubt that the chef who proclaimed that her chocolate cake recipe was better than an orgasm could top the sweets that conclude this meal!

Al enjoyed telling me about the night he came home from work, found the dining room table set with candles, music playing, and his wife naked. He doesn't need to know that this is Standard Operating Procedure for women who understand and use secrets. Let him continue to think his wife is the only woman who came up with this. "She handed me a towel," he began, "and told me to get undressed. We ate dinner, but she kind of teased me all through it. It was like a form of foreplay. It was a wonderful buildup. I'm never in the

mood just when I come home. Peg knows this and tends to
have to be romantic and set a sensual atmosphere. I really
liked it, and thought she must really love me to make me feel
so good. It's nice to know that someone cares that much."

Don't overdo this one, even though it is easy and the
results rewarding. It can become routine and lose its value
for breaking old patterns.

TAKING TURNS AT PLEASING

There is one basic point that still needs addressing. *In
many relationships, one person generally assumes the position of
pleaser—one who hands out most of the pleasures—and the other
the pleasee—one who receives most of the pleasures. You should be
aware of which category you fall into and make a concerted effort to
reverse them now and then.* Don't be complacent about this.
"Selfish sex" is okay for breaking patterns but not on a
regular basis. Resentment can rear its head if everyone's
needs are not tended to.

Here's how it works. If you know you have been slow to
climax and your husband spends a lot of time to excite you
with foreplay, one night tell him to lie back and enjoy two or
three times the amount of foreplay you usually give him. If
you have gauged it right, he will be ready to explode. "Take it
to the max," Stephanie told me. "Ronny kept saying, 'I won't
last. How much longer?' The countdown was tense."

If the tables need turning in your favor, speak up!

LONG-LASTING TREATS

A good way to incorporate all of the secrets we have been
talking about and to intensify a sexual experience is by
developing a thirty-day LOVE CALENDAR. I did this months
ago and gave it to Mark. I can't count the number of
unsolicited "I love you's" that were showered upon me
during that month. I think it was one of the best things I ever
did in breaking our sexual routine. I played it to the hilt from

LOVE CALENDAR—THIRTY DAYS OF SEX

SUNDAY	MONDAY	TUESDAY	WEDNESDAY	THURSDAY	FRIDAY	SATURDAY
	1 First Night Treat Let me guess 2 of your favorite tricks	**2** Anywhere but Bed Your Choice	**3** Rub-a-Dub-Dub 2 people in the tub	**4** A Quickie I'll take top bunk, you relax	**5** Ladies' Night Your turn to hand out the pleasures	**6** Fantasy Night Plan together during the previous week
7 Selfish Sex For *you*, dear!!	**8** A Treasure Hunt Exploration for hidden treasures and buried erogenous zones	**9** Bonus Night A half hour of your choice of foreplay; mix and match if you like	**10** Warm up with kisses and wine	**11** A night Off To prepare for a weekend whirlwind	**12** Lunch Break, TGIF Starts early	**13** Date Night A boudoir feast
14 Breakfast Sex You serve me coffee in bed, thanks!	**15** Selfish Sex For *me*, dear!!	**16** Double Your Pleasure 2 times please	**17** Careful, Touching only on this eve	**18** A Quickie, Build up steam for the weekend	**19** Your Choice 2 of 3 Massage, oral sex, hand job	**20** You Treat, I Treat Night at local hotel, dinner by room service followed by all-night gala
21 Night Off For good behavior	**22** New Position Anyone's suggestion	**23** Your Turn To be creative	**24** A Night of Pure Rest	**25** Wanna' Try Another Fantasy?	**26** My Turn For 2 of 3	**27** Show Stoppers I went shopping
28 You come, I come We both come together	**29** Movie Time	**30** You'll Never Guess	**31** Grand Finale I'll surprise you if you surprise me!			

the beginning. I called Mark during the day and told him I had a really great present for him. He couldn't wait. "What's this thing you have for me and when are you going to give it to me?" he asked the moment we saw each other that evening on our way to a concert he was not in the mood for.

I told him, "Don't worry, it will keep. It lasts a long time." Over a drink at dinner I handed him the paper and he loved it! It read "Love Calendar: because you're special and because our sex life is only as good as an eight." Halfway through the calendar month, it moved steadily up to a ten. The first night's activity said, "After Concert Reward, Your Choice." Is that killing two birds with one stone or what?

I have prepared a sample calendar for your use from the suggestions of the women and men I interviewed. (My calendar is private. Yours will be too.) I hope your husband enjoys it and calls you as much as mine did asking, "What are we doing tonight?" The anticipation and buildup before sex increases the desire and lengthens the pleasure. If you can't really deliver on this, an alternate route is a creative deck of cards from which he can pick pleasures sporadically. Calendars and cards also make fantastic birthday gifts for the man who has everything.

There is nothing wrong with proposing to your husband that he follow your lead and make up a calendar of delights for you.

FANCY NEW DESSERTS

Feeling pretty smug because you have tried menu changes before? Great, but don't forget *everyone can use some fancy new desserts*. There is no end to the creativity necessary to qualify as happy playful partners. Just give it a try.

A forty-year-old husband married eighteen years is bummed. "Prior to being married, experimentation played a big part in my sexual relationship with my wife. I feel that

now she associates marriage with maturity, and maturity with being conservative sexually. I don't!"
Well, in case she's reading, here are some remedies.

- **Anything is new if you haven't tried it.**
- **If you are racking your brain and can't come up with a thing, there are good books to get you started. Go through them and make a list of the things you want to try. Lots of couples get those X-rated films we discussed just for this purpose.**

I can't imagine any couple who doesn't need outside help in researching this one. A woman married over thirty years who told me she enjoys sex and is willing to try anything is not lackadaisical in her continuous investigation. One of her favorites is a book about driving your husband crazy in *bed*. She took it along for a road trip and read it out loud to her playmate. "We had to pull over and stop," she told me. Guess that bed isn't the only place it works.

Since the wife who gave me this one can't remember where she discovered it, I'll pass on the details. "There was an article on how to improve your sex life, and it was over a matter of a two-week period. It might have been called *Fourteen Days of Sex*. You were supposed to do things step-by-step, but you weren't allowed to have intercourse until the last night. It was supposed to teach you how to control your body, the highs and lows of orgasms. You were supposed to do massages but not touch any sexual areas of the body. By the fifth night we had sex anyway. It was one of our better times."

Set up your own NIGHT OF SEXUAL EXPLORATION. Make it a contest with ample prizes for the one who discovers the most new tantalizing areas on each other's body. No limits, and no rules provide the optimal conditions for this uninhibited treasure hunt.

You probably have many of your own fancy desserts. Those sexual fantasies you have been storing away, hiding from each other, is a place to begin. They don't always turn out great, but they are new and worth a try if you both seem to be of the same mind.

BACK TO THE CONSENSUS

Keep these three points in mind as you work on the secrets in this chapter:

1. Sex is a powerful, playful experience among happily married couples.

2. Sex should be mutually satisfying, creative, and expressive of love.

3. Reaching a sexual consensus is one step toward keeping love on track, altering the attitude of the man about the house and promoting a monogamous relationship.

Remember: *Sex affects your entire relationship so make sure you and your partner are getting enough equally satisfying sex to float you over the rocky passes.*

4

Love Talk, Small Investments With Big Returns

"The secret of my good marriage is that I court my wife," confides a man who is still happily married after thirty years. His terminology may be a bit outdated, but the essence of his words has survived the test of time. According to *Webster's*, those who go a courtin' shower flattery and attention on another person, wooing themselves into favor. Why abandon a strategy that makes you fall in love?

Love talk should be an integral part of your game plan long after the wedding bells have rung and the honeymoon photos are developed. It keeps you on your toes, reminds you to stay on your good behavior, helps you over the rough spots, and clearly demonstrates an appreciation for your spouse. Why should romance and all of the amenities end just because the realities of daily life set in? It hasn't for many of the married couples I interviewed who make a real effort to keep Cupid's arrow pointed in the right direction.

Chip, married for twelve years, is determined not to fall into a trap. Keenly aware of the absence of love talk in too many relationships he says, "The only thing wrong with marriage is that people slack off and treat each other like husbands and wives." If you and your husband are one of those couples Chip is referring to it's time for a mutual reeducation in love talk.

LOVE TALK

This section is dedicated to two women who suffered a terrible absence of love talk. In response to my question, *"What is the most romantic thing you ever did for your husband?"* a forty-year-old woman married nineteen years responded, *"I'm drawing a blank on this one."* A teacher with twenty-five years of marriage to her credit wrote me, "After thinking about this question for four or five days, I realized I need to work on this!"

LOVE TALK TAKES MANY FORMS:
1. **Love messages**
2. **Romantic overtures**
3. **Stimulants to stir dormant emotions**
4. **Responsive love acts**

Most of those who subscribe to these secrets say you get satisfaction back tenfold: Love talk begets more love talk. *It is a cold-hearted man (or woman) who finds it easy to resist passionate reminders of what he means to you.* You may choose to use love talk for pure pleasure, as a means of expressing love and appreciation, as a persuasive device, or as a practical tactic to cause contentment. Any which way, it adds sparkle to everything in your love life.

Large and Small Love Messages

Love messages, large or small, are gestures of generosity that bring enormous returns. They benefit the giver and the receiver.

Love talk worked its magic on a confirmed thirty-two-year-old bachelor who four years ago was in need of some management. "Meagan was determined to make things work after we started dating," he says about the woman who finally snagged him. "I wasn't so sure I was ready yet to settle down. But she knew I was the one she wanted. I couldn't help but be swayed by the energy she put into our relationship. She sent me packages, cards, and flowers. There were moments I thought I just wanted to date around, but she had a real sweetness and I finally had to admit I was attracted to her. I was always kind of looking for the perfect woman, sexually and otherwise. Meagan encompassed most of these things, maybe not in all aspects, but she sure came as close as anyone could. She hasn't stopped putting that kind of energy into our relationship."

WHY THEY WORK

Love messages keep veteran couples responsive and loving. A woman who admits to a deliberate daily regimen of love talk finds that the articulation of her feelings reinforces for her how much she cares for her husband. "There is no taking him for granted when I say those endearing words to him every morning. When I tell him I love him, it reminds me that I do and that I should."

"I-love-you" presents, candlelight dinners, daily hugs, flowers, and seductive grabbing motions are good for the home front, and love talk is also a prudent way of keeping in touch with your honey when he or she is out of sight. Plunging into the fun of love packages gets you both thinking about each other, a healthy habit for sure. Whether it is a note in a brief case, a card, a gift in an overnight bag, or a call at the office, love talk assures that you will be on your spouse's mind. If you are creative and playful, you may want to try one of Halley's tricks: Prepare a love tape for your lover. Put it in the car tape deck and wait for the surprise to unravel. Stick by the phone. You'll get a call when your partner arrives at his destination, if he can wait that long to tell you how much he cares.

"Things like that always put me in a good mood. They are very important," attests a man who missed these little touches in his first marriage and now enjoys their effects in his second.

Paula used to show Norman how much she cared by lighting a candle in the window when he came home from business trips, to show that he was special to her. He demonstrated his love the same way one winter evening when she was experiencing an acutely tough period with her son and was down in the dumps. She came trudging home from a school meeting to find a lit candle in the window and a warm dinner on the table.

Bee's Bait and Other Gifts

Herb had no problem demonstrating his appreciation after his wife, Bee, who had her own business and a large pocketbook, surprised him with more than a little bauble.

The Scene: The parking lot of a local restaurant one evening after dinner. Herb spots the car of his dreams.

"One of these days I'm going to have a car like that," Herb says, looking enviously at the sleek beauty on four wheels next to his tired wagon.

"Why don't you get in?" Bee suggests.

"Oh, right. So the next guy out of the restaurant can throw me out."

"Well it's yours," Bee says coyly, dangling the keys in front of her disbelieving husband.

When I asked Bee how he showed his appreciation, she grinned like the cat that swallowed the canary. "He made love to me all night," she said.

Bee's story makes me think the man who told his wife he wished she had nude modeled the fur coat he bought her got shortchanged. I know a couple of ladies who would accommodate him and even wear the coat in the raw to the grocery store. I wonder what would happen if one of them showed up at her husband's job that way just to say "Thanks a heap!"

Love messages don't have to be elaborate. If you have forgotten the value of little gifts, show up with some new golf balls, a gag T-shirt, or a slice of your spouse's favorite type of pie. Just make sure the gift reflects some insight into what your partner likes so he or she can recognize the thought behind it. This may seem commonplace, but it's not if you are on the receiving end.

The lesson is clear from a woman who inadvertently bought her husband a small love package. She was at a men and women's boutique and spied a great-looking fishing cap with a patent leather beak and a khaki twill base. She thought her husband might like it, and if he didn't, she would gladly appropriate it for her own use. When she gave it to him with a little note that read, "To the best fisherman in my life," the gesture seemed too small to be important. Later that night when he said he really appreciated the hat, she thought he was joking. "No," he said. "Not many guys have a wife who thinks about him and would do such a nice thing."

Even though the bait was not intentionally set, he took it. It was a good reminder to her and all of us that we should put that line out more often!

BE ENCOURAGING

Never, but never, miss the opportunity to show your spouse how much you enjoy a gift that was meant for you, even if you get a tennis shirt and you don't play tennis, or you love red roses and keep receiving African violets. Encourage your partner to use love talk. **Make an adequate fuss or this could be the last love package, large or small, that you find on your doorstep!** (You will soon know enough secrets to remedy any improper selections anyway.)

Sammy derives great pleasure from giving love talk to his wife by going to all kinds of trouble planning fabulous anniversary outings. "I go to all the trouble because I really enjoy her response. When a woman responds by getting giggly and excited, a guy thinks, 'Wow, that was neat. What can I do the next time?' Her response is what turns everything on. If women could only understand and accept that all they have to do is respond the same way they would when their little boy brings something home from school. Simply get elated and excited. Nothing goes farther!" There you have it. Straight from a forty-year-old husband's mouth.

With a heart full of love, the next three types of love talk should be a natural.

Romantic Overtures

There is no doubt that an overwhelming number of couples I encountered use romantic gestures, a major category of love talk, as a prelude to sex. And we all agree on what sex means to a marriage relationship!

SHORT AND SWEET LITTLE NOTHINGS

When I asked women how they encourage or keep romance in their marriages, they admitted to sexy nightgowns, perfume, provocative underwear, seductive evenings, and nights away from the kids. Here is how it works for them. "It was his birthday," wrote a bride of three and a half years. "I waited for him to come back from work. We had set a date at a certain time. I undressed him and brought him into the bathroom where the tub was filled with warm water, fresh lemon and lime slices, and rose petals. I served him wine. Let him relax. I dried him, put on his bathrobe, and served dinner. We finished on the living room floor drinking wine, talking, and then falling asleep in each other's arms."

"The most romantic thing I have ever done was for Bruce's thirty-seventh birthday," explains Linda. "I took him to a cabin for a weekend. No television. No electricity. No distractions. I took all the food and a little nightie. We stayed in the cabin all weekend."

What kind of impact did this have on Bruce? "The weekend made me feel great," he says. "It was a real nice present. I didn't have to do anything. Everything was arranged. I was surprised she went to this much effort. I probably didn't show her just how much I appreciated it. But we were both in a good mood for at least a month."

Simple getaways provide the necessary privacy for romantic overtures and are worthwhile at any time. A young medical professional says this type of private time enables her and her husband to make love day or night. A game of tennis followed by a shower is often a natural prelude to an afternoon of love making.

Husbands aren't necessarily concerned about where the idea for your romantic gesture originates—just how it proceeds. Lucas guesses that his wife must have been talking to some of her friends and found out that she was one lucky lady to have a husband—younger at that—who still found her attractive and worked hard to provide for her. Her show of gratitude included wearing a red teddy to greet Lucas at the door. "You bet these things make a difference," he says. "What a surprise!"

Roxanne's Tonic

Roxanne was game for an elaborate scheme and thought her romantic overture would serve two purposes: 1) quench any thirst for an extramarital affair; and 2) fill glasses to the brim with a flavorful new drink of romance.

"Every time I heard one of my friends or one of their husbands was having an affair, I would tell Donald about it. I did this as a form of therapy, but I started to notice he became very interested in the details. I think he felt he was missing out on something. This could have turned into a dangerous practice. So I decided to play a charade and be his mistress for a while. I invented some ground rules. I would never play mistress at home. It would have to be something we did away from home to get the real forbidden flavor of it. It seems strange, but I thought: **If he wants to know what it would be like to have an affair, it's better for him to have it with me.**

"I saw the excitement in his eyes from the time I mentioned that his mistress was going to call, and he loved the flowers in the hotel elevator. He was pretty concerned about how I knew so much about day rates, though. It's kind of kooky, but we are both so attentive at our rendezvous that I don't think either one of us wants to give them up. We each know who we are. It's just a game we like playing for the moment."

Not a bad suggestion for love notes guaranteed to stir slumbering emotions either!

Stimulants to Stir Dormant Emotions

If you are suffering signs of marital stagnation—a deteriorating goodbye kiss that feels like the brush of a feather, a half-hearted "luv ya," a muffled night repose into a pillow by a semiconscious spouse—*get to work on some love talk to reawaken some of the passion of your youth!*

My Own Secret About Jealousy

About six years ago my relationship with Mark was registering a slow, comfortable simmer rather than a mad, passionate boil. Then we each bumped into old flames.

Thirty-five thousand feet up in the air aboard a 747 over the Atlantic Ocean, my husband sat engrossed in his newspaper. Next to him, I fidgeted restlessly waiting for the beverage cart. I looked up to assess the progress of the flight attendants and noticed a gentleman in a suit assisting her who introduced himself to other passengers as Antonio.

Suddenly a bell went off in my head. My memory stirred, and I was a fresh college grad touring Italy. There I was sitting in my yellow bikini on the edge of a swimming pool in Rome being harassed by a very insistent and rude older man. A young, moderately attractive Italian male by the name of Antonio rescued me. To reward his gallant behavior, I joined him for an evening tour of Rome. Since he was the one and only continental man who crossed my path, every detail of this romantic episode clung to my then-impressionable mind.

Returning to the present, I blushed and told Mark, "Do you remember the Antonio I have been talking about for twenty years? Well, I think that's him," I said pointing ahead of us several rows.

Not believing the story in the first place, my husband motioned to bring over the man in question. "What can I do for you? My name is Antonio, and I am in charge of international in-flight training."

"Were you living in Rome in 1966?" I asked him. "Did you have a brother in the NATO forces? Was your favorite line, I mean song, 'Call Me'? And do you remember an American girl in a yellow bikini at the Rome Hilton pool? I was the yellow bikini," I gushed.

There was no doubt he did not have the foggiest who I was, but all the other identification was confirmed. Antonio's response to this giant coincidence was of no consequence to me. Really! It was my husband's reaction that counted. He suddenly became very attentive and looked at me closely. It was an attitude that followed him off the plane.

Several weeks later, I understood what he must have been thinking. A bubbly blonde approached him at a friend's party. "Do you know who I am?" she giggled childishly. "I was sure I was going to marry you after we met during my freshman year at college."

Blankly, my husband stared back at this woman while I looked at him with daggers. "No, I don't," he replied with little *savoir faire*. She produced clue after clue until finally he said, "Oh, yes, you were from Utah." Wrong.

Wrong or right, bikini or no bikini, blonde or brunette, French or Italian, Utah or Florida, my passion was aroused!

It was good medicine for both of us. I had forgotten just how appealing my husband was to me and to other coeds in our youth. I had forgotten this man did not always belong to me. I had forgotten how miserable I felt when we broke off our steady relationship for the twentieth time. I had forgotten how thrilled I was when we set the wedding date.

He seemed a little more precious to me after this episode. And I had an insatiable desire for him. I couldn't keep my hands off him for months. I had shivers imagining that I might have let him slip through my fingers more than twenty years ago. I pictured myself sadly pining away for the one man I had loved in the world.

Each of us was now aware that jealousy set the stage for this rash of love talk that turned up the heat even more. When the effects of our encounters wore off, we each casually slipped in a little nudge about our past, just enough to light the embers but not extinguish the fire with our jealous natures. I have even been tempted to book another flight based on Antonio's schedule if things ever get too dull.

CAUTION: JEALOUSY CAN BE DANGEROUS

Lots of spouses out there acknowledge that jealousy can be flattering and may act as a catalyst to renew heightened interest in their partners. **Use it wisely for maximum results.** Instead of allowing renewed passion to take over, Keith and Fred's wives take jealous feelings too far and leave the love talk behind.

Keith says, "I used to think it was cute and kind of fun if

my wife thought someone was attracted to me at a party and got jealous, but she takes it too seriously and makes me feel untrustworthy."

Fred identified jealousy as one of the things he likes least about his wife. "Most of us experience some form of jealousy. If not, most likely there is no love involved. I think it is a matter of degree. The thing that bothers me most is that jealousy upsets my wife so much. I've tried to convince her that there is nothing to worry about, no basis for her jealousy. I finally had to give up. I was never able to convince her. Somehow, she either eventually let go of it or suppressed it."

Fortunately, Fred's wife was no stranger to love talk, and this one glaring fault did not overwhelm her efforts to be his adoring and loving third wife.

RESPONSIVE LOVE ACTS

Responsive is the key word here. There is nothing that has a greater impact on trying to create a permanent match than responding to your partner with genuine love, respect, and appreciation.

SHOWING KINDNESS

Juliann completely understands the essence of responsive love acts. She agrees that they must be performed out of love, not duty. No one derives real happiness from them any other way. Married the first time for fifteen years, she looks back and says, "I tried like a puppy to make my husband happy. I thought that was the role of the wife. He expected me to do things for him and was furious when I didn't perform." Now remarried for several years, following an eleven-year stint as a single woman, Juliann has a healthier perspective toward love talk. "I do things for Chris because I like him. It can be going somewhere with him or baking his favorite pie. I know if I don't do them, it is okay too. But I think it is extremely important to show those little kindnesses to each other. I care enough about him that I want to spend time doing things for him. I think there is entirely too much selfishness in some marriages."

SAYING THANK YOU

Jake uses his own brand of kindness to repay his wife for the respect and consideration she has shown in welcoming his fourteen-year-old son into their home. "I tell her time and time again how much I appreciate what she is doing for me and Jimmy. I try to be real attentive to her and pitch in to do laundry and dishes. We work as a team, but still I know it is hard."

Whether there is Jake's son to deal with, his mother's care to oversee, or his wife's father who was seriously ill five years ago, the duo can count on each other to help. Some husbands and wives make the mistake of underestimating their partners' needs and miss the opportunity to prudently indulge one another in the kind of love talk that conveys appreciation and gratitude.

PUTTING THE OTHER PARTNER FIRST FROM TIME TO TIME

A big issue is always the in-laws. I cringe when I hear of couples who do not attend family events together because they just can't take another hour of that woman called his or her mother. Now, Bob, Dick, and Martha may not express any dissatisfaction when Sally, Jane, and Harry do not accompany them to their folks' houses—but come on. Imagine how much better they would feel if they had loving partners who made this part of their life easier, simpler, less complicated, less stressful.

Putting your spouse's needs first from time to time conveys a wealth of love.

ACTING IN A CONSIDERATE AND APPRECIATIVE FASHION SHOWS YOU ARE GETTING THE HANG OF LOVE TALK.

It is also mandatory if you are going to create the most rewarding permanent, lifelong love match.

"Tom treated my mom like a queen when she lived with us for nine months," reports Jennifer. "I always tried to let him know he was good through all of that."

The message was received. "I can tell Jennifer appreciates me," confirms Tom.

Now that's a smart wife. What better motivation for all of the things he enjoys doing and providing for her? Jennifer may have found him considerate and giving from the first date, but her marriage strategy certainly has nurtured these fine traits. "He gives more than I do," says Jennifer. "He is always willing to go out of his way to make me happy, even if that means taking a video back at midnight. But I try to give back and take care of him mentally and physically. I don't take any of this for granted," she says, referring to the living room around her with a sweeping gesture. "My parents fought all the time and never did nice things for each other. I always said I was going to have it all!" It is out of love, appreciation, and a practical attitude that she enjoys keeping her big beautiful house clean, their two young kids in order, and his favorite foods on the table.

Jennifer was not always this little, loving angel. "I had to grow up," she confesses. "I never used to have any patience if he left things out or worked late. Even though I hate both of those things, I nag him less and make sure I give him a good life, too."

What a contrast to the scene I witnessed at a country club swimming pool one summer Sunday afternoon! A very spoiled, pampered young housewife stormed into the snack bar and pitched a loud, unbecoming fit in front of embarrassed bystanders. "I have been sitting and baking in the sun all day at the pool watching the baby while you have been playing golf and tennis with Mike [apparently their other child]. You take care of this baby!" she screamed, her golden, tanned face getting slightly flushed.

Perhaps if wedding vows included the phrase to "love, respect, and appreciate" each other, and a pledge that couples commit to the use of "responsive love acts," those who take the plunge into matrimony might have a better understanding of how to have a lifetime love affair.

Why and How You Can Enjoy the Power of Loving Communication

What love talk can and should accomplish is now apparent. What still needs clarification is that love talk is a total attitude. Don't ration your allotments. There is no way one can go overboard on love talk.

How Kelly's Clever Attentiveness Works for Her

I met a bubbly young blonde with one overall object. No helter-skelter love talk for her; no stabs in the dark; no miscalculated efforts. Her eight years of marriage read like a manual on love talk, much of which she had learned from her mother. Love talk is just what Mom prescribed for Kelly to handle the young man she brought home one weekend from college.

"I was worried about how it would work," admits Kelly's mom. Her son-in-law, Patrick, had witnessed only the unhappiness of his parents' union, and his brothers and sisters followed suit: They all divorced. "But Kelly has created a comfortable home, a real haven. I always told her that home is the place where men should feel the most comfortable and happy, and that she would have to go overboard with Patrick to teach him that and to make family life important to him. They are a real happy family, and that is largely due to Kelly."

Kelly's mom, married over thirty years, the mother of three, an independent career woman and the wife of a very satisfied husband, has earned the right to bend our ears a little with her philosophy. "A woman has to be clever in a relationship," she says. "Young women who don't think this is necessary are losing the battle," she emphasizes. With this in mind, we can begin to get a glimmer of the attitude that has made Kelly dedicated to using love talk and a myriad of Marriage Secrets.

Evidently Kelly has learned her lessons well. According to Patrick's testimony, "My marriage is a ten because Kelly makes it a ten. She makes me feel like she is glad to be married to me. I have never felt so loved before. She tries hard and is pleasing and is very affectionate. All her little tricks keep me straight. I am definitely content with Kelly. I couldn't love anyone more, and I wouldn't jeopardize that."

It took time, however, to get Patrick into this shape. "The minute I met him I was nuts about him," Kelly admits. "We fought because he wasn't ready to commit to a serious relationship. I said, 'Fine, you don't want to get married. I will date other people.' I had a boyfriend for three years, and he still called me. Patrick knew it. So, on the Fourth of July, I disappeared after a fight. There were all these parties I was supposed to go to with Patrick. I was always available even after a fight, but I went out of town and didn't tell him. He came to pick me up, and I was gone. He called everyone till he found out where I was. He was beside himself. He slept in the car outside of my apartment waiting for me. He has been great ever since."

There is never room for complacency in an intimate relationship, according to Kelly and her mom. *"You have to make men feel loved. It is the only way to have security. I never* let my guard down," says Kelly. Even at her youthful age, Kelly has become a master of love talk. It isn't hard when you are as crazy about your housemate as she is about Patrick.

Don't go overboard. Some of Kelly's early antics were a wee bit overzealous, even comical. A devout practitioner of never looking like a complete slob in front of her pal, Kelly overdid this during her first several months of marriage. "I would get up before Patrick in the morning, put on makeup, do my hair, get back in bed, and wait for him to get up," she confesses. Fortunately she has relaxed since then.

You probably suppose there is never a dull moment in this loving household. How true. Kelly is thinking all the time. "I play games," she reveals without embarrassment or hesitation. "I'm not ridiculous. *I kind of flirt with Patrick.* It is genuine. If we are out with friends at a restaurant and I see him come in, I still get that feeling that I did when we were dating. I usually tell him this. I went away for a week with the kids and my parents. When Patrick got there, I was all over him. I was nuts about him. He loves it when I act like that. That is the whole deal. It keeps our marriage fun and exciting. He probably knows what I am doing, but he likes it. When my three kids are a little older, I want to get a job in public relations. I am probably using a little of this on Patrick now."

Wild Antics

Here are some ideas from women who seem to have thought of everything. A few more of those wild antics ought to motivate you to come up with some of your own.

The frolicking and teasing never ends. Always warning her husband to be wary of the "Seven-Year Itch," Penny planned a surprise to mark the day of potential reckoning. "Today is the Day!" she announced to her husband that morning, packing him off for a memorable surprise trip. With three children now inhabiting their love nest with them, Penny and her husband have initiated Wednesday-night dates. They keep them even when they are pooped from their own hectic schedules.

Exhaustion is not a word in Brandy's marital vocabulary when it comes to dinners out or sex. "There are times I don't want to have sex but will even initiate it. I will think it has been a few days. I better keep this going." So one night to spice things up, Brandy called Joel to meet her at a hotel restaurant pronto. "I told him I had a baby-sitter for the evening. He was so excited he could hardly stand it. I told him at dinner that I had something exciting on under my clothes. I was even five months pregnant, but I had bought this sexy new underwear. We ate dinner and then went up to the room. We were getting undressed to take a bath together when the fire alarm went off. Our clothes were everywhere, and a voice was booming over the loud speaker, 'Go to the steps, please use the steps.' We ran down seven flights of stairs. I felt like everyone knew what we were doing up there. After we got outside, Joel turns to me and tells me I have my dress on inside out. My shoulder pads were flipping straight up. When we got back upstairs, we had wild sex and went home."

Not everyone puts so much energy into love talk or their marriage. But these wives admit that they have fun doing girlish kinds of things and can't understand the questioning looks they get from other women when they reveal their secrets. "They have such boring marriages and tell me this kind of behavior won't last, that it will wear off," Brandy says.

"Marriage might be a drag without all these games," says one very active player. *"All these little pranks allow me to be the monster I really am without disrupting the spell that my husband is under."*

Balance the Act

There is only one inherent danger in the overachieving player's insatiable drive to act out all kinds of love talk:

BE SURE TO LEAVE ENOUGH ROOM FOR YOUR SPOUSE TO GET IN ON THE ACT. LOVE TALK SHOULD NEVER BE SPOKEN ONLY INTO ONE EAR.

I sure hope that the men who couldn't come up with one tiny example of using love talk, or the guy who admitted that he had been stagnant in this department since his honeymoon, were merely experiencing a lapse of memory when I posed the question. As the recipient of love talk, I can only tell you I would never want to live without it!

Although I was not able to find one husband who could compare with Kelly's sustained zest for love talk, I did speak to a good many happily married men who seemed to have the knack for coming up with a variety of intermittent love talk. Aside from plentiful flowers, surprise parties, daily hugs, repeated pronouncements of their love, and unexpected tokens of appreciation, there are a few more creative secrets that are worth revealing.

RANDY is definitely a romantic who wants his wife to know how very much he cares about her. He has been steadfast over the last fifteen years in acknowledging in some romantic way the anniversary of their first date. He has also learned the value of love talk to weasel out of uncomfortable but unavoidable situations. Randy demonstrated a sensitivity to his wife's unhappiness over a prolonged business trip. "I left about twenty-five notes all around the house. Each one had a message of love and a clue to where to find the next note. The last message told her to play a certain song that holds a sentimental meaning for both of us."

KENNETH'S wife had a difficult pregnancy, complicated by

an overactive toddler running her ragged at home. Before she even delivered, he decided he wanted to show a special expression of his love for her when she came home from the hospital. To accomplish his mission, he purchased several pieces of jewelry, wrapped them elaborately, and put them in strategic places around the house where she was sure to find them.

MY OWN HUSBAND must have gotten enough pleasure out of my candlelight dinners to reciprocate by surprising me with one after a particularly harried day. The pride he took leading me to a table set with candles, flowers, linen napkins, wine, and a warm meal was amply apparent from his smile.

PICK A SECRET

You should be full of ideas by now. Move ahead systematically.

1. Test your talents and monitor the results.

2. Use the powerful secret ingredients of love talk in your mix of Marriage Secrets to help revive and solidify your partnership.

3. Advance at a moderately slow pace, unless you are willing and able to keep up the racetrack speed of someone like Kelly. Nothing is worse than turning love talk on and off like a tap.

4. Try a secret from each of the categories of love talk, spacing them a week apart.

5. After you see some real progress, begin to suggest ways in which your spouse can heighten the return on your love talk investment. This will spur you on to indulge your relationship with rigorous and thoughtful new secrets.

Before you know it, you will both be speaking the language of love, giving each other the warmth, respect, and appreciation basic to any relationship built to last a lifetime.

5

Stroking and the Ego Connection

Affirming your partner's good qualities, his or her strength and importance to your life, is nourishing to your marriage. This caressing, soothing, gentle, emotional, and physical handling provides food for the ego. When dispensed in just the right amounts, stroking not only helps to ensure that your partner will keep coming back for more but that neither of you will need to go elsewhere for comfort, love, sex, support, or a positive self-image!

MAKING THE EGO CONNECTION

Everyone needs to be reminded of how wonderful they are. Men, in particular, need to feel they are special. If they don't get these vibes from you, make no mistake about it—they will look for them elsewhere. No one is exempt. The healthy condition of your partner's ego is one of your most important concerns. That is, if you are willing to really work at making this a permanent love relationship. Consciously or unconsciously, women in happy households regularly give off signals to their guys that make them feel powerful, successful, and desirable. All three qualities are vital *ego builders*.

84

An enduring testimonial to the ego connection came from seventy-seven-year-old Sam, married fifty-six years, with a *ten and a half* level of marital satisfaction to his honey. When asked if his wife, whom he says he loves one hundred percent, takes care of his emotional needs, he responded, "What do you think? Positively!" There is no way his wife, "the love of his life," slipped up in this arena. "I feel like I am everything to her," says Sam, proud to admit that he is still on that "cloud ninety-nine" he ascended to when his wife first professed her love at the tender age of sixteen.

TO MAKE THE EGO CONNECTION AND LOVINGLY NURTURE YOUR SPOUSE—INSIDE AND OUT—YOU MUST WORK CAREFULLY AND WISELY, RECOGNIZING ALL HIS OR HER FRAILTIES AND INSECURITIES.

If done well, this can be mutually beneficial. If done poorly, excessively, or not at all, this effort can be disastrous, as we will soon see.

According to the women in this survey, husbands are most insecure about the level of their economic success. Whether justified or not, they are rarely satisfied with their current earning capacity. And believe it or not, the close runner-up in this department is men's worries about losing their lady love. In third place was a deficiency in self-confidence that manifested itself in social situations.

Recognizing how vulnerable your husband can be, even if he looks like a professional linebacker and acts like Atilla the Hun, should motivate you to accept the updated adage that a *man and woman's* home is their castle. After all, where else in this competitive, grueling, dog-eat-dog world, can either of you be accorded a position of royalty? Furthermore, your castle should be absolutely the *one and only* place your man feels that he is king and where the woman beside him is the queen. When you accept the wisdom of this powerful secret,

you will be ready to make the ego connection and award
your spouse a status of royalty.

The Royal Treatment

All too often we tend to overlook and minimize the impact
of little strokes. Don't make that mistake! Unless your
partner is a real oddity, he or she needs your *admiration,* your
attention, your *pampering,* and your *respect.* **Men will even
admit they don't care how blatant the dishing out of sweet
accolades are. They just want them to keep coming.**

OBVIOUS PATS

Don't neglect to use simple loving strokes. Tell your
spouse how great he looks even if you've just run into his old
buddy who has the hair your hubby has lost and lost the beer
belly your hubby has found. Remember, your young or
middle-aged resident jock likes to be told he's great after a
Sunday racquet ball victory that comes to you complete with
play-by-play description. Nothing gets to the core of the
male ego more, or goes further with a man, than talking
about his accomplishments in the presence of others. And
for heaven's sake, act proud to be with him.

SHIRLEY doesn't beat about the bush; she gives Arnie just
what he wants. "I treat Arnie like a king, literally and
figuratively," she says with the authority of forty years of
marriage. "He always gets the best cut of meat. I know he
likes to be catered to. Sometimes he doesn't even know I'm
doing it, but I'm the one who benefits." Treating her man
like royalty has *helped to make Shirley the queen* with all the
trappings of her power.

BETH begins the royal stroking the moment Lenny walks
through the door. "I get home before Lenny does. No matter
what kind of day I've had, and even if I don't mean it, I stop
what I am doing for a moment when he comes home and give

him a kiss. I tell him I've missed him. It never fails to bring a smile to his face. He once brought someone home for dinner, and I went through my usual routine. When I went in the other room, I heard our guest tell my husband with envy that if he was treated like that, he might make a point of coming home every night. According to what my husband had already told me, that would be quite a switch for this Casanova."

SUBTLE SOOTHING

The wives who keep tabs on their men's morale and act on this information belong to a corps of ego boosters. Peg was particularly aware of Howard's fragile ego when he decided to interview for a new job. "Several times Howard came home really down in the dumps. I knew he thought he was going to be warmly received by many companies. When it didn't work out like that, he got depressed and embarrassed. I bought him little gifts to show him how important he was to me. I also put the kids to bed early and didn't work overtime for a while so I could be there if he wanted to talk. I think this helped him stay on at his old job and feel happy about it too."

TAMMY was willing to tell us that she does get a little tired of cheerleading. Her husband's incessant grumbling about not being rich enough seems ridiculous to her at times. *"Sometimes I lose my patience, but I hold my tongue.* Greg needs someone to pick him up. He is particularly aware of the neighbors' riches and wants an even bigger chunk to his own credit. He has lots of insecurities. So I do a lot of cheerleading. His complaints are predictable. They usually start off like, 'We haven't come any further in five years.' I tell him we are doing great. I will point out the nice house we live in and his successful law practice. But he needs to be wealthy. I really think he has an obligation to keep himself mentally healthy, because I don't need another child. So I tell him to stop worrying and enjoy himself."

Tammy says *there is a reasonable limit to her stroking*—and there is. The next two tales of woe show us that.

BE WARY OF RAISING YOUR PARTNER'S PEDESTAL TOO HIGH

The object of stroking is to nurture a healthy, independent ego. But miscalculating the fragile nature of the male ego has the dangerous potential of weighing his crown with a burden that may be too heavy to handle.

What Happened Because Glenda Couldn't See Her Husband's Instability

I was at a cocktail party out of town where I encountered a prime example of this delicate issue. My hostess knew that I was writing a book on marriage and had given me several personal clues about guests who might make good candidates for an interview. It was up to me to make my intentions known. I identified a couple that had suffered a major trauma a few years back. I was intrigued by how attentive they were to one another, holding hands and sticking close together. I had my chance to talk to the Mrs. when the Mr. left her side to get a refill of his drink.

I approached this woman quickly before her husband's return since my policy generally is to interview women first, sometimes with and sometimes without the knowledge of their husbands. I introduced myself and wasted no time explaining my mission, promising total confidentiality and anonymity. She agreed with little hesitation but qualified that this would be our little secret. No husbands, please!

When I went to her home several days later, we casually sat in her large Florida-style kitchen sipping coffee and getting to know one another before I began the process of excavating the buried feelings of her private life, which had taken a turn for the worse several years earlier. The first part was easy. In twenty-six years of marriage, the first two decades had gone by without a blemish.

"Nolan was a very successful corporate attorney for a tremendous developer of planned communities. Our marital problems started as soon as he decided to buy his own real estate company. Once we had ownership, we thought, 'Oh boy, this is it. This is what we have been working for all these years.' Several months later, we realized what garbage we had bought. We had put up our entire life savings, plus borrowed a fortune, to finance a huge parcel of useless land. All of a sudden my husband was thinking, 'Maybe I'm not so smart.'

"He never admitted to me he had these doubts because I had him up there on a pedestal and whatever he said was gold. I trusted his judgment implicitly. Meanwhile, he is in a hole and digging himself deeper. But he never brought any of this home. You figure it's a new business with problems, but I had no idea how shaky it was. He never told me we were close to losing it.

"I never really knew what drove Nolan so hard in his work. It wasn't until after we separated that he admitted it was, and still is, the fear of failure that drives him. He is still struggling with the idea that he didn't have the affluent life-style growing up that most of his friends did. He suffers from the notion that he has to try harder than everyone else, because he doesn't feel equal. Believe me, I had no idea he felt that way! Six years ago, I never sensed his insecurities. We never communicated our feelings. I thought the marriage was on solid ground. But the fact that he didn't feel comfortable coming home to tell me this blew this cover.

"His project manager, a woman, was aware of what was happening to the business. He didn't have to explain to her what was going on. He had had an affair with her for about two years. He had nothing to hide from her and felt relaxed when he was with her. He thought he was in love with her. I had been afraid for some time that he was fooling around, but he would look me straight in the eye and tell me it was the business that made him so distant. But I didn't like how things felt. I was really getting mixed signals. There was sex but no love. He would throw in jabs that hadn't been there for twenty years. And yet, some days he would come home and hug me for no reason and tell me how happy he was that I stayed with him during the rough times. I finally couldn't take it any longer and told him I was moving out.

"He insisted that he be the one to do it. He told me he was going to a hotel for a few days. He needed to think things through. It came out later that the reason he wanted to leave first was that his *ego* couldn't take it if I was the one to walk out on him. He really was in torment and knew what he was doing wasn't right. He knew he needed room to get his head together. I'm sure the other woman was putting pressure on him too, but of course I didn't know any of this at the time.

"For three days after he left, I didn't know where he'd gone. I told our three sons he was away on business. On the third day, I started calling local hotels looking for him. I found the one he was registered at, but he wasn't in. I called all night. Finally he answered at eight in the morning."

At this point Glenda takes time to collect herself. The difficulty of going on is apparent before she tells me she still gets a bad feeling in her body when she recalls their conversation and the weeks that followed. The pain caused by Nolan's indiscretion still hurts five years later.

"I said hello," she resumed. "He acted surprised to hear from me. I asked him how he was feeling and expected him to say better, and that he was coming home. He said he wasn't good and that it was not an easy time. I thought, 'Oh, my God! What is happening?' I just had this real sinking feeling. I don't remember what I said. He says that I told him it was over. I do remember not being able to slam the phone down in his ear."

Within days, the details of Nolan's lengthy affair became

known. Without a hint that they would ever reconcile, Glenda announced her separation to her family and friends, a separation that lasted less than six months. How she came to terms with the blow she suffered is the subject of Chapter 10, "Drifting Apart and Back Together Again." What is important for us now are the things she found out about her husband during the months spent living without one another.

GLENDA'S LESSON: It does no good to shake your finger at Glenda and tell her she was much too trusting and naïve. She would agree with you on that score now. All of the signs of Nolan's infidelity and the problems within their marriage glare at her in retrospect. However, only conversation and intense listening—after they decided to talk to each other in an effort to patch things up—revealed the most important lesson about Nolan.

"He got all of his ego gratification out of his business," explains Glenda. "That is why he could tell me about the affair finally. But he couldn't tell me that the business was about to fail. He even admitted that he had hoped I would hear from someone else if he went into bankruptcy. I had always raised him onto such a high pedestal I never saw his vulnerability. I think I was a little blind. I don't think I was a very aware person."

By now you may be saying, "Come on, he was out there for sex, for lust. He has fed you a bowl of beans." Glenda herself will tell you that was her initial reaction. Her clergyman even told her, "Glenda, sex is a powerful thing." But no, after seeing the situation with the lights on, Glenda says it was a matter of ego. She is thoroughly convinced of that. In rebuilding her marriage, she was careful not to construct any tiny platforms that he could easily fall from. Her eyes are now wide open.

If this unsettling story distresses you, it should. If you are blaming Nolan, blame him for his indiscretion. But don't blame him for a fault in our society at large.

> MOST MEN HAVE BEEN TUTORED, REARED, TRAINED, AND
> BRAINWASHED INTO BELIEVING THAT IT IS UNMANLY TO
> BEAR ONE'S INSECURITIES AND BETTER TO HIDE ONE'S
> WEAKNESSES.

If you are blaming Glenda, don't. No one told her pedestals are dangerous. No one told her about egos, and that it is hazardous to have all of your husband's ego gratification tied up in one place. That is why it is particularly important to key in on the status of your partner's ego. The healthier your spouse is, the greater your chances that your relationship will stay fit.

How Marissa Overparented Her Husband and Created a Monster

Marissa started out her three-year marriage with the wrong notion about egos and admits that she got stroking and parenting mixed up. In the end, the little boy in her husband surfaced too often to handle.

"I became Stewart's mother when we started living together. He was twenty and I was twenty-one. I rescued him from a terrible situation at home. He wanted to be with me and came with me when I moved out of state. I felt responsible then for him to finish college. My family helped support him financially. I supported him emotionally and gave him the encouragement he didn't get from his own family. He saw me as his savior, and to this day what I have to say is considered gospel."

In her overzealous attempt to protect him and support him, Marissa started parenting Stewart. Instead of constructively stroking him and helping to build an ego rich in self-confidence and self-esteem based on his own handling of events, she took charge of his life and compensated for his insecurities through her own strengths. Marissa was even willing to become submissive and subservient to his immature mood swings. To put it bluntly, she *overdid* it, and

Stewart's weak ego gave rise to childish, rebellious, and even verbally abusive behavior that cost the relationship dearly.

"For two years in a row, Stewart created a problem over the Christmas party at my office," Marissa explains. "The first year I stayed home with him and felt terrible." The second year Marissa wised up when he pulled the same thing. "He got into a fury, had a tantrum like a child, and threw things in the kitchen. I went upstairs. I put on a black velvet dress. I came down and got into the car. He ran out and said if I would wait ten minutes he would go with me. That broke the pattern. It was a really big moment.

"I used to like the power I had over him," says Marissa, placing some of the blame for his malfunctioning ego on her own needs. "I liked being needed so much. But Stewart can be so taxing that I go to the office to relax," she told me only half in jest. "Everything I say can be monumental. He even asked me to verify that his personal feelings toward his family were legitimate."

It is not uncommon for husbands to enjoy mothering and for wives to dish it out. One such gentleman admits, "Men have very delicate egos. Even though we are mature, we still have little boys in us. It is important for women to understand this. My wife always indulges my opinions, even the ones that are rather childlike. I know I am acting kind of foolish, but she just lets it ride." Unfortunately, his wife has never told him just how annoying this childish behavior is to her. Of course, we all know about the Little Boy Syndrome, witness it from time to time, and act the mom at prudent moments. But I never thought so many men who exhibit this childish need to act spoiled, indecisive, immature, and irresponsible would acknowledge this to me with such little hesitation.

The question is: Do we want boys or men? The best marital relationships call for two mature adults. No wonder in the beginning Marissa's level of marital satisfaction was no more than a disappointing four. Today, with new insights, it is a seven, looking forward soon to the heights of at least an eight.

MARISSA'S LESSON: With the benefit of hindsight, Marissa is more realistic in her approach to Stewart and strongly advises against mothering. To put things on the upswing, Marissa had to go back to the beginning. She had to nurture that old male ego at the same time she tamed the monster she had inadvertently helped to create.

Although it got pretty rocky for a while, she wasn't ready to call it quits. "Stewart has a number of saving graces. He is bright, fun, interesting, does things I would never think of, and he loves buying me great gifts. I've gone pretty far to make this marriage work. It is getting much better. The peaks and valleys are starting to even out.

"Stewart needs to see to some of his own insecurities himself. I am beginning to set boundaries and limits on how far I go in taking care of him. A counselor I went to for six months helped me get a different perspective on the situation. She made me see what I was doing and that I could make the choice to continue babying him or walk out and go to a movie. Protecting him is not wise or productive."

Instead, Marissa uses secret prudent stroking to help him overcome his shyness in social settings. "I usually do reward him once he gets out. I try to make an effort to steer him to people he knows and who make him feel comfortable. That helps."

When Stewart pouts about his work load, Marissa is right there to tell him, without going overboard, "Honey, I know you can do it." No more staying up all night to write cover letters and thank-you notes when he decides to engage in a new job hunt, she says.

Bad patterns are hard to break, even in a thirty-year-old male. Stewart still tries to provoke Marissa into responding when she refuses to solve a problem he should work out himself. Fully aware of the dynamics, Marissa now answers these questions with a noncommittal, "I don't know." She would rather endure his complaint that she is "cranky" than sound like a parent by coming right out and saying, "Honey, I want you to figure it out on your own."

Now that Marissa has her own ego in check and doesn't require or want Stewart to be so dependent, they are both making strides in their personal happiness and in their love relationship.

Stroking interspersed with too much mothering can result in the creation of a dependent, adolescent-like male. Ego-building binds your spouse to you in a loving, healthy, appreciative way. Too much mothering fosters a dependence that becomes wearisome for you and generates anger in your spouse.

EGO COMPLICATIONS IN THE NINETIES

The times they are a changin', and with male egos still so wrapped up in their jobs, a new dimension to the ego connection is making its way over the horizon. One of the most fundamental changes in today's marriage relationships is the preponderance of married women in the work force who provide financial support to the family. The implications are far reaching, even threatening, to the male ego. According to the 1991 figures from the Bureau of Labor Statistics, one in four working wives now earns more than her husband. The statistics are the highest in wives between the ages of twenty-five and thirty-four, a time when many marriages are fresh and mates are inexperienced in dealing with matrimony and secrets.

The nineties woman needs to develop more wisdom in dealing with the nineties man, who, though evolving, is still lagging behind in his acceptance of women's increasing power. So pay attention to the prudent, artful behavior outlined in this chapter. **If you want to have it all, there is no way to do it without enlisting the support of your man's ego.**

Several Women Offer Their Views

IDA, sixty-seven and married quite happily for forty-five of those years, feels comfortable assessing the failure of her son's first marriage. "Basically, things have not changed when it comes to handling a man. They still have those egos. A man has to feel like he is in charge even if he shares that power today. That is what caused my son's divorce. He no longer felt in charge. His wife was a vice-president in an investment firm. I think if she had built up his ego somehow, they might have saved the marriage. A man's ego needs tender love and care. I always told my husband how great he was and asked for his help even if I didn't need it."

MARY JANE, a forty-something mother of two, owns her own business and is a partner in a blissful marriage. Her twenty-eight-year relationship with Ed does not go unnoticed by her friends. "Mary Jane runs the show. She knows how to work her husband," they say. Obviously, there is nothing passive about this woman who knows her own mind and that of her husband as well.

Mary Jane hopes to be able to convey some of her secrets to a young daughter-in-law entering the family picture. "My husband is pretty spoiled. It comes naturally to me to flatter him, hold his hand, and make him feel he is terrific. He likes it, and I get it back. He does thoughtful things for me. I sense that he really cares, and we are good friends. You can't buy these things. I am old-fashioned in that I wait on my husband. My daughter-in-law is reluctant to do that. Instead, my son waits on her all the time. He needs back up at home. I think eventually he will resent her for it. There are limits."

Don't start arguing with me yet. Don't put up your defenses. Wait until you see the whole picture.

HANNAH, a corporate president, complains, "I have two women in my company who are finding it hard not to intimidate the men they date and are having a tough time

finding someone to share their lives. It seems women almost
have to apologize for their high incomes and success." On
the other hand, this woman has found the magic formula
and agrees with me that **part of the problem lies in
forgetting to leave the executive at the office.**

Formulating love relationships and successful marriages
has been a greater challenge for women of her generation,
Hannah believes. "The reason is that *Mom said the man will
support you and you will take care of the children. That's not the
way it worked out* for me and many others. All of a sudden you
are trying to figure out how you are going to deal with
something quite different. There is no school to go to for
this, no text book. *You just have to learn each day and through
each encounter.*"

Hannah has a great marriage, exceptional career, and
earns more dollars and cents than the man in her life. What
are her secrets?

Striking the Right Balance

Hannah and her husband, Cal, have been able to have it
all in the last five years—gratifying careers, family, love,
and play time.

He Keeps Her Ego in Check and She Doesn't Step on His

This is a significant accomplishment for Hannah and Cal,
especially since he earns less than his wife and is employed
by the company she heads and owns.

Cal and Hannah met through a mutual friend after each of
their attempts at marriage had failed. Hannah's ex couldn't
seem to accept an aggressive, successful wife. Cal, on the
other hand, lived with a woman who was as productive as
he but had less zest for life as a whole. When they met,
Hannah's retail and mail-order gourmet food business was

making great strides, and Cal was satisfied with his lucrative factory rep job. With an eye for business, he saw an
opportunity to expand her business into the wholesale and
corporate marketplace. They hoped it would speed them
toward achieving their common goal of financial security.

If you think marrying the boss didn't carry the potential
for trouble despite the benefits he could bring to the business, think again. Cal was and is accused by others of taking
a free ride from his spouse. But since this was a sensible
partnership on both sides of the bargaining table, one of the
first discussions Hannah and Cal had before the business or
personal knots were tied was about his ego.

"I think you hit it right on the head," Cal told me right off
the bat, explaining the basis for their successful marriage
and working relationship. "It is about ego, but I can put it in
check when necessary. I had to come to terms with it because
Hannah's business was already established by the time I got
here."

Hannah admits that their mutual respect and sensitivity
make the business and love arrangement work. When I
called and asked her for an appointment and told her that
the topic of our conversation would be how she handled her
husband's ego, she replied immediately, "CAREFULLY."

In person she added, "I tell Cal that sometimes our
colleagues don't see the bigger picture." Referring to the fact
that it took several years before his division proved its
worth, she is careful to point out that the rumors about his
free ride were hurtful and false. The proof is that his
corporate sales division is so successful now it may overrun
the retail and wholesale division. "My advice to him is
always to be patient," she continued, admitting that talking
to him about the way to do his job is a very touchy matter.

The situation Cal walked into may have been easier for
him to take than it would have been for other guys because
he had already proven himself to be a "hustler" in the
business world. He was self-confident. "But there are
times," he reveals, "that my ego gets a little stomped on and

I'll go home really pissed. I try to take a little time to think about it and its overall meaning. *Who am I being judged by? Is this worth getting mad about? What will I gain if I yell and scream about it? I realize there are things that can't be changed and I'm willing to accept this part of the total package.*'

Cal is not reluctant to admit that in some working arrangements his wife has accommodated his personality, workstyle, and needs. Their differences in management styles, he says, would probably make it impossible for him to work for Hannah if this had been purely a career decision. But working together gives Cal the opportunity to build their future together, the freedom to manage his own schedule, the liberty to pursue his individual interests, *and the time to help with parenting, household chores, and grocery shopping.*

Hannah makes some special concessions in order to keep Cal and his ego healthy and happy.

"When I came to the conclusion that managing people and being a hands-on detail manager wasn't going to work," explains Cal about their early business relationship, "we decided we basically needed to find the right area for me to participate in. I moved into the wholesale side of it, which is back to being pretty much a lone ranger when it comes to selling. I moved out of the building and attended staff meetings occasionally. I chose to work here because I can act independent of the business and because I am good at going out and finding customers. As long as I stick to that and bring in dollar volume, I don't care what anyone thinks. I have no desire to be the boss."

Hannah is smart enough to recognize where Cal's ego gratification lies and to put her ego aside and not force him to operate solely by her rules. It is this same sensitivity that makes her more accepting than most women would probably be of his passion for car racing. "I think each guy, if they are involved with someone successful, needs something they can hang their hat on," affirms Hannah. Racing provides Cal with an extra measure of ego gratification, they both agree.

Cal appreciates Hannah for leaving her ego and business persona at the office. "She is a tough woman. She will rip off your head and spit down your neck. That is what makes her successful. She plays tough. She is sort of schizophrenic. No one would believe me that when she gets home she turns the business side off. The only time I have to keep her ego in check is when she makes judgments about people without digesting all the facts. People with strong egos think they are right all the time. I just offer suggestions."

A big secret that Hannah seems to have under her belt is Cal's belief that **just because some of the rules have changed doesn't mean that the intimacy between a man and a woman in a love relationship has been completely altered.** Cal may be willing to do most of the grocery shopping and assume his fair share of the baby-sitting, but he believes "a woman still needs to be a woman in a relationship. I need a woman who can show admiration, who makes me feel like I'm hot stuff once in a while. Some of that may be acting but it is gratifying. *What's gained if people succeed in business at the expense of a happy relationship?"*

The CEO side of Hannah would tell you she has learned to balance her priorities and manage her time by giving her whole attention to the business during seasonal peaks, to her toddler son during off months, and to Cal intermittently during the year. *The warm and loving side of her would tell you,* "We get up in the morning, take a shower together, and talk. We try to have lunch together, and we never refuse one another's sexual needs. The little moments during the day are what he needs from me."

MAKING SACRIFICES FOR LOVE

Marcie and Abbey's Generosity

Marcie's remarks to her daughter, Abbey—who is engaged and completing her medical training—reveal much about her own marital relationship in which love compels her to take stock of her husband's ego: "Abbey and her fiancé applied to the same hospitals for their residency and were both accepted. Abbey was also accepted at a more prestigious institution, but Jeff wasn't. She struggled over what to do and asked my husband and me to give her our opinion. I told her that as a professional, she was making a decision that could compromise her career; but if she felt she wanted to do that for love, that was fine. She should just know that. I think she was really tortured, and I think her decision for them to be together was the right one. I would have thought that as a modern woman she would have gone the other way. But she thought about what it meant in terms of love, and that's what she wants. That's the most important thing."

I pressed Marcie to be more definite about what she really thought. "Did she do the right thing in your book?" I asked.

"Unequivocally, it was the right answer for them. She was able to do it because she has such a good sense of herself," she retorted. In exploring the issue in greater depth, Marcie admitted that her daughter, who is much like herself although she appears to be more overtly aggressive, always wanted to marry a man like her dad. That was exactly the type she picked—a warm, loving, supportive family guy who will be proud of her and her accomplishments. Now mom and daughter are off on the same footing, using the love they have for their mates as the guidelines for their actions.

You can easily sense the love, concern, and consideration that Marcie has extended to her husband before and after she started her own career. "I always supported Henry. Early in our marriage I was willing to move wherever he wanted. If it didn't work out, okay. It's no disgrace. I believed in him. I never wanted him to say, 'What if?'"

Astute in her ability to read people, and especially attuned to her husband's self-doubts about his ability to measure up to his older brothers, Marcie has always given

Henry every opportunity to show his worth. When he
openly berates himself for not completing college, Marcie
won't let him get away with it. "Wait a minute," she says.
"Because you didn't finish school you're not as smart as your
brothers? If you went back today and finished, you would do
just as well as they did. You didn't know what you wanted to
do. I'll put you up to them anytime." It has always been
Marcie's aim to build Henry up, and in return, she sees all
the support she gives him coming back to help her in her
own profitable career.

In my view, as an objective observer of her marriage, I
think Henry is able to boast about her successful public
relations and marketing firm—which brings in the largest
portion of the couple's annual income—because **his ego is in
good hands.**

To make this part of their history short, suffice it to say
that twelve years ago Marcie went out and got a job at a
public relations and marketing company, that she left six
months later (taking a majority of the clients with her), built
her own lucrative company, coped with her husband's loss of
employment, and funded a new business for him. Any of
these events could plunge a marriage into troubled waters.
But not Marcie and Henry's. Why? Number one, because
"Henry's love and pride make it easier," says Marcie. *Her love
and respect for Henry prompt her to use adequate ego management
to make sure Henry is feeling okay about himself.*

Number two, **even** with so many cards in her hands,
Marcie remains a woman with a relatively small ego and no
need to prove she's the boss. In fact, she says that in their
private lives, she and Henry carry on a rather traditional life-
style. Marcie is also a woman who requires the support and
stroking of her husband. "He is the rational one, the one
with clarity. He can easily suggest a way to handle a problem
I encounter at work. We are a team." Perhaps this is why
Henry is so proud of their success. Sounds as if this is

indeed one strong partnership, no matter who tips the scales from time to time.

CREATING YOUR OWN SUCCESS STORY

Now it is your turn to create a success story.

- **Identify your partner's insecurities. You may even want to draft a list, but make sure it's never found—ever!**
- **Ask yourself, What kind of insecurity am I dealing with? Is it affecting my marriage relationship? Is it diminishing my personal happiness?**
- **Is there any stroking I can do to raise my spouse's ego to a healthier level?**
- **Does his ego need a little trimming?**
- **What about your own ego? Too big? Too little?**

This simple exercise will *begin* your attempt to make the ego connection. Take it seriously. To *further* your exploration, try these steps:

1. **Determine which type of stroking will most benefit your partner. Try out a few.**
2. **Be discreet. He is more sensitive than he appears.**
3. **Be aware of your own frailties.**
4. **Don't be afraid to ask for help from your spouse. This deeper level of honesty and understanding will promote a closeness that is a reward in itself.**

Stroking hardly seems burdensome or manipulative when motivated by practical considerations and by love. Your genuine concern for your spouse will eventually turn stroking into an automatic response. But no matter how much energy or skill it requires of you, *stroking is an absolute must. It is one of those little secrets that tightens your bond to each other.*

6

Tips for Creative Communication and Effective Combat

If I had any doubt that communication was one of the most important ingredients of a healthy marriage relationship, it was entirely dispelled after reading the comments in my surveys. If you are under any illusion that good communication is a natural, simple function, take heed: "It doesn't come all that automatically," admits a thirty-one-year-old wife and attorney who gets paid for her communication skills in the courtroom.

It is well established that men and women communicate differently. Signals get mixed, interpretations get snagged, and emotions get stirred.

To make communication work for you and your spouse, you must make a concerted, conscientious effort to get your partner to listen objectively, to understand thoroughly, and to speak often. This may take some artful maneuvers. They will help you to know *when to, how to,* and *what to communicate.*

"But," you may insist, "communication should be straightforward." Read on. *The couples who rated their mar-*

riages at the top, reveal that communication can be tricky at best. To ensure their success at communicating with each other, these couples use secrets to make hot, warm, and cold confrontations productive, effective, and satisfying.

LIFE WITH AND WITHOUT GOOD COMMUNICATION

To begin with, let's take a quick look at Kate, whose love story was full of dangers, and Brenda, whose husband walked out after twenty-five years. Their stories illustrate the difference between life with and without good communication.

Kate: Up Front and Out in the Open

Thirty-three-year-old Kate knows there is no substitute for squarely confronting issues that can affect the fate of a marriage. In fact, she had a *whopper* thrown in her lap right off the bat! Never queasy about stating the ground rules or expressing her feelings, Kate had to face some pretty unusual conversations after she fell for a guy who had a pregnant ex-girlfriend on the sidelines.

"I had gone out with Howard three or four times and knew that he had previously lived with someone else. But I knew that they were in the midst of going their separate ways," she says. "Then he found out she was pregnant with his child. He wanted her to get an abortion, but she wouldn't. She was supposed to be on birth-control pills but had stopped." Nonetheless, without any reservations, Kate told him to go back to his former girlfriend, work it out, and forget her. He couldn't and wouldn't.

"When he decided they weren't going to get married, but that he would support his family, I felt comfortable with that. She had the child, and I stuck it out. I was crazy about him. He would sit down with me and say, 'You don't have to put up with this, but I appreciate it so much.' I had to put up with it because I loved him."

What enabled Kate to come out ahead and jump this hurdle was her ability to face conflict head on: to talk about it, and get her husband to respond.

According to some family therapists, couples who are less willing to face trouble, who never argue, or who fail to confront one another, place the marriage in greater jeopardy than couples who do. Avoiding this pitfall has helped Kate and Howard to achieve a happy six-year union, despite obvious hazards.

After Howard's baby was born, although Kate and he had made a commitment, Kate expressed some fears. "I told him I felt insecure before, during, and after the baby was born. I was afraid Howard might sleep with Lana. I would tell him I was nervous and afraid they would get together when he visited the baby. I am not very jealous. I was just a little worried, particularly when the baby and his mother moved out of town and Howard went to visit. He constantly reassured me, but I remember I ate a box of cookies and drank a bottle of wine when he left.

"As time went on I felt I had a right to know. If we hadn't talked from the beginning, I would have been miserable, afraid, or suspicious of his whereabouts. If we both didn't communicate, our marriage never would have happened. I left no stone unturned, because if I didn't ask, it would eat at me and make me crazy. Things finally fell into place over the years. We realized we still had to keep talking because it was a hard situation. How can you suppress things? It's impossible for me to imagine."

Kate has maintained her directness in charting a clear-cut course for Howard. **"I feel I trained Howard by telling him what I expected out of a relationship,"** explains Kate, one of those business women who is well served by her ability to use authority and delegate work. "If he couldn't comply, then 'goodbye.'"

Wanting to make sure that past and present messages are heard loud and clear, she explains, "I'll say, 'I am talking to you. I really want you to listen.' It sounds like I'm talking to a kid, but it helps him to know it's important. **If he gets that distant daze or seems to be shutting me out, I snuggle up and kiss him to make him listen,**" she reveals. For added emphasis, when Kate is out of sorts with Howard, she uses the old secret of the silent treatment to initiate some serious negotiations. Silence is more than unusual in this talkative lady and catches her husband's attention in a flash.

Whether it applies to her stepson, her own two children, or Howard, there is no substitute for stating the rules. "When we were thinking about having a child, I said this is how it is going to be. I set the standard before and said if he could pitch in and help, okay, otherwise, I couldn't handle everything myself." It paid off. Her self-employed husband has learned to adjust his schedule to accommodate wife, kids, and work.

Brenda's Mistaken Assumption That Her Husband Would Automatically Know Her Needs

Kate is a verbal communicator. Her marriage, even with the extra baggage, reads like a "How-to-Talk" manual. Brenda, without Kate's natural skills, was not able to steer her marriage in a similar direction.

Somehow it didn't matter that Brenda and Sam inhabited the same house, said a pleasant "good morning," sat across from each other at meal time, shared the same bed, raised four kids, and traveled and socialized as a couple. They never developed an intimate level of communication. For the sake of brevity and emphasis, this simplified description of their complicated relationship will suffice until we meet Brenda and Sam again in Chapter 10, "Drifting Apart and Back Together Again."

Brenda and Sam were equally guilty of silently harboring growing resentments. Sam, feeling cut off and out of touch with his wife, retreated into the arms of another woman. He left the house. You know there wasn't much communication when Brenda says she was hesitant to express such a simple preference as wanting to eat before eight o'clock, a dinner hour set to accommodate her husband.

"I held everything in and didn't assume any responsibility for communicating," acknowledges Brenda. "I think we were caught in a marriage where *I* felt *he* was taking more than giving. *He* felt *I* was taking more than giving. But this was something we never discussed." **She, like many wives and husbands, suffered from the delusion that marriage partners should be clairvoyant about deciphering one another's needs.**

Once Sam came back and they both tried to reconcile, Brenda was astute enough to recognize that a whole lot of communicating better begin. After she identified her own needs, Brenda proceeded cautiously and protectively in order to engage in forms of verbal, sexual, and emotional communication that were formerly taboo and missing from the relationship. How did she know she was getting her message across? Simple. There were obvious changes in Sam's behavior.

She must have discovered the right formula. Thirty-seven candles on their anniversary cake signifies a degree of success. "It came to a point where each of us could express our needs and listen to each other. It has made all the difference." In Brenda's opinion, there aren't many good communicators among the couples she knows. She feels fortunate; despite the pain both she and her spouse experienced, the temporary split was the catalyst that made them finally address the lack of communication in their marriage.

Now that Brenda has become more candid in speaking with Sam—forcing him to face a more outspoken partner— communicating can still be a delicate issue. So Brenda is alert and open-eyed when it comes to being effective in the exchange. "For starters, I do a lot more listening," she says.

Instead of falling back into a defensive mode when a suggestion does not strike her fancy, Brenda backs away and offers to give it some thought. This gives each of them time to think, to put things in perspective, and to imagine how the other partner feels about the issue.

Brenda's story is a good example of how vital a factor communication is in marriage. The secret, though, is to communicate effectively and creatively.

To communicate with real success as well as finesse and to increase your influence over the course of your marriage, you have to do more than just talk!

PRUDENT COMMUNICATION USING ARTFUL MANEUVERS

Skillful communication requires attention to a number of things: **what you say, how you say it, and when you say it.** If you can put all of these factors together, you can develop an active habit of prudent communication.

When You Say It

Whether your *mission* is to clear the air of misunderstandings, bargain successfully, discuss the budget, be a pal, or state your needs and desires, **start by being an expert at getting your spouse's undivided attention.** Separate the mundane daily chatter from serious conversations and use whatever ammo you need to draw that uncommunicative housemate into a real exchange. If I've heard it once, I've heard it over one hundred times. *Men are poor communicators. They don't like to communicate. They don't communicate on the same level as women.*

Many women I spoke with make the mistake of asking their husbands to have a heart-to-heart talk or deliberately stalking into a room to pick a fight while their husbands are watching TV or are otherwise engaged. With this technique they're bound to hear any number of discouraging replies, including "Okay start talking" or "What do you want to fight about now?" or "No psychoanalyzing. I'm fine. Things are just horrible at the office."

If this strikes a familiar chord, pay special attention to the next few paragraphs and begin enlisting the magic of the secrets in Chapters 3, 4, and 5!

There are other ways to get your spouse's attention than leaving or administering threats. Browse through this list of attention getters.

- **Make communication pleasant** and try to achieve an atmosphere that is conducive to serious conversation.
- **Make sure the house is calm,** the kids are asleep, and your husband is in a decent frame of mind before commencing serious negotiations.
- **Consider setting aside ten minutes** a day to clear the air so you can solve simmering problems before the weekend.
- **Try airing your disagreements** before going to bed so they don't linger till the next day.
- **Maybe your partner requires a more focused situation** in order to pay attention. Sit on top during sexual foreplay and begin a discourse, not an intercourse. The chances of anyone getting up and walking away are pretty slim! One thoroughly scrubbed woman said she gets her husband to sit with her for hours in a bubble bath for their talks.
- **Suggest a long drive.** If you don't have a destination, invent one.

• **Walk around the block,** take the phone off the
hook, or lock the bedroom door. There has to be a
private niche somewhere that custom fits the two
of you.

It is hard to imagine, but if these tricks of the trade don't
work and your mate is still unreceptive, *you may need a more
demonstrative approach.* Pick a fight, bang the pots and pans,
try the silent treatment, or slam some doors. Hang a banner
that reads "Communication Needed" or issue a formal
invitation for his presence at a bar or restaurant for some
"Serious Conversation." You will undoubtedly arouse curiosity and interest.

**Once you get your spouse's attention, make sure you
make the most of it!**

How You Say It

COMMUNICATING THE WRONG WAY CAN SACK A GOOD
ATTEMPT AT VERBAL INTIMACY AND MAY UNWITTINGLY
START FRESH CONFLICTS.

Of the women I approached to ask permission to interview
their husbands, most replied, *"Sure, you can call my husband,
but I don't think he will tell you much. He doesn't like to talk."*
This gave me pause. I wondered if this wasn't an indication
that their attitudes were part of the problem.

You can imagine how surprised I was time and time again
when their husbands answered my questions, volunteered
more information, and offered to chat again if I found it
necessary. Certainly I had to take into account that my phone
interviews were not threatening in the way that conversations between married partners can be. But their
willingness to open up, even in this unusual situation, is
worth some thought.

Here are some points to consider:

- **Listen to yourself very carefully.** It takes work in many cases to decipher the tone of voice, the choice of words, and the posture that encourages your mate to talk.

   Take notice when your spouse tells you that you sound annoyed, displeased, or angry when you speak. You may inadvertently put someone off or clam them up by your manner. Even if it takes sounding sickeningly sweet, try it. Chances are he will stop and notice the change of tone. Sit back, relax. Be easy. The more you do it, the more spontaneous and natural this mode of communication will become.
- **Whatever you do, don't sound critical.** A good suggestion came from a woman addicted to self-help tapes. "If I want to change my husband's behavior," she begins, "I don't make him feel wrong about what he has already done. Instead of saying in a naggy, bitchy voice, 'Don't do that anymore,' say, 'I know you didn't mean to do this, but it hurt Don [one of their kids]. Or, I know you didn't realize this, but you upset Don. Maybe you should try to talk to him this way.' It is like dropping a pebble instead of a boulder."
- **Drawing a visual image may help to avoid conflict.** When you want to tell your partner how you are feeling but are fearful of sounding like you are attacking him, try a visual image or project a hypothetical situation. One woman who complained of feeling unimportant and neglected in comparison to her husband's children, expressed it to her husband this way: "If there was a burning house, I feel you would save the kids and then maybe think of me." It was a

startling revelation to him, she reports. Words were empty, while the image had clear emotional content.

- **Bring him into the act of communicating.** "I don't think I am communicating this very well to you," is one lady's tactic to encourage her guy to react to and try to understand what she is saying. So she asks him questions, which he then has to answer. This is a terrific little secret that not only gets him to open up, but gives you a chance to find out his level of understanding.

- **You may not be hearing the same message.** According to Deborah Tannen, author of *You Just Don't Understand,* men interpret words differently than women do based on a masculine perception of the world. The "mixed messages" that can be given and received are problematic indeed. I met a woman nearing fifty who thought that her husband might have been suffering from a case of impotence some years before. Actually, what had happened was that he felt she had not been responsive or sympathetic enough when, after six years of marriage, he told her he thought he had gall bladder trouble and would need surgery. He made the announcement while she was feeding three children under the age of five. Her choice of words evoked a screaming response from her very stubborn husband, who said he would never again tell her when he was ill. P.S., he never had gall bladder surgery and purposely failed to tell his wife that he was temporarily out of commission due to prostate trouble.

BECOMING AN A+ LISTENER

Listening is not a one-sided affair. If you aren't going to listen to what your partner has to say, there is no reason for

**anyone to start talking. Remember: You want the informa-
tion your partner can give you.**

If you can, stop what you are doing. Look at your partner.
Show interest and give attention. And don't interrupt once
the motor starts until the other person gets the hang of
communicating. Otherwise, it might stall permanently.

To test how good a listener you are, practice on your mate,
your friends, and new acquaintances. After an encounter:

- **Ask yourself what you learned about and from
the other participants.**
- **Try to remember who did the most talking and
decide if the conversation was balanced.**
- **Practice holding off your comments until you
are sure other people are through talking.**
- **Identify questions you could or should have
asked.**
- **Then be sure to use this analysis and become an
A + listener with your spouse.**

Several years ago I spoke with a woman who revealed that
her marriage was on the rocks. In a last-ditch effort, she
decided that if she could get her husband to talk, they still
had a chance. In an honest self-appraisal, she saw the
obvious, that she herself was at fault for inhibiting him.
After weeks of letting him say whatever he wanted, with no
interruptions and no negative comments, the climate
around the house improved.

What to Say (and What Not to Say)

*You can put on a see-through negligee, dim the lights, tone down
your voice, and still lower the boom if you say something too raw
and honest.* For too long, professionals have been touting

total, unadulterated honesty in communication. But there are limits.

DESTRUCTIVE CANDOR

A woman with firsthand experience in this area admits, "I blew my stack and said things I shouldn't have in my first marriage. I was so frustrated that it led me to overextend the boundary on how far I wanted to go." After experiencing more success and gentler communication in her ten-year second marriage, she adds, "I caution old and young alike to be sensitive to other people's feelings; we all know how much another person can take. People who are terribly honest can be brutal. I saw that occurring in my mother. She felt because she was just a terribly honest person, she had the license to say anything."

DON'T SAY THINGS THAT CAN BE POTENTIALLY DESTRUCTIVE TO YOUR RELATIONSHIP.

Your watchword should be "constructive communication." There is no concrete formula for determining the difference between the two. That is where, once again, knowing your spouse well can be of greatest help.

Nonetheless, I can tell you that a host of men and women who participated in my marriage survey said they refrain from saying hurtful things to their spouses. The men stay away from innuendoes and comments that reveal they notice their wives are aging or losing some of their natural beauty. If she is a bad cook or annoys people by being too talkative, they are kind enough to keep it to themselves. Women tread carefully and try not to disclose their husbands' physical defects as well. These well-meaning women keep it hushed up if their pals aren't the world's greatest lovers, show signs of getting chunky around the middle or losing their hair, and just aren't as handsome as the guy on the movie screen. These seem harmless enough flaws to tuck away and file.

At the same time you are trying to establish an intimate level of communication, **don't forget to respect your partner's right to privacy.** A guy in his late thirties is grateful his wife cares so much about him but wishes she would stop being so nosy and insisting on knowing the feelings behind all of his moods. *"My wife likes to get to the bottom of everything, and I try to be honest. But there is a point past which I can't go. I have to retain something of my own. If I were completely honest with her and divulged all of my private thoughts, she would be appalled."*

It is an absolute necessity—when it comes to more significant issues—for each partner to know exactly how far he or she can go in exposing innermost thoughts. A good rule of thumb is to be careful and soul-searching before broaching a topic that could cause harm to your relationship and set you adrift.

SEX AND HONESTY

Nan, a therapist, had a problem that she eventually shared with her husband. Bringing him into her confidence on this matter was delicate, but, she said, *"I knew my husband could handle this kind of honesty."* She was finding it hard to accept that her sex life would forevermore be exclusively with her husband since she had never had another sex partner. Brought up in a highly restrictive home, she had not developed a healthy attitude or an interest in sex until her fifth year of marriage. Her commitment to fidelity precluded the possibility of any experimentation outside of marriage and the satisfaction of a budding curiosity about sex with other men.

The first time she suffered such pangs of regret followed a weekend at a folk-dancing retreat. "All of these guys were cute and great dancers. I was really in a funk. I said to myself, 'I am married to this man for the rest of my life, and I'm never going to get through this.' So I allowed myself to fantasize about all these other guys. Eventually, I got tired of it, and it worked itself out."

When the problem presented itself again a number of years later, however, she was not able to shake it so easily. "Recently, I regretted never having sex with any of the guys I dated. I realized that the choice I made then meant I would never have new opportunities because I am not going to have an affair. So I was really mad about that, and I was really mad at my husband. For a while I took it out on him. I was pissed at him, aggravated with him. He couldn't do anything right. Finally, I got to the point where I guess I had resolved it enough in my own mind that I was able to talk to him about it. It was awful. And he was a wonderful person. I was crying and carrying on. It was kind of painful for me to say it and acknowledge it, to realize where my anger was coming from.

"The miraculous part of talking about things is that you do feel better when you don't deny them. I knew my husband could handle this kind of honesty. I realize not everyone could. I was concerned how he would feel. He wasn't thrilled, but he understood. Experience told me my husband could take this."

DETOURS AND ROUNDABOUTS

Detours and roundabouts are particularly handy when the person you are talking to is not responsive.

IT DOES NO GOOD TO KEEP RUNNING INTO A STONE WALL. APPROACH YOUR SPOUSE IMMEDIATELY FROM ANOTHER HIDDEN DIRECTION.

For instance, instead of appearing too nosy and pressing, don't try to get closemouthed partners to answer. Instead, *entice them to answer your questions by purposely making a miscalculated statement. Have you ever noticed how people need to defend their position when it is inaccurately assessed?* Try something like this to loosen up a response: "Sorry you are so down in the dumps tonight. Your boss must have really come down on you at work today." You might say this when you know it's not the case, and then walk casually away.

Roundabouts and detours are more frequently used by women. But I did indeed encounter some happily married men who have maintained harmony by using this technique to evoke a specific response they could not get by a direct route. Here are some examples that might ring a bell.

"When I want to instruct but not criticize my husband," explains Pam, *"I make an example out of someone else's husband.* I do this most often when I have something to say about his parenting skills, and I know it would cause an argument. Like I told him the other day, 'Can you imagine that Linda's husband says he is baby-sitting when he takes care of the kids? How can he be the baby-sitter? He's the father. She doesn't say she is baby-sitting all day long.' I think he got my drift."

Making him think something is his idea is a notion that has been handed down from mother to daughter for generations. I like the one about the couple who couldn't agree on what kind of dog to get. She wanted a Dalmatian. "Absolutely not," he told his wife adamantly., "That is the one breed I dislike."

"I subtly left pictures of Dalmatians around the house but said nothing more about the dog. Several days later, he said he thought he might be interested in looking at a Dalmatian," reported this satisfied wife and dog owner. The power of suggestion is mighty.

Howard wears his wife, Tobey, down with roundabout jabs making her feel guilty until he wins his way. Several months ago he wanted to go camping with the kids. He also wanted Tobey, who preferred to stay at home, to come along. "I kept telling her how important it was to spend time with me and the kids. I left articles around the house that talked about the value of family vacations. I do this sort of thing whenever I really want my way."

Effective Combat

The purpose of good fighting is to clear the air, not to knock out the opponent. There is nothing wrong with you if you and your spouse like to fight. Many loving couples do. It feels good and signals extra passion about a subject. You can fight playfully; it can be an exciting way to communicate.

"I have screamed, thrown shoes, slammed doors shut out of frustration and anger," reveals Judy, married more than twenty-five years. "I think it was healthy and helped us to work things out." Robin says, "A good fight clears away the cobwebs. We recognize what is going on and try to figure out a solution. Although I am not madly in love right after a fight, I feel much better. **After a good fight we usually find a solution.**"

To come out feeling as positive as Robin does, pay attention to the rules and the secrets of the fighting ring.

THE GOLDEN RULE OF ARGUING:
NEVER, EVEN IN THE HEAT OF BATTLE, OVERSTEP BOUND-
ARIES AND BLURT OUT DESTRUCTIVE STATEMENTS AND
INSULTS. JABS BELOW THE BELT KNOCK OUT THE OPPONENT.

Innocent fights can all too easily become monumental. We've all been prey to arguments that start with a simple matter of what to eat for dinner and end up with sweeping declarations about one another's mishandling of the children or money, nasty gripes about in-laws, or painful attacks on one's insecurities or failures.

SECRETS ABOUT FIGHTING SMART

Here are two tried-and-true secrets to prevent your arguments from turning into knock-down-drag-out fights:

1. Next time you find yourself in a situation when the tension is inordinately high and you are just about to strike, pull back and **bring out the humor.** Couples who can laugh at themselves rarely spin out of control into the danger zone.

2. One of the most important secrets to fighting the good fight is to **stick to the issue at hand.** Never bring up extraneous beefs. This is an absolute rule of thumb for most happy couples.

My Way

Personally speaking though, when Mark and I fight, *I want to get the most out of it!* I don't stretch the issue, but I sure do stretch the results if guilt is running high. We used to fight more often in the early years. Typically for the married population, we fought over money, kids, and in-laws. Today when Mark and I fight, it's usually because one of us doesn't get our own way. I agree that this is pretty silly. That's why I make it count. If I make him regret that he stepped on my toes, I'm in the driver's seat. However, after twenty-five years it seems he is catching on, and every now and then I get the feeling he is reversing my strategy.

Confused? Maybe an example will help. After a golf game with Mark one evening I was feeling the need for a chiropractor. There is one who lives near the course and is wonderful at getting the kinks out of my neck caused by bending over the word processor, two visiting college kids, a thoroughly aggravating round of golf, and a slightly pinched nerve. Mind you, we were playing on this weekday because we were to entertain a client of Mark's who canceled out on the game and dinner just before tee time.

When I asked Mark to accommodate me, grab a quick dinner, and stop at the chiropractor's office—which would get us home no later than eight-thirty—he flipped negative. *He* wanted to get home. *He* wanted to relax. *He* wanted to eat later. *He* said he had already played eighteen with me. I suppose *he* interpreted this as a favor.

"Okay, buddy," I said to myself. I got home, jumped in the shower, ate in a drive-through, and drove an extra forty-five minutes to get to the doctor's office. I purposely stayed out late treating myself to an ice cream cone, licking it slowly in the car. If I know anything, I know Mark doesn't like to be left alone at home!

By the time I got back, he apologized, vowing to act differently if the situation ever arose again. The taste of one victory made me go for more. It just seemed like a good time to reinforce three points: **a)** that I am worth all sacrifices; **b)** that he should savor the time we are together, even on the golf course; and **c)** he can't always have his way.

"Aren't I worth a few sacrifices? And I resent your saying you took time off to play golf with me, like you did me some big favor!" I ranted with restrained fervor. "I'll just find some other partners during the summer for a late afternoon game and meet you at home *after dinner.* No one says I'm a charity case you have to play with. Go play with the guys as much as you like. I'll do my own thing."

I'm not a shrew. He has his games with the boys, and I am happy that he does. But he hasn't protested a round of eighteen with me in several weeks, and in general I would have to credit him for a spurt of genuine accommodation, which *I* reward generously!

All is fair in love communication as long as it serves the partnership.

Keep the Lines of Communication Open

The best way to explain this is by making the comparison between two very different women's approach to communication. Bonnie has been married over thirty years and can spend an entire evening with her husband sitting at arm's length in stony silence. On the other hand, Ann's relationship is all about talk.

How Bonnie's "I'll Get You Before You Get Me" Approach Shut Down Communication

Why the bleak scenario in Bonnie's house? Bonnie has followed a plan initiated early in her marriage: *attack and counterattack.* It has had a disastrous effect. When she found her husband refusing to discuss and negotiate issues with her, she attacked him vehemently. There is no doubt that she and her husband have numerous differences, but handling them this way closed all doors.

"It began to some extent, because **I thought I could get a rise from him when I made him angry. I always struggled to get him to communicate. But it didn't work. Instead, it changed into a dangerous reflex. We became addicted to it."** What Bonnie is talking about are major "put downs." *She went right for the jugular.*

"Norman hates to spend money. So when I decorated the house and he said it looked terrible, I said, 'You don't have good taste. You don't understand. You wouldn't know if anything was good if it hit you in the face. You only like things that are falling apart like your parents' home.'"

Heard enough or do you need more?

"If he turned me down sexually, I would shout, 'You must feel inadequate as a lover. You're not the most satisfying thing around anyhow.'"

When he complained about work, Bonnie might tell him: "You don't have the balls to go out on your own. You're afraid to do it."

Today, she realizes that there is a better way. But the mood was set, and the damage done by their "I'll-get-you-before-you-get-me" style of communication was beyond repair. Bonnie and Norman still share the same house, but rarely do they share a shred of conversation.

Self-restraint and an awareness of the consequences of malicious talk could have benefited Bonnie and Norman like they did Ann and Chip.

Why Ann Put the Brakes on Some Justifiable Anger at Her Husband

Ann's self-control was certainly put to the test. It's a test not many of us, I venture to say, would have reacted to so prudently under the set of circumstances she faced. But fortunately for Ann, her cautious, calculated behavior left the door open for continuous exchange and the opportunity to make amends. What is her reward? A loving husband, companionship, a great life-style, and a family-centered existence. They are all things she wanted for her future.

After seven years of marriage and the addition of two children, Chip came home from a month of extra legal training with a confession that could blow the lid off the best of relationships: A round of tennis and a dinner for two led to a quick, brief sexual encounter. Initially in shock, Ann cried. Chip cried, understandably disappointed and upset, yet aware of the implications.

"I listened to what he had to say," Ann explains. "I believed he felt guilty enough without me telling him he should feel that way. **It took all the control that I had not to lash out and say some really mean destructive things that could have made us lose all respect for each other. I could have picked on all the things that bugged me. By not doing this, I believe, I saved my marriage without being too accusatory.** I did tell him that my trust was shattered. I never doubted he loved me, but I was determined to find the cause of his behavior. We spent weeks talking about it. I wanted a reasonable answer I could live with."

After weeks of hashing out the problem, Ann decided that Chip's lack of early sexual experience and a decline in their sexual intimacy since the birth of their second son were two contributing factors. She was finally able to pass it off as something inevitable, almost necessary for his ego, since he had been socially awkward in high school.

"When I look back on it," Ann adds, "I think it is pretty amazing. I'm glad he told me and kept the lines of communication open after the incident. If I had found out some other way, I would never have been able to trust him again. I wasn't going to let him off the hook completely. I brought it up for at least six months. I let him know I wasn't stupid and that he had better be careful because he could be tested again."

In Chapter 12, I'll talk more about betrayal and adultery.

STAY IN TOUCH

There isn't any substitute for staying in touch! In a recent survey, 54 percent of the respondents said a cellular phone had a positive effect on their relationship with their partners; we can optimistically conclude that this gave couples more time to communicate. Over the phone or face to face, whatever you prefer, select the modus operandi that gets the job done, and COMMUNICATE.

7

Move Over, Rover,
I Have a Best Friend

I wonder if the fellow who first called the dog "man's best friend" was married? For the wife who told me that their giant German shepherd was sometimes successful in its nightly challenge to her own rightful position beside her husband in bed, there might be some truth to the statement.

THE MAJORITY OF HAPPY COUPLES I SPOKE TO SAID THAT OVER THE YEARS THEIR SPOUSE HAD BECOME THEIR BEST FRIEND.

Friendship is such a vital component to a good marriage that as far as I'm concerned it should be part of the vows exchanged at any wedding ceremony. If you don't pledge to be his friend and he yours, you might as well cancel the reception.

THE FORMIDABLE POWER OF FRIENDSHIP IN MARRIAGE

There is something irresistible about friendship. No wonder so many of the young, middle-aged, and older couples I interviewed described a relationship that began as a friendship. A good friendship takes acceptance, support, generosity, and trust. The glue that holds a marriage together is made of the same qualities.

The intimate familiarity that goes hand in hand with a genuine friendship is comfortable and cozy. "It's almost like having a good girlfriend," says one contented lady about the man in her second love match. "I think it's why our marriage works."

For Anita, an attractive widow in her fifties, friendship beat out the competition for one of her city's most eligible widowers. "There were a lot of women looking for this type of man," admits Anita. Initially, she only formed a friendship with Dave; the loss of her husband was too fresh to jump into a more romantic attachment.

Social acquaintances before their spouses' deaths, Dave offered to drive Anita to and from the support group they attended for new widows and widowers. "It gave us time to talk," explains Anita. "We had a lot in common. We had both recently lost spouses. Our children were the same age, and we had similar problems. We formed a friendship before we ever started to date. Dave would call and ask me how I and my children reacted to a holiday gathering without their father there. He was also having some real problems that I helped him with. When we finally started dating, it felt comfortable."

Married now for ten years, Anita rates this marriage—which is full of love, companionship, fun, and innumerable family joys—a zealous ten and a half. And yes, Dave is more than a friend. He is her "Best Buddy."

Best Buddies

Becoming each other's Best Buddy is the secret at the very heart of some of the most successful partnerships I encountered. It is a relation worth striving for. Don't expect a

genuine camaraderie to evolve to its fullest potential without maturity and conscious effort. Being an irreplaceable Best Buddy is a position earned over time.

The test of how close you are to becoming your partner's best friend depends on the *degree of compassion, the tone of intimacy, and the amount of companionship* offered to a spouse. We are talking megadoses here, more than anyone else could possibly provide you or your spouse. Pretty hefty requirements. Well, plain old friendship isn't quite enough if we are going for the *best* marriage relationship. Let me reiterate once again: This is not a book about mediocrity. This is a book about getting every sweet ounce of pleasure out of your marriage and your mate.

Being a Best Buddy is a tall order for anyone, husband or wife. And if your spouse is not basically predisposed to extending himself into the arena of friendship, I hope you have paid very close attention to the previous chapters. It is no accident that I've brought up the topic of friendship in marriage after conveying the powerful secrets that ought to help manage your partner's more basic needs. **Once basic needs are met your spouse will be softened up, more willing to please and appease, less selfish, more available for compromise, and in the mood to act like your friend.** If you are successful in using these irresistible secrets, your pal should care enough by now to give you the very best! That is what is required of any best friend.

COMPANIONSHIP

Not only is it fun, but it is imperative that you and your partner spend plenty of time together.

COMPANIONSHIP IS ONE OF THE BEST REWARDS OF A MARRIAGE RELATIONSHIP AND ONE OF THE EASIEST WAYS TO ENCOURAGE THE GROWTH OF A FRIENDSHIP BETWEEN THE TWO OF YOU!

No, this doesn't mean always giving up golf games or tennis clinics and evening dinners with friends. I'm not suggesting that being best friends means giving up individual activities or separate friendships. Don't take it to the extreme! *Just make sure you have plenty of time to enjoy being friends with each other.*

Quite a few years ago when I was first married, I remember listening to a talk show about marriage. A stately couple in their mid-fifties made a lasting impression on me. Each confessed they had become too absorbed in activities that took time and attention away from one another. Both the Mr. and Mrs. felt that they had lost sight of the value of their relationship and the importance of sharing time together as friends and lovers. They were quick to get back on track, rid themselves of some extraneous commitments, and reaffirm each other's place at the top of their list of priorities. They looked and acted so happy that I have tried to emulate their secret of success. I can happily report good results.

What I Get Out of Going to Great Lengths

I have gone to great lengths to try to make myself a good companion. Good enough to replace my husband's old fishing buddies. I'll never forget our Alaskan fishing trip which called upon my utmost courage, humor, and determination. It also reaped great rewards.

I was petrified for months before our departure, contemplating a ride in a single-engine plane into remote fishing grounds, the prospect of coming face-to-face with a bear, and the idea of being cut off completely from the civilized world. I got to the cabin in one piece. Later in the day, I was captured on film frantically floundering about in a freezing, rushing stream, grabbing for my rubber pants which had slipped down around my ankles as my fishing pole floated away.

Not to worry. I retrieved both, and three days later when I finally hooked a prize salmon, I could readily enjoy the admiration and approval I had earned from my husband. The picture of me and that fish is prominently displayed in his office, and I have become his regular fishing buddy.

I am not the only woman out there tromping around in the wilderness who has learned to like fishing for her man's sake. I am acquainted with a fifty-year-old wife who has overcome her fear of snakes, heights, and mountain roads to hike with her partner to his heart's content. I also interviewed a woman who admitted, "I am not a terribly happy camper, but the summers belong to my husband at the lake." She gets her rewards in the winter when he follows her a little less begrudgingly to flea markets and restaurants of her choice.

Fortunately, these couples have **accepted the art of compromise and appreciate the importance of trying anything and everything in the cause of cultivating shared interests.**

One Novel Attempt at Togetherness

But who says you have to be doing exactly the same activity at precisely the same time to achieve shared moments? It is one of Stephan's secrets that you don't. His creativity is impressive.

"It took me more than half my married life to realize that being together was more important than what we were doing," explains Stephan, whose creativity in the art of companionship derives from more than twenty years of marital experience. "Here, let me explain. My wife always came with me to a variety of sporting events. I am a loyal, super fan of our local college teams. On the other hand, I often told her to get a friend to go with to the movies. She never argued with me, just left me at home more and more. I realized she relied on her other friends to accompany her most of the time. I didn't feel quite right. I'll admit the thought crossed my mind that she might look for another man or just bump into one if I kept refusing to go."

What did Stephan finally come up with? A compromise that modern technology made possible. When his wife chose to take in a matinee on a Sunday afternoon and a big game was being televised, he went with her to the theater and sat in the back row. In one hand he held a mini-TV screen. On his head he wore earphones. And on his shoulder was his wife's head. She got it right. Her intentional snuggling made his sacrifice well worth it. Obviously, Stephan sensed her appreciation: "This seemed to make her happy, and it was kind of fun."

Hopefully she too made some concessions during football season.

Companionship is one of the most delightful benefits of being married. In the relaxed atmosphere of walking through a park or fishing in a stream, there is the added opportunity to appreciate one another, setting the stage for greater intimacy.

If you haven't found ways to enjoy one another's company besides eating, sleeping, or making love together, experiment until you do. Get with it! This is the first step in becoming Best Buddies.

SOUL MATES

There is more to being Best Buddies than the fun and games of playing together. A good friendship is also built by tenderness and sensitivity, by unspoken kindness. There are moves you can make, specific maneuvers that cultivate this kind of friendship.

How Sammy and Elly Became Friends by Sharing Deep Feelings

Sammy and Elly were both definitely in need of a good friend when they met. Sammy's wife had recently left him with three children under the age of ten while he was in the hospital recuperating from cancer surgery. Despite the weight of this tremendous responsibility, dumped at such a precarious time in his life, Sammy was probably better off without his wife's unrelenting verbal abuse. Elly's first husband abused her physically, impregnating her with their second child during a rape. She walked out of the door with a gun to her head, and two children, ages two and four, by her side.

The friendship between Elly and Sammy has developed over the fourteen years of their marriage and has been built on their caring efforts to heal one another. Baring their souls with brutal honesty, they have nurtured an acceptance in each other that is of immeasurable comfort. But it takes more than a pouring forth of past heartaches to create the intimate bond of friendship these two have. *To repair the damage it takes consideration, given generously in the form of gentle love talk and soothing strokes.*

"When I met Sammy he felt guilty over the separation with his wife; he was still paying all her living expenses even though the children were with him," Elly begins. "He thought it was all his fault. His wife had given him an inferiority complex because he was not able to maintain the style of living she wanted. I had been through so much physical abuse that I learned to box in my first marriage. I had to defend myself. But Sammy's verbal abuse was just as bad. Even now, if our money gets tight, he feels like he is a failure. I have to tell him to look at all he has and all he has accomplished. I have to work him like that a lot."

Fortunately, this is secondhand to Elly. Intuitive, good-natured, and a professional counselor for women starting their own businesses and seeking better employment, Elly knew just the right buttons to push on Sammy to get him to open up, communicate, and be her friend. It took her two years to raise his level of confidence before he could really open up, but her steady, ardent persistence paid off.

"Friendship is a matter of being able to share and confide real deep feelings," she tells me, while we are sitting in her front yard. "Some men won't share the fact that they hurt or cry. But because Sammy was so open, I was open. I think that helped to take care of the bitterness. Pouring your heart out has to be mutual. We were gun-shy in the beginning because that is what got us into trouble with out first spouses. We gave all we had to give to them, and they threw it back in our faces. It took a good five years before he communicated everything about the past. But *once the trust is there, you can share anything."*

And once you arrive at this intimate understanding of one another, friendship may even be communicated in silence. Elly explains: "Now neither of us is lonesome anymore. **When I was married the first time, my husband was not a friend, and I was lonely even when he was at home."**

In attempting to describe the essence of this friendship, Elly appropriately feels that she and Sammy have an intimacy that is just as potent as their loving sexual encounters. However, instead of being connected through the intensity and passion of sex, they mesh tightly together in an emotional union, getting immense comfort from the close support and understanding they offer one another.

Other couples described the same phenomenon to me by calling each other "soul mates." No matter what name you give it, it describes a relationship in which you know one another well enough to anticipate each other's feelings or to read the meaning behind a touch or a glance. You've experienced this secret meeting of the minds, I hope. **Haven't you taken your husband's hand when you can feel something is wrong and are confident he understands and received comfort from the gesture? Hasn't he offered a smile of reassurance at just the right moment?** "It is the icing on the cake," Elly says.

A BEST BUDDY IS THERE WHEN YOU MOST NEED ONE

There is no better feeling of security and comfort than knowing you have a Best Buddy on call. Life's difficulties

and demands are not only eased by compassionate acts of friendship, they nurture its very growth.

Stephanie expresses this succinctly. "We've been through an incredible amount. That is probably why we are best friends. Within six months of my husband's father's death, his mother spent every weekend with us. I got a form of hepatitis and thought I might not be able to practice medicine again. So that was a tough time for me. The good news was that we had a new baby girl. But then, within nine months, we lost three people who were very close to us. My mother-in-law died of cancer, and my sister was killed in an automobile accident. On top of that, my husband's favorite aunt passed away. Hugh and I were very supportive of each other," Stephanie remembers thankfully.

A gentleman married for the second time told me how he tried to be particularly attentive and comforting to his wife after his stepson committed suicide. As tragic as it was, he admits it brought them closer together. Undoubtedly, seeing her suffer moved him too, and she accepted and appreciated the warmth of his genuine response.

THERE IS A SENSITIVITY AND RESPONSIVENESS YOU RECEIVE FROM A BEST BUDDY WHEN YOU MOST NEED IT THAT PAYS BACK EVERY OUNCE OF ENERGY AND EFFORT YOU PUT INTO MAKING THE FRIENDSHIP WORK.

Once, when on assignment for a magazine story, I attended a session of a support group for men whose wives were suffering from Alzheimer's Disease. This was particularly traumatic because my father had died of the disease. With tears streaming down my face, I returned to my desk and immediately called Mark. He briskly said, "I'm busy, I'll call you later." Within seconds, the phone rang and this time he said, "I'm sorry. I forgot how difficult that must have been for you. Is there anything I can do?"

Now that's a quality friend!

The more of life's experiences you face together as a team, the more you meet your children's dilemmas as a pair, the more you band together to combat the struggles of career wins and losses, and the more disappointments and joys you suffer through hand in hand, the more tried-and-true your friendship becomes. Your shared history builds a base of understanding and appreciation which serves you better and better each time you call it out of reserve. It is one of the most valuable and satisfying benefits of a mature love relationship, and it offers you one of the most meaningful rewards for the hard labor of keeping marriage and love on track.

Treat Your Partner the Way You'd Treat Your Best Friend

There are more than enough daily opportunities to show our readiness to be a sincere best friend simply by being considerate and caring.

If your spouse ever says, "Hey, you treat your friends better than you treat me," back up and take a good look. Make a list of all the nice little things you do for others over several weeks' time. Then make a list of all the sweet things you do for your spouse, such as running errands without complaining, giving a compliment, or making a daytime phone call for support. Place the lists side by side. Whose list is longer? It should be your household partner.

Don't forget the simple lessons of your own friendships at school, work, or play. Apply these rules *first* to your spouse if you want him to be your Best Buddy. He should get your ultimate attention and respect.

THE GOLDEN RULES OF MARITAL FRIENDSHIP ARE:

1. NEVER TAKE YOUR FRIEND FOR GRANTED.
2. TREAT YOUR FRIEND LIKE THE PRECIOUS GIFT HE OR SHE IS.

3. BE A FRIEND IF YOU WANT A FRIEND.
4. FRIENDSHIP GIVEN IN EARNEST IS ITS OWN REWARD.

"If you want to make friends, you have to reach out and be a friend," agrees a smart female tactician. "Don't look at it as making your husband a friend just to get something back. See it as how you want to be treated yourself. Give it first. It works for all types of situations. I want to be treated with that high degree of love, compassion, and verbal caring—the all over thing. I want that back, and I have to give it first, or else I'll never be able to get it." Both partners come out winners by this captain's rules of the game. And after all, that is precisely what secrets are all about.

WITHOUT A BEST BUDDY

If I had designed my own experiment to emphasize the impact of friendship on a marriage relationship, I couldn't have come up with anything more to the point than the set of circumstances peculiar to Vivian. She had two diametrically opposed relationships at the same time: 1) a marriage without friendship; 2) a long-term friendship with another man.

Until I met Vivian, I may have taken for granted the significance of the intimate marital friendship. A pretty woman in her late fifties, Vivian has a gregarious personality and risqué sense of humor that made me feel she would be receptive to an open discussion about marriage. "Sure," she said. "I'll do it." I learned a lot about friendship that afternoon and about how a beautiful love story can turn bitter.

Try not to be judgmental here as you read Vivian's story. You may sense along the way that she gave up prematurely on making her husband a buddy. The lesson, however, remains the same and illustrates the emptiness and pain that come when living with a spouse who never becomes a friend.

Vivian Learned From Another Man's Friendship What She Couldn't Have With Her Husband

"I don't think I ever loved anybody in my life as much as I loved Harley Rath," Vivian said about her husband.

Did you catch the past tense?

Recollecting the early days of her thirty-odd years of marriage, she began, "Harley didn't know how to be a best friend. He chose his mother over me. We were temporarily living with his folks while we looked for a home right after he got out of the service. Harley denied who I was. He never stood up for me in front of his family to demand they accept me for who I am. He never came through for me. He pretended I wasn't Catholic and that I didn't drink or smoke—all three things his folks didn't like. When I had a fight with his mother, he stood up for her, not me. I moved out in a hurry and told him when he found a place for us I would come back."

Unfortunately, that didn't solve the total problem for Vivian. The friction over loyalties was there to stay. It intensified as her anger mounted; out of spite, her husband rejected her. As a defensive mechanism, each withdrew into silence, shielding and protecting their innermost thoughts and feelings from the other. Intimacy eventually became out of the question.

"No, we are not friends. We definitely are not friends," Vivian repeats, in a hard, bitter tone. *"I didn't know at that time that what I really wanted was for Harley to be my friend. I didn't understand that until I had a relationship with another man."*

"I met Doug when I was traveling regularly for my job. He was a great friend. Our relationship made me see what was missing in my marriage. Doug and I had a sporadic affair over eight years from the time I was thirty-five. We would have dinner and talk on the phone. I would lie through my teeth to be with him. I did go away with him, but we never had a sexual relationship. It was a platonic affair, long and loving. We talked about our jobs. I gave him advice, and he listened. Harley never asked me anything important, and here is this guy, the vice-president of a corporation, talking about his business with me. Doug told me intimate things. We shared our feelings. It was the greatest affair I ever had in my life."

Actually, it was Vivian's only affair. **But the good feelings she derived from the intimacy of the friendship were so nourishing, so loving, that she contemplated leaving Harley when Doug separated from his wife.** She was thankful when Doug remarried and removed the temptation. Committed to religious doctrines that forbid divorce, and wounded as a youngster by her own parents' divorce, Vivian faced burdensome internal conflicts.

Once tasting the intimacy of having a buddy, however, Vivian knew what she had missed. **"Friendship means being able to bare your soul to one another and opening doors to let each other in. This is the most important part of marriage,"** she now says. **"You have to be best friends. I wanted to be able to come out and tell Harley, 'I have this guy I can talk to. He's replacing you, and I don't like it.'**

"I wish I could have told him that, but I didn't, and it was too late. He would never have forgiven me for it. Because if we weren't best friends then, it was not the time to try and start a friendship. If you have a friendship, you can get through anything. If I had it to do all over again, I would take the chance. I would jolt his ass right out of the seat and take the consequences. After all, I made them. When I was with Doug I learned how to share with someone. It made me a better person."

Vivian attempted to patch up her marriage and sought

counseling. Harley reluctantly went for a brief time. After one of the sessions, they came home and lay down on their bed together. "We didn't touch or anything," recalls Vivian. "He said, 'I really love you.' It was the first time I saw a tear in his eye, and he told me some very personal things about himself. I don't think I was ever filled with so much love and compassion. I think if we had done that all the way through together, we could have been like the Rock of Gibraltar. Without this kind of trust and sharing, it's like living with a stranger."

Unfortunately, it seems too much damage had been done to repair their relationship. "We are like two lost souls who can't go back," she says, obviously saddened and hardened by the reality. "We do very little together. I would give up everything today if he would be my friend. He would be my top priority. I still love him, and I think he would say the same of me. But I'm not so sure we like each other anymore."

Every now and then, Vivian tries again to make headway and turn Harley into a friend by starting from scratch. Her offers to be a companion and accompany him biking or rafting are accepted but not reciprocated. She has the right idea, but her timing is way off. This would have been a good place to begin building a friendship thirty-five years ago.

The Friendship Checklist for Husbands and Wives

The weight of the secret in this chapter should be pretty clear by now. But if you're not sure just how you and "Buddy" are doing, take time out to test yourself. I recommend that *each and every husband and wife* participate in this exercise. If either of you have more than a few "no's," start mending your ways before you find yourselves in Vivian and Harley's boat. The checklist will get you started with a meaningful evaluation. It provides both of you with a place to begin exchanging thoughts on what you can do to keep

love on track, to speed your relationship to greater heights,
and to have a lifetime love affair.

QUESTIONS FOR HUSBANDS AND WIVES:

Yes No

1. I recognize the times when my spouse needs
   the special touch of a caring friend.
2. If my spouse says he needs me, I drop
   everything.
3. When someone else asks me to go to a movie I
   know my spouse wants to see, I refuse and
   wait until I can go with my spouse.
4. My spouse doesn't have to ask me to do small
   favors for him or his parents; I do them on my
   own.
5. I have tried many activities and gone many
   places with my spouse just to be with him or
   her.
6. I am not hesitant to ask my spouse to be my
   friend and help him or her to see what that
   means.
7. I treat my spouse with just as much or more
   consideration than I give to my other friends.
8. I want to share my innermost feelings with
   my spouse. I encourage reverse sharing.
9. I thank my spouse verbally or in other ways
   for acts of friendship.
10. I want to be my spouse's Best Buddy.
11. I hope my spouse wants me to be his Best
    Buddy.
12. I can give several examples of how I compro-
    mised on something I wanted to do to be with
    my spouse.
13. I try not to take my spouse's gestures of
    friendship for granted.

14. I save the best of *me* for my spouse.
15. I am always loyal to my spouse and take his side in an outside dispute.
16. I try to be considerate in dealing with my spouse.
17. My partner can count on me and knows it!
18. I do not sit and stew when my spouse fails to act as a friend; I use secrets to get him back in my corner.

If you have racked up at least 66 percent "yes's," you may already be a Best Buddy. Anything less means you have some work to do! Keep this list of words in mind as you go about the task:

Accepting
Supportive
Caring
Sharing
Giving
Trusting
Loyal
Compassionate
Intimate
Considerate
Compromising
Reciprocal
Appreciative
Sensitive
Responsive

FRIENDSHIP GETS YOU THROUGH THE WORST

To be or not to be a Best Buddy is not even up for debate among those couples who have achieved true companionship. Being a Best Buddy is an integral part and mandatory parcel of a marriage relationship that makes the grade as a permanent love match.

Friendship provides the sturdiest foundation and delivers an immeasurable return on the investment of effort. *It builds your relationship. It nourishes your relationship. It solidifies your relationship.* It emanates happiness, security, and comfort for you and your spouse. **Friendship enhances the best of times and gets you through the worst. It is worth all the effort.**

8

Stay Close, but Give Me Space

Everyone needs room for independence in a relationship. But sometimes having too much or too little space in a marriage may wreak havoc on the most well-intentioned partners.

Finding the very best ratio enables a couple to stay close, yet gives each person the room to grow. The way to do this is one of the toughest secrets to master. Prudent men and women know the value of independence to a good marriage. They know how important it is to have freedom to pursue their own interests. They artfully formulate a mutually satisfying equation to establish a safe balance between their individual needs and the needs of the partnership.

You have to sit up and take a long steady look at the space you and your partner require in order to reach fulfillment in your marriage, your career, and even your leisure hours. Allowing each other space, which has become one of those positive buzz words of the eighties and nineties, may sound simple enough, but there is a trick to doing it right.

How to Determine How Much Space Is Enough

The primary yardstick to determine whether the space you and your partner seek is on target is the effect it has on your marital relationship. In the ideal case, the independence you give each other should be comfortable, productive, and mutually agreeable to each of you. This is rarely a simple matter. **The power struggle in a relationship where two independent people attempt to mesh their lives always appears with the conflict between selfish desires and selfish needs.** That's when secrets really come into play!

Two people never see things exactly the same way all of the time. So beware that achieving the right balance might require finesse: *a hidden agenda packed with artful maneuvers that follow prudent guidelines.*

Allowing too little space may result in a rebellious, angry, resentful mate. But too much space may alter the kind of commitment required in maintaining a truly satisfying lifetime marriage.

Juggling Independence and Togetherness for the Working Woman

Undoubtedly one of the greatest changes taking place in American society and the American family today is the increase in the number of working wives and mothers. Through a combination of a desire for career, economic necessity, and economic security women have joined and are climbing in the work force at all levels of society. At the same time a *New York Times* poll reveals that 26 percent of the women and 20 percent of the men sampled felt that marriages were receiving less attention from working women. We all know by now that marriage requires a huge amount of attention; and 77 percent of the adult participants in a national survey by the *Roper Report* counted a *happy* marriage as part of the "good life."

This does not signal an end to *"having it all"* or indicate a retreat of women from the workplace. But it does mean that there is a greater challenge and new stresses and strains to cope with. This calls for new strategies. We have touched upon this in our discussion of the ego. We have even mentioned women who use the secret of ego massaging and bolstering to enlist a husband's help with household chores. On the whole, studies show that women are making strides in getting men to pitch in. What is needed, however, to bridge the gap between achieving success at home and at work is a deeper look into how this new separation and space can affect a marriage. To achieve a balance satisfactory to *both* men and women requires greater compromise and accommodation than the word "space" has previously implied. This is essential if you wish to be a working partner in a healthy, sound marriage that can ride the many waves that will no doubt come crashing to shore.

THE BABY DEBATE

The debate by married couples over whether *to have or not to have* children is in part an outgrowth of the vast number of women who have joined the labor force, opting for full-time careers. *In order to accommodate husband, wife, and the partnership, the issue of space will assume major importance under these circumstances.*

How Patty and Rick Made Room for Each Other *and* Their Baby

Rick and Patty are both professionals, married for almost fifteen years. The Baby Debate almost ended their happy marriage several years ago until they made the kind of concessions that would allow Patty enough space to pursue her career uninterrupted.

"When we married, I knew that Patty was not ready to have children," Rick admits. "I did go into this marriage knowing that she might never want them. I thought she would change and become a fine mother. **But we came to a point in our marriage when we began having real problems because of it. I wanted children and she didn't. It became such an explosive issue that we weren't able to talk.** We went to a group therapy session called 'The Baby Debate' with five or six other couples. This helped us to talk about our feelings and our needs. Patty was able to express her fear that motherhood would change her life. We were able to face these issues together."

Patty and Rick were able to work out a compromise based on flexibility, insight, honesty, foresight, and love.

In 1989 when their daughter was born, Patty went back to work after eight weeks and Rick became part of a growing minority of stay-at-home dads. In 1975 there were only 61,000 men accepting the position of primary caretaker. In 1990 the figures increased fourfold. Still, this is less than 2 percent of all fathers.

Rick, raised in a liberal intellectual atmosphere and surrounded by women with feminist leanings, had no problem with their compromise. "I had been teaching for ten years with no sabbaticals," Rick explains. "I was getting stale and needed a break. The fact that I could take a ten-month maternity leave with benefits and a small amount of pay was great. I think what made the difference was when Patty was convinced I would stay at home and that I would be the nurturer and not dump her with the responsibility. I was thrilled to do it."

Prudently, Rick accepted the guidelines that would enable him to be a dad, save his marriage, and allow Patty to be the primary wage earner. Artfully, Patty recognizes, "There are times I need to pamper Rick. There are times when I have actually brought him flowers. I admire and appreciate him for being able to do all of this."

Understandably concerned with her career aspirations, time constraints, and impressive earning power, Patty currently sees her job as a number one priority, with Rick and the baby a close second. On the other hand, Rick puts his family first and his job second. When Rick is disgruntled with Patty's extended work hours, week long trips, or inequitable handling of household chores, it is not a matter of ego. Rather, he is expressing the loneliness he feels and the concern that he and Baby Jessie are getting shortchanged when it comes to Patty's attention. In this case, some kind of real adjustment of each partner's space needs to be made.

Determining the right amount of space for a couple is an ongoing process that demands continuous attention. The following section reveals an important secret which spouses ought to consider when going back to the bargaining table.

A Matter of Priorities

It is practically unanimous:

HAPPILY MARRIED COUPLES, MEN AND WOMEN ALIKE, LISTED THEIR LIFE'S PRIORITIES AS FOLLOWS: 1) SPOUSE; 2) CHILDREN; 3) JOB.

The only exceptions were mothers and fathers of small children who gave the entire family unit top billing. *There seems to be little room for deviation of priorities if your goal is to emulate the rewarding relationship of these successful couples.*
Each partner must be careful of the other in the quest for self-fulfillment and self-expression. You are striving to achieve a love relationship that is mutually satisfying and exemplifies the best marriage has to offer. You cannot toy with this delicate balance.
Looking at partners who stray from the priorities established by successful couples indicates that too much latitude

is counterproductive. **When a marriage is twisted into too many awkward shapes it loses its center and falls apart.**

Dwayne and Audra Squeeze a Marriage Out of an Unconventional Setup

I met a couple several years ago who suggested they were quite happy in their marriage and made no apologies for their mutually-agreed-upon order of priorities: 1) children; 2) work; 3) spouse. When I began planning this chapter, I searched through old notes until I found their phone number. Curious about the survival of this marriage, I first called the wife and then, with her permission, I called her husband.

Now in their late forties, Dwayne and Audra have been married for more than twenty-five years. They live approximately eight hundred miles apart and depend on the engines of jets and the wires of telephones to keep tabs on one another. They launched their relationship in a conventional fashion. Dwayne was finishing his Ph.D. in genetic engineering, and Audra was teaching school the year they exchanged vows. Two years later they moved into a midwestern community and settled down for a life together until Dwayne was required to fulfill two years of military service in the South. This began their first go-round with a commuter marriage.

Dwayne's move came at an important juncture in Audra's new career. She was up for promotion in a brokerage firm and did not want to sacrifice the prospect of advancement to go with him for his two-year stint. "Dwayne was supportive and recognized my aspirations. We agreed to try it," Audra told me. When he missed her so much that he asked her to join him after a year, she took a leave of absence and was by his side.

As planned, they moved back north, where Dwayne started a three-year research project. Audra advanced to a better brokerage firm, where she was the highest-ranking woman by the time she became pregnant with her first child. "I felt compelled to be the best role model and put the company's interests above my own," she explains. "I worked up until I was ready to deliver and came back to work five days later." The second time around Audra surpassed this record by delivering on a Friday and returning to work on Monday.

It wasn't long, however, before this united household suffered the trials of putting work ahead of everything else. Dwayne got an offer for an important new position on the East Coast, but the area did not appeal to Audra, who by now was up for a promotion to VP. It was back to the commuter track for Dwayne, until the space they agreed on was no longer comfortable. "Enough of this," he said two years later. Then it was Audra's turn. The children moved East, Dwayne bought a house, and Audra comes and goes on Friday and Sunday evenings.

Why do they do it?

"The whole reason is that each of us wants the other to be very happy with their lot in life and develop their full potential," Audra offers. "Everything was carefully planned. There were some lonely nights, and I thought, 'Who am I? And why am I doing this?' I had to critique my own life. I have to be an individual, self-sufficient, and contribute financially. There are trade-offs, but I speak to the children once or twice a day. They know they are loved. My husband and I call each other three times a day. My drive to remain challenged has intensified over the years, although I miss the aura of love and the closeness of being in a home with my family."

How has Dwayne fared? "When I moved east after fifteen years, our relationship started to change," he admits. "I felt I wanted a conventional marriage, and so we separated for a period. It was a rough time. We still wanted to keep the family together, so we sought counseling. We aired some of our differences. There were issues that were apparent to me. I was tired of commuting and felt it interfered with my work. You grow apart and become independent. I don't think Audra really cared about that but blamed me for leaving the house. There was a lot of pent-up anger. There were things both large and small that bothered me. The need for companionship and affection got suppressed. There was a lack of affection that I felt should be in the marriage."

Audra acknowledges that. "Dwayne always had a greater need for intimacy and closeness," she says. But both partners have remained faithful despite the weekly separation and shake their heads at the prospect of an affair. Despite this admirable attempt to remain loyal partners and responsible parents, *their marriage has become mighty close to being a nonmarriage.* Too many of the qualities that maintain an intimate bond and a healthy, supportive friendship are missing from this relationship to allow it to work.

"If you had asked me twenty-four years ago what I would have expected out of marriage, I would have said more personal affection and companionship," Dwayne says. "I wouldn't have envisioned this kind of marriage. This relationship was born out of events, so we have adapted to each other and our needs and the opportunities that have come along. We wouldn't have chosen this if we had written our own fate. I would not recommend this type of lifestyle; it is not easy to get through. If it weren't for the kids, the marriage probably wouldn't have survived. I hope we will grow closer, but separation has put a strain on that. As you get older, I think you need more emotional and physical closeness."

Despite the burden placed on their marriage, neither Audra nor Dwayne has opted to sacrifice a slightly diminished professional status for positions that would bring them together in the same city and that might allow them to renew that closeness that seems to be fading. That may surprise you; it surprised me. Dwayne says it is not a bad marriage. He rates it a seven and is relatively satisfied.

WHAT KIND OF SATISFACTION ARE YOU AIMING FOR?

"The unemotional part of our marriage is functional," Dwayne reveals. "My options are limited. I think we do love each other, not a puppy love like we had when we were young. I know some people still have that in their eighties. We don't. But it is not a determining factor in our relationship anymore."

The quality of marriage certainly can be a subjective matter based on individual needs. Not everyone wants the same thing out of it. Nonetheless, I can't help but feel that *the amount of space that these two people have given one another cost their love relationship dearly. What is marriage without companionship, passion, and time to treat each other to the secrets we have discovered?*

The true essence of a marriage relationship is the enjoyment and fulfillment of each partner. The gifts of closeness offered to someone you love restore that bond between you. The secret of a terrific marriage relationship is putting husband and wife close to the top of the list.

This is not a gender issue. It applies to both men and women. Marriage, a really special marriage, requires that both careerists make their commitment to one another and the family the most important appointment on their calendar.

ALLOWING FOR BREATHING ROOM

Breathing room is a healthy concept. It does not run counter to the importance of taking time to become one another's friend and companion. Nor does it compete with the priorities we have established so far. *Allowing sufficient breathing room is a safety hatch that ensures neither partner suffocates.*

Time Out: How Mimi and Eric Spend Their Summer Vacation

Summertime separation has been a positive experience for both Mimi and Eric over the past several years. Married six years and with a combined average level of marital satisfaction settling just under a nine, Eric explains, "It is just nice to take a breather from each other. We are both dominating people. Each usually likes his own way. Usually by the time Mimi is packing up the kids for the two months to go and stay with her folks at the beach, we are at a point where we are really stressed with each other."

"We are both Scorpions," says Mimi with a laugh. This follows a full description of what sounds like a genuinely wonderful young marriage with all the ingredients for staying power. "Scorpions are not supposed to marry each other. I think if we didn't genuinely like each other so much, we would drive each other absolutely crazy. There are times we do that. Last year when I left, I couldn't stand Eric. I was so glad I was leaving. He was having a hard time and had been feeling disappointed in himself. He has these great expectations and some are unrealistic. He wasn't happy, and it made me unhappy. I think I was mad at him for not being happy with himself."

"What about staying home and helping this cute young husband out of the doldrums?" I was thinking to myself. Eric cleared up my concerns on that front. **"Space is very important to me. I like being independent, I always have. I play solitary sports and I work alone. I have the lone wolf syndrome."**

Sounds great in theory, but what about in practice? I waited until the middle of the summer and called Eric back to see how the breathing room felt. No problems at his house. It was a particularly hectic time on the work front, and he did not have to face the guilt he might have felt for neglecting his wife and kids if they were at home. Besides, he was making the nine-hundred-mile trip the following weekend to vacation with his family. No doubt he would be met enthusiastically by Mimi, who confesses she really missed him. "The separation makes it worthwhile when you get back together," says Eric as he looked forward to the reunion.

How Sally Turned Mac's Solitary Adventure Into Her Own

The need for space takes on quite a different meaning for Sally and Mac, a middle-aged couple happily married for over twenty-seven years. Sally, who thoroughly understands the dynamics of space, is a perfect role model for us.

"About a year ago it was Mac's fiftieth birthday," she says. "He always said he wanted to take time off, kind of drop out for a period when he hit this stage. The time came. He planned to go to a small, very modest apartment we have in Utah for several of the winter months. I didn't want to stand in his way, but I was against his going for a two-month stretch. I have my own business so it was out of the question for me to go with him. He expected me to make frequent trips to visit him."

Family members misconstrued his need for space and thought it was a trial separation. Far from the immediate truth, Sally says, "Any time you do this sort of thing there is the danger that it could happen, that we could both find out that life was better without each other." Nonetheless, she is filled with trust, had no serious reservations that his departure was going to be final, and knew that his business could be safely conducted from Utah. **"My biggest gripe was that he announced he was going rather than asking if he could."**

Prudently, with an edge that maturity and experience provide, Sally gave him the yellow light—not the red or the green. She had the right secret ammunition to handle his mid-life fantasy, which might get out of hand. "I decided I should be an integral part of his plan. I didn't want him to leave on a sour note. I was careful to add a little glue to our marriage rather than create a rift," she says. *Putting her foot down and shouting a big boisterous "no" would have generated a spark of resentment and made it look as if she didn't trust him. Allowing him to take off with no strings, no guilt, no worries would have encouraged him to behave like one of their excessively carefree college children.*

Keeping her cool enabled Sally to handle her husband skillfully. "Besides," she adds calmly, "Mac isn't the kind who makes friends easily or likes to be by himself. I bet on him lasting ten days at the max." To ensure that Mac proceeded with caution, Sally calculated her moves, which were designed to convey a specific message. Several months before his departure, she went to Utah with him to purchase a few things for his "den of self-evaluation," as he called it. First on the list was a not-so-comfortable hide-a-bed. Three weeks before he fled their conventional world of suburbia and work, Sally purposely introduced some disquieting ideas. At dinner one night with another couple, the wife provided just the right opening: "Won't you be afraid or lonely without Mac for such a long time?"

"Who said I'll be by myself?" she retorted.

When it came time for him to leave in February, she nonchalantly took him to the airport with a promise to visit, but did not set a date. She reacted enthusiastically to his first call about his two days of reflection and skiing. By day four she sensed his loneliness and ignored his complaints of a head cold. She talked on about how busy she was before cutting the conversation short. "Sorry, I have to go. They're honking for me. I'm going out to dinner," she told him. Whether this was fact or fiction makes no difference.

At week's end, he began asking her when she was coming to visit. "I didn't want to give him a date to hang his hat on," Sally revealed. "All I said was when I could get away I would, but things were too busy to commit. I let him know it wouldn't be as soon as he wanted."

Day nine he called to say that since she couldn't come to Utah, he would come home for a few days. He never went back. Mac later told the friends who inquired about his self-searching that he had had too much work to allow him to return. With a self-knowing chuckle and a look at Sally, he also admitted to them that he missed his wife too much and that he had had just enough time to find it out.

He lived out his fantasy, but Sally admits that he came home too soon. "In my mind I had set up that I would have some freedom too. I looked forward to that freedom and thought it would last longer. It was going to be a time to spend with my friends here at home."

Sally was smart to turn Mac's adventure into her own. That is a good secret to keep in mind.

Winning Tactics: The Illusion of Space and Others

The real secret here is making your partner *think* he or she has enough space. **More than 90 percent of the men in my cheery sample felt their wives gave them ample room.** I doubt this means their sweethearts let them go on their merry way or surrendered their claim over all leisure hours. *Rather, these women are masters at judging the space their husbands need, creating the illusion of space when they request too much, and gladly waving goodbye at the door when space is well deserved.*

Making an illusion of space is preferable to the age-old play on guilt, which backfires too easily. **Don't be too harsh on your partner's request for space, especially if it is infrequent.** Have compassion for your partner who labors for the good of the family, loves you most of the time, and is generally a pretty darn good person. There is only so far one can or should go in saying "no" to some genuinely deserved *legitimate* space.

SPACE DEPRIVATION

Keith qualifies for a deserved vacation. In pursuit of space, he drove from Oregon to Southern California with a fishing buddy but his wife, Jackie, made it difficult for him., "Jackie didn't want me going down there and played this mind game on me. It worked. I came home irritated at myself and her. To this day I tell her, 'Never do that to me again.'" Jackie stepped on his toes, hurt his pride, and embarrassed him in the presence of his male buddy by pulling in the ropes and depriving him of his space. Naturally Keith got over it. But just imagine the points Jackie missed on this one by not using the methods Sally called on to weather the Utah gig. In Sally's case, she fostered the notion, trusted her husband's decision, and understood his need for space. Because of this she held the best cards.

MAXIMIZING RETURNS

Another tactician instructs, "I use every opportunity to make it look like Kevin has all the freedom he wants. Last year when the guys were planning a golf vacation Kevin had some previous business commitments which prevented him from going along. I wouldn't have wanted him to go because I was interested in taking a vacation with him. I kept making the point, *after the fact*, that he should have gone on the trip with his friends, and what a shame it was he had to miss it. I can always say I never held him back if it comes up again and poses a conflict with other travel plans. It seems like I am always giving him breathing room. When he has a so-called business golf game in the middle of the week, I make a fuss about how wonderful it is that he got a chance to get out of the office. **Somehow when I condone or approve of an activity, even when I have no control over it, it looks like I'm the one giving him room to do what he wants.** Then when the weekend comes and he wants to play again, but I want him to baby-sit, he thinks he owes me one. So far, so good."

A DELICATE BALANCE

How much space can you and your partner handle and still keep love on track? I hope you have enough insight now to answer this question.

Perhaps I should add a qualifier to the end of this: The need for space changes continuously as one moves through the cycles of life. Therefore, don't forget to run periodic reevaluations and checks.

Of course, knowing the answer and persuading your partner to accept your measurements may be two different things. Take your lead from the suggestions given in this chapter, and then go back and pull secrets from the preceding pages that will reward, cajole, or convince your partner to accept the position which best ensures the survival of your marriage relationship. If this requires frank, forthright conversation, do it. Or, if being playful, even kinky, will get his attention, lasso him during sex and make a joke and a *point* that you feel some real concern about his need for independence or yours.

Just get yourself thinking about SPACE! It can make or break the best love match.

9

Living With an Imperfect Spouse in an Imperfect Marriage

I was sitting in a theater between my husband and the couple who accompanied us. The female lead appeared on stage, followed by an overly attentive, extremely solicitous, obviously loving man. Immediately my husband whispered in my ear, "Is that her lover?" Almost simultaneously my girlfriend asked the same question of her husband, who in turn asked me.

What did we all suspect? Each of us had been married for over twenty years. We knew very few, if any, spouses who acted so attentively, so textbook perfect. Consequently, we were less than surprised a few minutes later to find out that this man was an imaginary spouse, a husband entirely of the female lead's making. Her real partner was a self-absorbed intellectual, completely oblivious to her inner thoughts and feelings. Rather than face her disappointments squarely, the heroine of this drama retreated into a world of fantasy. That was not a wise choice.

She would have done far better to find out what could be changed in her partner and what was fixed, unchangeable, and off limits. Too bad she didn't know the power of a worthy captain armed with prudent and artful marriage secrets. She would have seen that **the biggest and most important marriage secret is to face reality.**

PERFECT MATE? PERFECT MARRIAGE? WHERE? WHO?

In reality, no one is married to a perfect mate and no one has a perfect marriage. Marriage is no place for fairy tales. Images of Prince Charming blur the real value of the regular guy you live with. It will set you up for dismal disappointment.

Accepting this secret, replacing fiction with fact, is paramount. Failing to recognize this truth can really weaken the fabric of your relationship.

TEN? ARE YOU SURE?

This question touched off a discussion of a funny situation between a husband and wife married for a quarter of a century. On this rare occasion when I interviewed a couple together, the question, "Do you think you have a perfect marriage?" brought up sparks.

The husband answered sincerely, *"We have a perfect marriage."*

The wife rebutted, *"It is impossible to have a perfect marriage.* Neither one of us is perfect, and our marriage is not always perfect. What about all those times you tell me I act like a real bitch?"

Obviously startled and a bit hurt by this response, the husband defended his position: "A perfect marriage is like a perfect football game. There is some defense with some obvious offensive plays. When the two teams come on the field, they play their game. The execution of plays is not always perfect, but the game is."

Matching my own confusion, the wife quizzically asked, "What on earth does that have to do with a perfect marriage?"

"We have our inevitable differences. Everybody has them. But we ultimately have a happy relationship and victory in the end. We have a good marriage. It is comfortable, and I love and respect you. It doesn't matter that each minute is not perfect; all of it is together. Knowing that we can reach this kind of happiness makes this a perfect marriage to me. Like now, it makes me happy you are listening to me, even though maybe ten minutes ago you were bitchy. Most of the time I really am happy. I don't always like you. But I always love you," he concluded, leaving his wife with something to think about.

Frankly, I was amazed at the number of people who boasted that their marriage was a perfect ten. I have to assume, however, that their response was more akin to this gentleman's, with all of its hidden qualifiers, that took into account that nothing really is perfect 100 percent of the time.

Still, I feel more comfortable with the evaluations of spouses who came up with a rating of nine and one half, indicating that there was always room for improvement. And I appreciate the honesty of the women and men who responded to this ambiguous question with an ambiguous answer: "Are you asking me to rate my marriage today or yesterday?"—noting the fluctuations in marital harmony.

A wife in her sixties discussed this very issue with her husband. Both decided they had had a good marriage for nearly forty years because more than half of those were clearly happy and fulfilling. Their reality barometer is still in place today. **If they find that they are happy at least one half of the time with one another, their apparent lifelong love match still qualifies as a good union.** Evaluate your own marriage and see how it stacks up along these lines.

The Best and the Worst

It's time to store the shining armor and put that spouse into the proper perspective. At a recent bridal shower I attended for two of my nieces, one of the clever hostesses wrote humorous verses warning the brides of the transformation that awaits their youthful grooms: balding, pot belly, inattentive, perfunctory lovers. An overstatement, I hope, but a fruitful look at reality nonetheless.

What was needed to fully complete the lesson were similar verses celebrating the virtues of the grooms that would blossom with matrimony. Granted, it is not wise to wear blinders to hide a spouse's obvious flaws; nevertheless it is even more advisable and less risky to concentrate on a mate's positive attributes.

Let's take a look at **the qualities that drive husbands and wives nuts and those that make them happy.** This is a handy comparison that will aid your reality check and clarify whether you or your spouse is getting a tad too picky with the other these days. You also might get some tips on how you should be treating one another if success is what you are after.

She Likes, He Likes

Why not start with the good stuff first!

Women report the following as the qualities they want most from their husbands:

Sensitivity
Responsiveness
Caring
Understanding
Patience
Honesty

Lovingness
Loyalty
Sense of humor

Men report these as the qualities they want most from their wives:

Lovingness
Caring
Attentiveness
Strength
Independence
Intelligence
Sexiness
Beauty

She Dislikes, He Dislikes

Women most dislike it when their husbands are:

Messy
Uncooperative
Stubborn
Overworked
Dogmatic

Men dislike it when their wives are:

Dogmatic
Fickle
Angry
Nagging
Procrastinating
Not listening
Siding with the kids
Making them feel guilty

REMEDIES

None of the negative traits listed above can't be cured with a few secrets. A couple of strokes, some "roundabout" communication and ego building, can remedy a number of complaints made by the men. For the women, creative love talk and fun-loving play might turn everything around.

These suggestions demand hard work. That's okay, as long as they are **directed at a mate WORTHY of such elaborate attention.**

Keep in mind that all of these grumblings were voiced by men and women who professed to be part of a love match that measured an eight to ten on the scale of marital satisfaction. Consequently, there appears to be pretty universal recognition that everyone and every marriage has faults. One husband hit it right on the head: **"No matter how bad things seem, I take a look at someone else's marriage, and mine looks a lot better."**

If you recognize yourself and your spouse on the list of favorable attributes, good. If not, draw up a list of likes and dislikes and encourage your partner to do the same. Exchange notes on what you like and dislike about each other. It can't hurt if you do this knowing you may not be thrilled by what you read but are willing openly and honestly to confront your differences.

A NOTE OF CAUTION

This could be more difficult than it appears. I was at a huge party recently where I was approached by a husband and wife. She said, "I'm sorry that I didn't send back your questionnaire, but Fred made me throw it in the trash when I rated him less than a ten."

I explained that the rating was for the marriage, not the partner. "I know that," she replied, "but Fred couldn't see it any other way."

Then Fred asked me, "Did you get any tens?"

Once again, I tried to explain the meaning of the rating. All he could say was, *"I don't know why she doesn't think I'm a ten."*

After he walked away, she said, *"I do all the compromising. That is why he thinks he is a ten."*

"Yes," I told her, *"he has no idea how much manipulation it takes to make him look perfect."*

She smiled in complete understanding.

If you are looking for perfection, you will have difficulty finding it in your spouse or within your marriage relationship. It is much more constructive to accept the inevitable imperfections.

LEARN FROM COUPLES WHO HAVE SHOWN WISDOM IN HANDLING AND CURBING THE MISBEHAVIOR OF THEIR SPOUSES AND THE FAILINGS OF THEIR PARTNERSHIP.

The following examples have been carefully chosen to illustrate these points. Take advantage of these lessons and save yourself and your partner some needless wear and tear!

TAKING CHARGE OF A LESS-THAN-PERFECT MARRIAGE

The secrets to tuck away here are:

- **Know** when to put your foot down.
- **Take action** when your spouse's behavior no longer seems reasonable because it calls for too much compromise and threatens your own well-being.
- **Acknowledge** your partner's imperfections.

- **Utilize** all available means to make an imperfect marriage work.

If you haven't already faced these issues, you will. Everybody does at one time or another. You won't be spared. And if you don't sort out the answers in time, you will find yourself identifying with the couples in the chapters on "Drifting Apart and Back Together Again" and "Doing It Right the Second Time Around."

Sally and Jake's Thirty-Year Secret Accommodations

Sally and Jake, a West Coast couple, have a thirty-year marriage that invites envy, but it wasn't always that way. "I was married at twenty during my second year of college," Sally begins. "We weren't thinking of what it was going to take to make it work. I'm not so sure it just wasn't a case of love and lust. At first it was easy. We were students. We had no financial pressures. But then our first child arrived after college and twins shortly thereafter. There wasn't a lot of time for the next fifteen years to really work on a love relationship; it took a back seat to work and kids. We just kind of got through those years."

Sally's eventual ability to handle the imperfections in her marriage and in her husband was like putting money in the bank. The deposits she made over the fifteen years paid dividends and helped to ensure the survival of their marriage through the most turbulent times.

One of the first things to contend with was Jake's enormous temper. Second, Sally had to learn how to handle his domineering, old-fashioned attitudes. This took longer to master, and Sally had to summon all of her assertiveness to do it.

"I can drive him crazy, too. Jake is a perfectionist, and I'm just the opposite," Sally says. "He thinks if you wash the floor it should be the best job. I could give a damn, but he's mellowed. **You better understand each other's idio-syncrasies and accept and respect them. You're just kidding yourself if you think you can reconstruct a person and make them into someone else. Remember that something in that person attracted you in the first place."**

Though this is certainly good advice, Sally found out that there are some things you just can't let your partner get away with.

"We were living in Seattle with four kids already. Jake used to tell me not to take his shirts to one particular Chinese laundry. My theory was, He Who Takes Shirts, Takes Them Where He Wants. So, I continued to take them there for convenience. One morning he was getting dressed for work, and I heard him carrying on. He was screaming in the bedroom. I looked in the door and saw him tearing his shirt to pieces. I thought, this guy is really sick. I need to get away from him. Then he screamed, 'Look at this shirt. It is all wrinkled. I can't wear it. I told you not to use that Chinese laundry.' He was absolutely in a white rage. I didn't even look at him. I ignored him and walked away. He was still ranting and raving when he went to work."

"Later that day he called and said, 'I'm sorry about this morning, but you don't get it. I have told you a hundred times not to take my shirts to that laundry.'"

"I said, 'Listen, take them wherever you want. I'll never take another shirt anywhere.'"

"After a couple of weeks of that, he said, 'Take the shirts wherever you want. Just please do it.'"

I applaud Sally's stand and think she was kind to resume her trip to the laundry! By putting her foot down, Sally finally got her husband's temper to a more tolerable level. **Temper tantrums are easy as pie to combat compared to trying to squelch that domineering machoism that so many women complained about in their young, and not so young, husbands.**

Jake was one difficult contender who didn't easily abandon his bossy ways. Sally found herself in other stews because she didn't know quite how to outsmart his attitudes. It took some time before she came to grips with his domineering personality. In fact, at one point in their married life, he attempted to move her around like a pawn on a chessboard. This episode taught her some very important lessons.

Sally and Jake were great tennis players. Jake Jr., their son, looked like he could be a real champ. Unbeknownst to Sally, Jake Sr. volunteered Sally to chaperone Jake Jr. on a year's intensive training and tennis education in Florida. After an unsuccessful protest, some ranting and raving of her own, and a "Hey, let's think about what is best for me," Sally packed up her son and youngest daughter and headed south. "He was used to bulldozing me, especially because he got away with it," admits Sally.

Trying to pack along a positive attitude as well, Sally thought maybe the change would be fun, after all. But Jake's latest treatment brought on one of those spells so common among women: *"It was one of my greatest periods of not loving him,"* she admits.

In an episode of "All in the Family" Edith Bunker told her daughter Gloria that falling in and out of love was a fact of married life. Archie may have called Edith a dingbat, but she was full of insight on this one. **Thirty-eight percent of the women who are presently in love with their spouse and rate their marriage at the top of the scale, when asked the question, "Was there ever a time you didn't love your husband?" answered yes.**

Approximately 25 percent of the men in the same category replied yes.

Women pinpointed this loss of love as occurring during the time they were raising their children, when his job kept him away too much, or when—like Sally's husband—he overstepped his boundaries. Significant numbers of husbands and wives told me that they may not have stopped loving each other, but that there were periods when they didn't like one another, and were disgusted with each other, or expressed disappointment in their relationship.

What can you do when you feel this way? Edith said it: "Ignore it. It will pass." Another couple gave me a secret rule of thumb. **"We both act AS IF we love each other, even during those times we don't.** Each of us has felt this way, and we both know this is the best way to handle it." I would suppose so after forty-odd years!

That leaves just two more choices: Say goodbye or try to change what is wrong. Each is a reasonable option. But you have to do the choosing. Sally opted for change rather than replacement when it seemed clear that the tough parts of the relationship were unbearable.

Sally Looked Deep Into Murky Waters

It didn't take long for Sally to reject the notion that her separation could be fun. She was lonely and wanted her partner to talk to. She was bored with just the kids. She missed her husband and their private weekly dates. She realized how helpful he had been coming home and taking charge of the kids now and then so she could enjoy a hot bath and a good book. "I got a real taste of being single," Sally says. "And I decided I would do whatever I had to in order to protect my marriage! I like being married. I like coming home and having someone there. I like sharing and spending time together. I need that companionship."

Here is Sally's prudent course of action.

• **"I accepted, after all this time, that Jake is the kind of man you have to exert power over. Without it, I would be eaten up.** He could be so controlling. I had to set him straight. I think one of my greatest strengths became my tenacity, my will to stick in there and make my point. I wasn't just going to give in any longer. He would have to start compromising. He knew I felt really strongly about something when I began taking that kind of a stand."

• **She became an amateur psychologist and tried to understand where his highhanded behavior originated.** The first clue was obvious: He was raised with the idea that men know best; to act otherwise would show unacceptable vulnerability. Clue number two: She saw that he feared her strength which she had tucked away in herself.

When Sally exposed this side of herself, Jake would ask her, "What the hell is going on here?" Now she understood that he was afraid to show weakness, afraid not to have all the answers, and afraid to appear vulnerable.

• **She empathized with the stresses and strains Jake felt in providing for his family and pitched in to help.**

The first things Sally had to change were in herself. "I have learned to think about him a little more. I learned a lot once I started working. Before I would hit him up with the things that had gone wrong in my day, whether it was the washing machine or whatever before he even took off his tie. Instead, I started to relate to what he was going through. Before I thought, whatever he had to say was no damn big deal compared to being home with these screaming kids."

Rather than wasting time over bitterness and resentment because of unintentional mistreatment, as unfortunately so many other women have, Sally remained clear-eyed and focused on making her marriage work. This enabled her to recognize Jake's insecurity and low self-esteem about the ups and downs of his business. Sally, or anyone with similar problems, should take another look at the implications of the ego connection covered several chapters back.

Rocky Beginnings, Happy Endings

It's too bad you can't start out with all this experience and insight when first going into marriage. You need it.

THE MOST LIKELY TIME FOR A DISASTROUS, QUICK ENDING TO A MARRIAGE HITS BETWEEN THE SECOND AND FIFTH YEAR.

The next five years are pretty tough, too, and add enormously to the high divorce rates. But the early years are mixed with confusion. It isn't unusual for men and women to wonder if they have done the right thing and if they really are in love with this person they are now supposed to live with forever after.

Consequently, the first several years require inordinate amounts of love, patience, and commitment to survive the adjustments of becoming a married couple.

Don't despair. There are happy endings. If you require proof, meet Patsy and Bill and Sonia and Miles.

How Patsy Zeroed in on the Strengths of Her "Family Man"

Patsy, now married thirteen years, introduces her story by confiding, "The first year was rough. Bill wasn't sure he really wanted to be married again, even though he loved me. I think he didn't want to be the one to call it quits. He made it so miserable for me thinking I would be the one to leave. We worked together as educators at the same school. He would get jealous and make accusations if he caught me even talking to another man in the hallway. I was afraid to talk to anyone. He really eroded my self-confidence. It was kind of cruel, but I don't think he knew what he was doing. I cried a lot that first year. He responded with coldness when I wanted him to respond by holding me.

"I believed once I was married, once I was in love, it would be forever," Patsy explains. "I wasn't about to throw in the towel. I never was a quitter. I thought, 'I'm going to stick this out, and one of these days he's going to figure it out and quit treating me so badly.'"

Finally, after eight months, little improvement, and tiptoeing around Bill trying not to get him angry, Patsy wisely said to herself, "FORGET THIS!" Bill would have to do some changing, and it would have to be sooner rather than later. She confronted Bill head-on with all the fury that had been building and let him know exactly how he was treating her and the damage he was doing to their once meaningful love affair. "I have had enough!" she told him.

This, apparently, hit him like a ton of bricks. He became upset, remorseful, and apologetic. "He didn't realize what he was doing. In a childish sort of way, he wanted to see how much I would take," Patsy explains.

Patsy was right to be so direct. Bill even admits that one of the secrets of their happy partnership is that Patsy is her own person. "She is very strong, very independent. I am a very dominant person, but Patsy doesn't take my crap. She handles me by arguing with me. But I won't argue with her anymore. She'll win, and I know it. She's bright and she's sharp. I bow to her better judgment. I think she has proven herself time and time again to be levelheaded."

A little shaking up helped him to see what he would be missing if he let this treasure go, and now he handles her with respect and care. "Patsy is as pretty on the inside as she is on the outside," says Bill. "She is such a genuine person and softens me up. I can come across like a real prick sometimes. There isn't anyone who doesn't like her." His accolades went on and on.

Patsy and Bill are best friends and have come through intact after some tough times imposed by health and financial problems.

But how did Patsy know that she would be able to change the situation and that Bill was worth it?

It appears that Patsy made it quite clear to Bill he was either in for change or he was heading out the door. A hard play to call, unless your partner is the marrying kind! That's what she was banking on. In her heart Patsy felt that Bill had the potential and the desire to be a good husband and family man. He just needed to throw out some baggage from his first marriage and his experience in Vietnam. She was sure his hard exterior would give way to the gentle, loving nature beneath.

A difficult bet to put odds on, but Patsy was right to the core. While I interviewed her, I caught glimpses of Bill playing outside with their two toddlers. She had him pegged just right!

Patsy was astute enough to notice that there was hidden treasure buried within Bill. He was loving and respectful to his mom and expressed a desire to have his own family. He certainly was generous and unselfish as a man and as a lover. He was kind and caring with the children he worked with.

If this sounds all too familiar, hopefully, you, too, can point to some hard evidence that your Joe or Jane is, after all, a marrying kind. Let's set the record straight here: Not every man or woman is.

Patsy saw some true indicators that Bill was. Some indicators that you are hooking up with a **less-than-marrying kind include:**

He or she:

- **never puts you first**
- **rarely consults your feelings**
- **acts totally inflexible**
- **behaves selfishly**

- has an uncontrollable roving eye
- is spoiled, immature, and uncompromising
- does not exhibit a basic respect and appreciation for the opposite sex.

For marriage to work, you have to want it to be an integral part of your life. **You have to be willing to change for the good of the partnership. You have to be willing to cultivate those qualities that make for a family man or woman. You have to want to give and not simply to take. If love and secrets won't get your partner in the mode to do all of this, it appears you may be stuck with the unmarrying kind.**

How Miles and Sonia Stopped Blaming Each Other and Took Hold of Their Marriage

Things didn't turn around quite so easily or quickly for Miles and Sonia, who left the port with few of the right conditions for a smooth sail. What were the strikes against them thirteen years ago? 1) Sonia found out she was pregnant less than ten months after meeting Miles; 2) Miles was in law school; 3) there was little income; 4) Sonia did not have a support system; 5) Sonia was depressed.

"I would ask her," says Miles, 'What's the matter? What can we do?' But I don't think she knew herself what to do. Neither did I."

"We talked about splitting up," Sonia tells me with tears forming in her eyes. "It was a very sad time."

This was a very emotional part of the story for Miles too, as he sat in his well-appointed law office giving me his version of their marriage, tribulations and all. "It was clear she was unhappy. I didn't want to be out of the relationship, but I realized something drastic had to happen. I can remember the morning and the situation. Our little girl was in the car. Sonia was dropping me off at work. I was telling her that I would find a place to live. For me, it was like the most important person in my whole life was going to die. Fortunately, we did not separate and moved on from there and began to look at each other differently. At least, I think we did. She began to see that I was really devoted to her and wanted to stay with her, that we had something of value. I don't think she doubted that I loved her. I think she doubted that I could ever provide the things she needed to be happy."

Just the thought of losing one another makes Sonia and Miles gasp for air. "It is heartbreaking to think of breaking up," Sonia says. **"We talk about how lucky we are that it didn't all blow up."**

Things surely could have blown up. Sonia got a job to ease the cash flow problem and found some attractive men to be quite a temptation for her ailing self-esteem and boredom. "Other people started to look more attractive to me. We both had relationships with other people, but it was just lunch and someone to confide in. I thought about having an affair, but I didn't. There was a man from the next office who would come in and talk to me each day. He made a lot of money but was a real phony, very flashy. I can see that today. He was enticing. He always complimented me and massaged my ego. The other man was just a good friend. I was looking for excitement and that early lust," she tells me in her hushed, shy voice that made it hard to imagine her having these cheating thoughts. **"It was really tempting to have an affair, and it frightened me."**

Thankfully she learned an important lesson just in the nick of time.

"My aunt invited me to go to Europe with her for seventeen days. It was the first time since I was married that I'd be on my own to do what I wanted, to have a little fun and to be a little selfish. I was able to look at the whole situation from a distance, and I missed Miles. I came back refreshed and revitalized," Sonia explains.

And Miles felt a renewed commitment. *"Before, I sensed that*

Sonia was ignoring me and blaming me for the way things were.
She changed from resenting me to wanting to hold me and care
about me. And at that point, I became more understanding that
things weren't so great for her. Typical of our relationship, Sonia
was the one who looked for a solution and sought counseling and brought me into it.

**"We began to see that we were in control of our marriage
and we could change the direction of it. Up to that point I
don't think that we had any idea that we could control our
marriage.** I really don't. I think this was a big part of what
was going on. We felt like everything was out of our control.
After that, things started changing. For Sonia's birthday I
surprised her with a night in a hotel. She started doing the
same kind of things for me too. I know it sounds sort of
corny, but those are the kinds of things you do to start
moving in the right direction."

Sonia also needed to sort out who she was and what she
could accomplish in order to clear up her own frustrations.
Miles understood this, even though it was tough when she
accepted a full-time job that required her to travel. **"There
were times I was probably not as supportive as I should
have been. I think I was occasionally nasty, to be perfectly
honest. But I learned to be more tolerant. You have to let the
other person do what they want."**

A Bigger Lesson: Make Yourself Happy

Free to explore her own potential, Sonia took charge of
making herself a more contented person and totally stopped
blaming Miles for her unhappiness. It was an internal
process. Sonia was more than competent at her work, she
was highly successful. Her self-esteem rose, and her attitude
at home improved. When the next baby arrived, several
years later, and she quit her job, Sonia's self-esteem was
intact. She no longer suffered pangs of inferiority or guilt

about being labeled a housewife staying at home to raise her children. She could comfortably reap the joys of her children, husband, and friends.

In the world of imperfect marriages to which we all belong, Sonia brought up a point that should not be glossed over, a point which is echoed below by many other women.

SONIA: "I started to take responsibility for my own attitude. I realized that even though I was married I was responsible for myself. I stopped looking for someone else to take control of my life."

JANICE: "I can't expect one person to be everything to me."

MARTHA: "If I am happy internally, I don't put expectations on anyone else."

CANDICE: "Making myself happy has in turn made my marriage happier. What was probably missing was something in myself. I had a lot of misplaced blame."

BEVERLY: "A therapist told me to get a life. My husband had one. Since then, I don't mind that he isn't the kind to praise me all the time or shower attention on me. He has his demanding career, and I have mine."

What they are saying about their imperfect unions is simple: **Look deep within yourself to see if that imperfection is his or yours.** I don't care if you are twenty-five and a young professional facing motherhood for the first time or fifty and harboring regrets of a lifetime. **Everyone, including you, is responsible for making themselves happy.** No one, not even the most near-perfect spouse, can give that to you. You have to do it on your own.

For Janice, it was finding more pleasure and support in female friendships. For Sonia, it was the opportunity to test her independence. For Martha, it was being a corporate head. For Candice, it was finding stimulation from a less-conventional social circle. For Beverly, it was getting accolades from the community sector.

First make sure your spouse's imperfection is not really your own. Then it's okay to get to work on your partner!

Sonia's Happy Ending

"We each verbalize how glad we are that we stuck together. We have become a great support and friend to one another," Sonia summarizes.

"There are still challenges and adjustments," notes Miles. "It's just that we're better at it now. We have more tools to do it with now. Sonia makes me feel wonderful. I can't imagine life without her. I adore her."

I could readily sense Miles's appreciation of how close he and Sonia came to the edge. I could see his gratitude for Sonia's love, now genuinely reciprocated, and her "quiet strength" which helped to hold them together. After meeting this couple—Sonia in her home and Miles at his office—I couldn't help but smile and enjoy the warmth of their relationship.

STAYING AFLOAT

Are you gaining a new perspective on those imperfections? Have you thrown out your wish list and replaced it with a memo on positives? Is this new picture of reality helping you to get love back on track? The correct answers for the above better be a screaming, blaring YES.

Only feet that are firmly planted in reality will allow both you and your partner to establish goals that are attainable and help you to move in the direction of success. Save the fairy tales for the kids.

10

Drifting Apart and Back Together Again

Most of us have drifted apart from our partners at one time or another. If you haven't yet, you will. When you do, be sure not to slam any doors shut, even if, at the moment, you have little intention of coming back through.

There will be many times when you are fed up and tempted to call it quits. But when life without your spouse, life without the kids, life with someone else, or life with the pleasures of a solitary, undemanding existence becomes appealing **keep that door slightly ajar until you are absolutely one hundred percent certain that there is no going back!**

Don't panic and make a rash decision if from time to time you find yourself asking: "How much longer can I stand living with this person?" Chances are it may be a whole lot longer than you think and just a matter of time until Cupid's arrow once again becomes deeply embedded. It is not unusual to drift apart and back together again. The secret is knowing how to survive when the ship is off-course.

RIDING THE SMALL WAVES, SURVIVING THE TIDAL WAVES

Riding the small waves is mainly a matter of luck, timing, and good judgment. It probably follows that order, UNLESS you are already well versed in secrets. Preoccupation with children and jobs, frustrations and conflicts over money, in-laws, and child-rearing strategies, anger over infertility or puzzling impotence, bouts of plain old boredom, and spurts of growth that put you out of sync with one another cannot be avoided. But if you expect and anticipate these momentary ups and downs and are determined to lick them before they lick you, the effects of these disturbances can be drastically diminished, even circumvented. If, however, you choose a less realistic attitude, you run the risk of being caught totally off guard and thrown precariously off balance when the inevitable small waves hit the deck. A tidal wave could easily flood your craft before you have the opportunity to grab the life vests.

The secrets revealed in the first nine chapters should, by now, have added not only significant pleasure but insight into your marital relationship, helping to keep the marriage craft afloat in troubled waters. Nonetheless, there are times when all of the indications seem to point to the ship's being swamped by a tidal wave. That is the time when every secret must be summoned. The couples in "Drifting Apart and Back Together Again" came dangerously close to divorce, opted to separate, worked their way back into each other's arms, and miraculously walked away with a happy marriage.

The following three couples describe their separations, which lasted from a few months to two and one half years.

They are survivors, and their sagas are instructive. If these couples can make it, so can you if you really want to!

Tackling the Other Woman

An interesting statistic on a talk show blamed extramarital affairs for three quarters of all divorces. In this section, though, you will hear the voices of *the victorious minority of women, those who have come face to face with their husband's betrayal and prevailed.* They have their man and a satisfying marriage, too. Unless you are willing to hand over your mate, pay close attention and prepare to set a better course!

What Glenda Learned While She Was Separated From Her Husband

You met Glenda and Nolan in Chapter 5. Nolan got into financial difficulty with his business and added to his problems by beginning an affair with an associate. His shaky ego prevented him from coming clean with his wife, Glenda. He walked out. She discovered the affair, but not the risky business mistakes until much later. We left them dangling after the split.

"They say it's not the affair that is so detrimental, it's the cover-up. It keeps snowballing and skyrocketing," explains Glenda, insinuating that it forced Nolan into more lies, more betrayal, and more deception, making the entire episode impossible to bear. "I wish I had known right away," says Glenda. "I think it would have saved a lot of heartache. I don't think he felt he was in love with her the first or second time. He called it a diversion from his problems. At first it *was* a diversion."

Still, the damage was done. Nolan's infidelity was a fact. Their relationship was torn apart.

There was nothing Glenda could do in the beginning but tackle each day, one at a time. "There were highs and lows when we separated. I had never been on my own, and for the ten months we were apart I handled everything." Glenda was one of those women who went from home to college to Nolan. "I learned that I wouldn't wither up and die. I was afraid financially when Nolan left. I kept the air conditioner turned off, I was very frugal and bought nothing. I was working at the time, and business was not that great, but Nolan paid me regularly to keep up the house and the kids. One time when we were making arrangements about the kids, I mentioned that I was looking for a new job. He said he wanted to help. I told him sarcastically, 'I can find my own job. I can take care of myself. I don't need your advice or anything from you.' This kind of remark was particularly hurtful to him because he was so nurturing and enjoyed the role of protector. *I always thought he was the strong one, and I would leave all the major decisions to him.*

"Being separated was the most difficult period. Friends told me to get the best attorney and the best therapist I could. The therapist helped, because I preferred talking to a stranger than unloading on my family. But the legal issues put us on opposite ends, fighting all at once. It was horrible. I shopped around for an attorney but didn't hire one. I still loved Nolan. You can be angry and mad, but you don't fall out of love. I even told the kids they should still have a relationship with their father.

"My friends said I got through this with dignity," Glenda explains with pride. "It wasn't easy hiding how I felt and keeping my composure. I couldn't eat. But I exercised and began to feel better. While I was working I was sometimes able to forget what was going on. People told me I was a model through this. I didn't curl up and go to bed for a month. I still worked. I was productive. I was careful who I went into detail with. It was hard. Some people would come up to me and say, 'I don't know whether to offer condolences or whether to offer congratulations.' That was stupid. This was my husband of twenty years."

Rediscovering her appeal to other men was a consolation and ego booster that helped Glenda during her separation. Fortunately, in her vulnerable state she did not overstep boundaries of behavior that she would have found difficult to live with later. "Realizing I was attractive to others changed my attitude; there could be life after Nolan. It helped me feel better about myself. I came close to having an affair two times. Both situations were with men I met through business. I became particularly intimate with one man. Now that we are back together, Nolan is obsessed with that man. We didn't make love. I went to this man's hotel room, and we became very intimate. It was dumb. I have told Nolan why and when and under what circumstances because he wanted to know."

The Secrets of Reconciling

A few months after his departure, Nolan had a change of heart. He said he had made a mistake. Glenda's deliberate course of action reveals critical secrets that affect reconciliation.

• **Maintain an open-door policy.** Glenda knew this intuitively. "I believe that Nolan could have gotten through his business failure without an affair if the other woman wasn't there to encourage the situation. He was responsible, though; it takes two to tango. Yet, I owed it to him and the kids and to myself to try to make the marriage work. There was still love." Obviously, Glenda made the right decision for her. "I feel this is where I belong," she told me, gesturing to her home.

Glenda practiced an open-door policy, which she viewed as the only option that could lead to reconciliation: "I could have shot him down and said, 'Hey, you made your bed, now lie in it.' I felt he was taking a big chance. I knew he was confused and mixed up. He asked if there was any chance he could put this marriage back together again. I said, 'It's not you, it's us.' Marriage was, and still is, important to me."

• **Don't dwell on the affair.** Be smart, like Glenda. She didn't let pride stand in the way. She knew what she wanted and what she had to do. She was willing to assume responsibility, put the indiscretion aside, and negotiate. All of these elements are common denominators among the men and women I spoke with who patched up their marriages after discovering their spouses had extramarital affairs. No matter how painful, how demoralizing, how disappointing, or how destructive, no one saw any benefit in dwelling on the actual affair: Was it love? How great was the sex? What did he like better about her? You may be curious as all hell. You may think you will be comforted by knowing the details. Take it from Glenda. She says you won't be. Throw it out, and reinvest your trust.

"My therapist told me one thing that took all the pressure off," she reveals. "She told me that while I would have to trust him again, I should lay ground rules. If it happens again, it's over. I said to myself, okay I won't wonder or be suspicious. You have to be able to put it away and go on. It took a long time. I am a lot more aware today and realize one should never say it can't happen to me. But if I dwell on it, I could drive myself crazy."

Whether you agree or not, and how you react, is not an issue, Glenda says. There is simply no predicting these responses. But once the shock of betrayal is over, what is absolutely certain is that *if you can't forgive and at least partially forget, watch out!*

The tidal wave will hit you squarely like it did Sharon, pregnant, twenty-eight, and married just a few years. Typically, indiscretions are less forgivable and less tolerated among younger couples. After receiving a phone call from a woman who confessed to having an affair with her husband, Sharon says, "At first I broke every dish in the house, and

then I screamed, 'Now I am going to get AIDS and die.'"
The stress and shock of her husband's behavior caused her to
have a miscarriage. "My husband sent diamonds and
flowers. He really tried to get me back. No, I couldn't go
back to him. I would feel like an idiot. I felt like he was out
there making a fool of me."

**WITHOUT PUTTING YOUR SPOUSE'S AFFAIR BEHIND YOU,
THERE IS LITTLE CHANCE FOR RECONCILIATION.**

• **Decide what you want**. Be very clear. Brenda, whom we
met in Chapter 6, knew this. She has an excellent suggestion
for the next step toward reconciliation.

"Ask yourself a key question," Brenda instructs, "when
your husband says he wants to patch things up: **Is it really
what I want?** If your answer is yes, then go for it. That's what
I did. I decided I wanted to be married. I wanted this
marriage to work. Why should I start over with someone
else? He is a good man."

There is nothing wrong with being practical. Even with a
cracked heart, Glenda, Brenda, and other men and women
can be practical and not blinded by shortsightedness. Naturally, happily married couples assert their intentions to
remain faithful to one another. Unfortunately, this will
become a matter of lip service to more than half. Peggy,
happily married and in her thirties, has an attitude that is
not all that uncommon in the face of such a possibility. "Mike
and I always agreed everyone is allowed one mistake. A one-
week or two-week affair can happen to anybody."

Once the affair is discovered, however, someone has to go!

• **Tell him she has to go**. Don't make any bones about it.
Glenda wanted Nolan back. She was willing to forgive, to
forget, and to listen to what he had to say. **She was strong
enough to deal prudently with his indiscretion.**

"Nolan came over right away," she says, carrying on with

her story and laughing at her own naïveté. "I said, 'We can work on it, but you have to end your professional and personal relationship with Maxie right away.' I figured he would go back to the office and give her two weeks' notice and we could continue as before. Of course, it hardly proved that simple. Not wanting to hurt anybody else, Nolan did not tell her that day. I'm sure he played both ends against the middle for a few weeks. It took several weeks. Because of the magnitude of her job, he gave her six months to find an equivalent executive position."

• **Patience is a virtue that is invaluable.** Hold on if you are squirming. Glenda owes her success to the long-term view.

"Nolan doesn't respond to threats and demands," she says, sensing my upcoming question about why she didn't give him an ultimatum with a strict deadline. "When we were together, it was so good, and I was okay. But I was afraid she would sabotage the reconciliation. I never knew what she was going to do. I found out later that this woman had had designs on Nolan from the first interview. At least six years earlier, she had told him that she divorced her husband for him. He said he never gave her any indication it would go in that direction. Although I was upset by her continued presence and the sexy way she dressed for the office, I knew I had to let Nolan find out for sure what she was all about. It took the full six months plus. My worst fears were realized. Just when Nolan was in the middle of an important bank closing, she sued him for sexual harassment. It almost blew the deal."

Patient or not, Glenda is the first to tell you she was angry for a long time. "I did put the knife in for at least a year. After the subpoena I would say, 'And you loved this woman!' On every anniversary I say we have to wait ten more months to celebrate because we were separated for that length of time. I keep it alive as a warning of what can happen.

Restarting the Marriage

Getting rid of the other woman does not result in an instant return to normalcy. But it is a good place to begin to restart the marriage.

DON'T WITHHOLD SEX TO PUNISH HIM

Like many couples who split and attempt to reconcile, dating is part of the process which reintroduces them to one another, helps them to make a fresh start, and begins the romance all over again.

"It was like having an affair together. There is an excitement to getting back together sexually," explains Glenda, a sentiment voiced by many other women. "I never said I wouldn't sleep with Nolan until she left the office. I felt that was dangerous. It was exciting. It felt good that he wanted to be with me. It was like a honeymoon. Just having him home in bed felt so good, so secure."

Glenda was giving in to her emotions, but why not?

To withhold sex or affection is to inflict more punishment than the fragile healing process can endure. It also reduces the chances of mending a love match that can last a lifetime.

SHAPE UP YOUR SEX LIFE

Brenda and Glenda both worked on their sex lives and became more assertive in their sexual likes and dislikes. "Before, I couldn't have said, 'Don't do this, or this feels good.' *Now I have learned it is important to say if something bothers me. I'm not prudish about anything,"* admits Glenda.

As a matter of fact, Brenda recognized her previous sexual inadequacy and vigorously went about correcting her mistakes. Yes, communication was a big reason for their split. But so was sex. Because of a strict religious upbringing,

Brenda never understood the pleasures that sex held for her or the importance of it in her marriage. She says, "I was pregnant a good deal of the first twelve years of my marriage. I don't know that I even remember sex at all during those years. I needed to understand my own sexuality. I needed to explore and even masturbate to learn how to build my own sexual response. And then, for seven years, every morning, we had sex. Sam was delighted. Of course, he was happy. Talk about playful; it was a great time of play."

How's that for a record high commitment?

"I knew I had to do something," Brenda explains. "That was all part of coming back together. **I rank sex way up there. Certainly sex is on an equal level with respect— respect for yourself, your partner, and his needs.** His needs are part of your mind-set.

What safer place to fill all of his sexual needs than in your own house?

DON'T KEEP HIM OUT IN THE COLD TOO LONG

Glenda understood the importance of timing. She allowed Nolan to move back in ten months later with no outstanding conditions. "I felt if it continued there was a greater risk we wouldn't get back together. It was acceptable to me as long as he was willing to try and make this marriage work."

"I wish my therapist had prepped me better for the day he moved in," explains Glenda. "It was really tough. We argued a lot. I don't feel we were prepared for the clash. He had accumulated so many things on his own. It was strange to have him bring so many things from this period into our home. When he moved back, our purpose was to try to work things out. We weren't simply back together. There was still a trial period to see if we could relate. I was scared, but I knew I didn't want to live the way I had for a year. There was

a definite 'let's make this work' attitude. It was good before.
We can make it that way again."

GO FOR A REAL PARTNERSHIP

Stepping back and evaluating her marriage before their
separation, Glenda rates it a five or six because of the lack of
in-depth communication, an ego imbalance, and too much
idol worship. "After our separation, I looked at Nolan
differently. **Before I kind of idolized him. It was a very
uneven relationship. He took care of me. It was not a
partnership. Now I realize he is a human being, and he can
make good and bad choices.** Now I love him differently, not
any more or any less, but it is a more realistic love. He still
likes to be the patriarch, but he realizes that is his own
problem. I think he still needs therapy. I try to tune in more
to what he is feeling and am much more involved in his
financial and business life. I try to understand the pressures
on him and share the ups and downs." She took this
opportunity to show me a card he had recently sent to say
thanks for understanding and putting up with the most
recent financial woes. "I don't sit and wonder where I would
be," she says. "This feels right, being here in this house,
with him. Having him come home feels right!"

ENJOY THE FRUITS OF YOUR LABOR

By chance the phone rang while we were talking. It
couldn't have been planned. Nolan didn't know I was
interviewing his wife. But his call convinced me that what I
had seen at the cocktail party when I met this couple and
what I had been listening to was an honest-to-goodness
reconciliation. Opting not to pick it up and interrupt our
session, Glenda and I waited for Nolan to record a message:
"I called to say hello and I love you."

Is Your Partner the Same Person You Married?

Are you? It would be extremely difficult to imagine that after five, ten, or twenty years you can respond with anything but "no." Whoever turns out to be the surprise package, be prepared to meet a challenge.

What Penny Learned by Changing Course

Penny says her marriage to Herb was a big ZERO and soared to a TEN after some shifts in the wind that blew both her and her husband off course and caused what seemed an irreparable split. But a two-and-a-half-year separation provided the impetus for setting a new course.

"Herb's one big condition before we got married was that I would never work. And I made that promise. I was twenty-one and just graduating from college. He was thirty-two and recently divorced. He felt his wife's decision to have a career was the cause of his divorce. I totally worshiped him. I mean, if there is such a thing as person-worship, it was me worshiping him. He was older. He was more mature. He was on his way to being successful. Anything he wanted, I was there, and my answer was always yes."

So begins Penny's story about her twenty-year marriage. But after five years of caring for two babies plus Herb's eight-year-old child and turning all other creative energies into tennis, Penny was bored and frustrated. The answer to her dilemma came in the form of starting her own business.

"That was the beginning of the end," Penny believes. "To Herb, it was happening all over again. He was bitter and resentful."

Herb agrees. The "chief cook and bottle washer" he married was changing. The neat, precisely kept house he envisioned had turned into a disorderly mess. But nothing could stop Penny, who turned out to be a real dynamo, hardly afraid of work.

If she thought Herb was nonsupportive, uninterested, and lacked enthusiasm before, she had more coming when she conveyed the news that her business had failed and she was stuck with a $50,000 debt.

"Basically Herb said, 'It's your debt.' And he asked, 'How are you going to pay it back?' Our deal was, whatever I did was my problem and my life. He was one hundred percent nonsupportive all during the business. I guess the crushing part was when it failed and I literally sat on my partner's husband's lap and cried because Herb wasn't there. It was a big emotional letdown, and I thought for sure he'd come through. He didn't. After that I went and got another job to pay back the debt, which I did in one year. But all communication between us stopped. I hated him because he didn't support me. Looking back, I'm not sure he really cared. It was an attitude of planned avoidance. Finally, after we'd been married eight years, I said I wanted out, and it devastated him.

"We decided to go to counseling. The counselor made us realize how we had gotten to that point, and that neither of us really wanted to change. Herb didn't want to get a divorce. He didn't really want to separate either. He wouldn't move out of the house. I finally got to the point where I had had it and found a house to rent. After I told him about this, he moved out several weeks later. I had very little support from family and friends at this point because I had not discussed our problems with anyone. I cried the whole night and when I called my mother, she said, 'Herb was the best invention since peanut butter.'"

Penny wasn't buying that flavor.

"For the first three months we basically didn't talk. I had built up a lot of anger. I went to see a psychologist, which was probably the best thing I ever did in my life. The process started to bring about a lot of changes in me," Penny continues.

"We never could have worked it out if we had stayed together," Herb now believes.

Penny and Herb let go of the ropes and sent each other out to experience the single world they had left less than a decade before. Neither lacked for attention or dates. Quite the prudent businessmen, Herb recommends to anyone caught in this predicament "get a legal separation. Neither of us had to accept any responsibility for our actions during this period if we eventually divorced."

Penny admits that she knew Herb would be a very eligible bachelor, but she was devastated when she caught sight of him out to dinner with a date one evening. "I was demoralized. That was one of the worst nights of the separation," she says. "I didn't know at that point that he was dating. We had told each other that whatever we did was fine, but it was difficult seeing him with someone else and facing the reality of what had happened. Eventually, I had a serious boyfriend. He made me realize I could do anything I wanted. I will not ever forget his support. Herb was probably dating a different woman every other night.

"I finally got over some of the anger. I went out to dinner with Herb after about four months. *It was probably the first real conversation we had ever had in our lives. We talked about what went wrong and what was still problematic between us. We left dinner as friends for the first time. We decided to meet periodically to discuss the kids and to go to community and family affairs together."*

The notion of a divorce was shelved and stored by a well-intentioned lawyer who had a hand in keeping this pair together. "I never thought we would get back together, but Herb told everyone we would. The only times I talked about divorce were when I got mad about something, but my attorney said he wouldn't proceed until I called him when I was rational. We had been separated for two years and one month when Herb asked me out to dinner, which was no big deal because we did this occasionally," recalls Penny with an uncanny memory for detail. "He told me that during this whole period he still loved me and that he realized he had made a lot of mistakes. **He wanted to know what it would take to get me back. His attitude blew me away."**

Why the change of heart?

Secrets for Harnessing the Winds of Change

Three big secrets effectively helped Penny and Herb meet the challenge of change.

1. An Improved Attitude

Several things happened to Herb while he was out and about, according to his own observations and those of his spouse. For one thing, Herb had done some comparison shopping and realized that most of the women that appealed to him were active and productive. For another, he developed a new respect and admiration for women who celebrated the values of self-realization, productive paid or unpaid labor, and independence as a means for achieving a better image of themselves. "Penny wanted her own identity, and a woman with more identity is more exciting," Herb discloses with conviction.

But even with this in mind, total reconciliation did not come easily. It took Penny almost the three full months Herb gave her to make up her mind about asking him to move home and begin anew.

2. Renewed Commitment

"When we got back together, things didn't work out the way we planned. The first five months were horrible," Penny explains. "There was a huge wall between us. The children were gone for the summer, and we talked one night about getting a divorce. After that talk Herb left the house, and I cried hysterically for about four hours. Later, in the middle of the night, he came back and looked at me and said, 'I want it to work. Do you?' And here I am crying and saying, 'Yes, yes, yes, but it still isn't working.' But for some reason, that night was the real bonding, the beginning of the new marriage."

Let's identify the mandatory ingredient: COMMITMENT. Any marriage will sink without it. Penny and Herb were ready and sincerely willing this time to change and, according to Penny, to renegotiate a contract that would work to preserve and satisfy their marital relationship. Herb says, "We needed to figure out and decide if it could work and if we were compatible."

3. Setting a Different Course

Their compatibility depended on Penny and Herb's willingness to compromise, which is the best insurance against repeating old mistakes. "We are so much more secure with each other," says Penny of their current relationship. "Herb has no problem with me making money. When my new partner and I started our marketing agency a few years ago, I went to Herb and his attitude was, 'I think you are ready. I wish you all the luck, and anything I can do to help I'm there for you.' He was a totally different person. I think he has grown up."

Now Penny disavows the concept of the "captain," but she happens to be a natural. She has learned to be her own person, make her own decisions and stand by them. But she does not sacrifice the interests of her husband.

"Because it is real important to Herb—though I am busy with my own business—I take the time to do things with him and travel with him as much as I can. If he has business people in town and I am exhausted from my day, I will still come home, change, and be there with a smile. Our marriage has become an equal partnership.

"What I really feel is that we are two people who went

through a lot of pain together and changed. **People change when they want to change.** From my experience, when Herb decided he wanted to stay with me, I guess I decided the same thing. Together we decided we wanted a marriage that worked for us and that we would do what it takes. We go out of our way to please each other now."

Could she have made a better testimonial? I doubt it!

TRAGEDIES, THE CRUELEST OF NATURE'S FORCES

Some say it is a miracle that marriages survive at all, what with the many divisive forces that keep pounding away at relationships. One of the most devastating circumstances that turns even the best of marriages upside down is the tragic loss of a child. The combination of misplaced blame, personality differences, and the vicissitudes of the healing process all contribute to the decline of the relationship. Margo and Ray came close to ending their marriage shortly after the loss of their two-year-old daughter, but they kept the door open just enough to enable them successfully and lovingly to come back to one another after separating.

No Time for Honeymoon

A brief synopsis of the early years Margo and Ray spent together sound suspiciously close to the story line of a daytime soap opera. There was hardly a letup in the blows that hit this couple during the first decade of their married life.

Within ten months of exchanging vows, Ray graduated medical school and was shipped off to Korea. Margo followed shortly thereafter, living seventy-five miles from the base waiting for weekend visits. "It was an important time for our marriage because Ray needed me there, and I needed to be there. I grew up in a hurry," Margo notes, explaining that her sheltered, spoiled upbringing hardly prepared her for the traumatic turn of events that overtook her life. By the end of Ray's tour of duty, he and Margo had an eight-month-old daughter and were facing the prospect of a potentially fatal condition.

"Ray was twenty-seven when he discovered his melanoma. We didn't know if he was gong to live," explains Margo. "The doctors thought they had removed it all, but we were told to get our affairs in order. We went back to the States and decided not to have any more children, not to buy a house, not to do anything because we just didn't know what the future would bring. Well, I got pregnant. It was unbelievable. I was using a diaphragm. We were not ready to have another child, but we just felt that this must be a sign that everything was going to be fine. We proceeded with our lives, and I went through the pregnancy. Eighteen months later, our baby daughter got cancer and died at age two. We'd been married seven years at the time."

Each of these events, one more ravaging than the next, built up a terrible resentment in Margo that was compounded by Ray's inability to bring his emotions to the surface. She was open and expressed herself readily. "It was very rough even before our second child was born. Ray forbade me to talk about his melanoma, and he wouldn't talk about it with me. One day I cracked. I was terrified I was going to lose my husband. I told a friend. I needed a friend. Finally one day I told Ray, and he was furious with me."

"I was a very private person," Ray says. "My family was private. So I think I handled my malignancy the same way. This was hard on Margo."

"After he thought about it, Ray was able to discuss it with our other friends. That was an important step for Ray, because he kept things blocked," Margo offers as an explanation. "When our daughter got sick, we were our usual tough selves. When you are dealing with something like this, you have to get through the days. They were so stressful, so awful. We thought we were doing okay. In retrospect I think I was putting on the best face as the ultimate cancer-coping mom. It seemed at the time we were supporting each other."

Ray agrees, "We were together during that illness. It's so terrible, and to make matters worse you are not always in sync."

"It was after Sharon died that things got worse," continues Margo. "The first month was one of relief. 'Thank God this is over.' Then came the first holiday, Thanksgiving, and I cracked. I really cracked. I was weeping all the time. I went to a therapist. I knew I needed help. Ray refused. He said he was fine, and that set the bad tone. I couldn't grieve with Ray. He had nowhere to go with it either, and we couldn't talk about it."

"Sharon's death ravaged me," says Ray. "I was so close to the vest before, I never cried until I was thirty-two. I grieved by myself."

"I started a part-time job that saved my life," explains Margo. "I started getting involved with community groups. We would go about our own business. It was not a conscious thing. We just gradually withdrew. I would be at a meeting or a play, anywhere but with Ray. We both took our grieving different ways, and we were getting testy with each other. I was hating him because I formulated in my mind that this was his fault. I blamed him. There were a number of issues I was angry about. All of this was unconscious at the time, though. *He pulled away from me. That pissed me off. I needed to grieve. I couldn't lean on him. After a month or so, he turned off and buried himself in his practice and was removed from me emotionally. This apparently is very typical. Losing a child is not a bonding experience. I would stand in the shower for an hour at night because I didn't want him to hear me crying."*

In a sarcastic tone aimed at herself because of her misguided perceptions, Margo spells out the thoughts that surfaced in her after Sharon's death: "I had to go through Korea. I had to go through this melanoma thing, and probably because of his weak genes, our daughter gets cancer and she dies. And you know what, life with Ray is a piece of shit. **I was thinking if I could just get rid of him, this black cloud over our heads would go away.** So what I did was find reasons to dislike him intensely. Everything he does is wrong. I argue with him, pick fights. He can do no right. And I am thinking I don't love him anymore. And you know what? I never loved him, and I want out of this marriage. It will kill me if I stay in this marriage. I'm not connecting it at this time to the child we lost. I hate him. We are barely talking. It is very tense and quiet, and one night—this is so bizarre—I turn to him and say, 'You never read *Newsweek*. I want a divorce. You never read, and you're not stimulating enough for me. We have nothing to talk about. I want a richer life, and I want you to move out.' And he is looking at me, rightfully, as if I were insane. I had never discussed any of this with him before that night."

GRIEF, AN EMOTIONAL IMPASSE

Ray was no doubt bewildered at the time, although he sensed Margo's blame was displaced. He told me that almost 80 percent of the couples who lost children end up getting a divorce. Experience has taught him that every person must grieve individually and within his or her own time frame.

Yet he remembers his frustration a year after Sharon died. "I was trying to get beyond it. I wanted to come home to some happiness. I'm a doctor. I had been faced with death and dying all day long at work. But the sun had just gone down, and my wife had turned into a zombie. I would pull up the driveway and wonder what tonight was going to be like. There was a terrible pit in my stomach. I didn't feel sorry for myself. It was a shitty situation. It was a bad feeling. We had always, I think, shared a lot of things. I was really fed up at this point. She may have wanted out, but I was really pissed. I always loved her, but I was much angrier at her. She was angry at the whole situation. I thought this was uncalled for. I thought at the time that we had really come through some horrible events reasonably intact. I have to tell you, however, that the separation served an excellent function. We sold the house and we moved into separate apartments. It was the house where our child was born and died. Margo had horrible memories."

Sensibly, Margo and Ray drew up congenial terms for a separation, a separation that not only gave them the right to discreetly handle their private affairs but gave Margo the opportunity to discover what Ray really meant to her.

"We didn't go to court right away," explains Margo. The first three months were very bad, and we only talked when it was about our daughter, who was living with me. I thought, at that time, that if I saw Ray fornicating with some woman on the floor that I would just step over the bodies. That is how emotionally distanced I was from him at the time. I did date an old boyfriend who happened to look me up. I was very sexually attracted to another guy then, and it scared me to death. I hadn't been attracted to anyone in the entire time we had been married. It reassured me that I was right about our marriage going sour.

"Then some weird things happened. I tried to call Ray one day. I had to get in touch with him, and I knew from a friend that he was seeing someone. It didn't bother me—so I thought. I tried all night to reach him. I knew he was out with this woman, and he never came home. I went nuts. A light bulb was turned on. Was it that I didn't want him and I didn't want anyone else to have him? It was very strange. **One morning I woke up and I missed him. I was shocked. I**

**realized all the irrational connections and saw this really
wasn't about Ray. I was punishing him."**

Secrets for Finding Happiness

1. **Plenty of Talk**
"It was one of those bolts from the blue," explains Margo.
"I put on my wedding ring, and Ray and I started dating and
talking a lot. I found out how much I loved and missed him
when he wasn't there. I also realized it was going to be fairly
difficult to get this thing back on track. It still took a long
time to let go of the anger. I needed to talk about it. Things
we should have been talking about before started pouring
out. There were a lot of tears and difficult discussions. It
turned out that he felt guilty too. He felt maybe his genetic
history caused Sharon's cancer, and here he is a doctor and
he couldn't help her. I didn't even realize I harbored these
tremendous resentments over his not being there when
Sharon died or his not going with her for chemotherapy. I
forgot he had to make a living. If we had stayed together
with that tension, we might have grown to hate each other
and destroyed the marriage. I continued in therapy, and I
told him he had to keep talking as openly as we were then
for it to work.

2. **Building Trust and Understanding**
"It took a while for him to build up trust. I mean here I
had said to him practically if you touch me I'm going to
throw up, and don't want to see you again. I want you out of
my life. How could I be trusted? I had hurt him very badly
and, to his view, without warning. I said terribly painful
things to him. We spent a lot of time together, both the two
of us and as a family. He was willing to go that far. I said,
'Let's look for a house,' but he wasn't interested in looking
right away. He had more of a wait-and-see attitude.

"We got to know each other a little differently. **I think** during the grieving process I was waiting to be the recipient of all this understanding and nurturing without giving a lot of it back. I thought he knew the way I felt even though I wasn't telling him. It was quite clear we really loved each other and had this wonderful marriage and had an opportunity for an even better marriage. We set some new ground rules about talking and sharing."

3. Choosing Each Other

"I guess I made a pretty conscious decision. I could have gotten a divorce and started over, but I don't know why I would have done that. It would have been a dreadful mistake. There is no such thing as perfection, and there is no person who meets all our needs. So you can either take the time you've already invested in your first choice and really work hard at that relationship, or you can start over again with someone without a shared history."

The love has to be there in the beginning to get you through some of these things. "It seems impossible to look at how Ray and I were then and how we dealt with things," Margo says. "He is so much more open and in touch. Both of us are more mature. Life is so much richer. It feels so good to be that close to someone. I am sure of his love." Ten years after the split, Margo says, "I still grieve openly, and this is a little thing between us. He doesn't feel it. I mean, I can sit there anytime and weep profusely if our daughter's name is mentioned. It's not that it's over for him, but it is much less intense. Ray is the one I want to be with when something happens good or bad. He's the one I want to laugh with. I guess these are the ways you measure the success of your marriage. We are so tuned into each other now."

Short-lived or sequential marriages miss out on important experiences. Certain deeper feelings take time to develop. It's wonderful and so different from that first blush of romantic love. It's like the sheen that silver takes on after years of use.

"Now I have this partner who knows my intimate secrets. I have a wonderful friend I never expected to have in a husband," concludes Margo.

SAVING LOVE AND MARRIAGE

This is an emotionally exhausting chapter, but at least there are three happy endings. The doors of love were kept open. Each marriage relationship has turned out to be a permanent one benefiting from both partners' stepping back, assessing the situation, and coming to terms with painful emotions. Three husbands and three wives returned from stormy seas with fresh understanding, renewed commitments, and generous helpings of forgiveness. The pain of separation provided an impetus to work harder on the things that divided them before they drifted irretrievably toward divorce.

Whether it is a matter of getting back on track or starting over with a new love mate, one of the key secrets is not to repeat the same mistakes. This is a lesson well heeded by Glenda and Nolan, Penny and Herb, Margo and Ray, and the couples who explore their second go-rounds with us in the next chapter, "Doing It Right the Second Time Around."

11

Doing It Right the Second Time Around

Note: This is a chapter for everyone, not just those couples anticipating or working on their second or third marriages. The valuable secrets disclosed here can help any love match last.

If at first you don't succeed, try, try again. That is standard and sound advice, but this time add to try again, "with a new approach." People who are happy in their second round of matrimony have followed this prescription and beaten the dismal statistics that tell us 65 percent of such marriages fail.

The prerequisites for "Doing It Right the Second Time Around" are simple and straightforward: maturity, respect, commitment, self-esteem, and love. If you don't have them, you may be setting sail into the sunset once again with a mate who is not seaworthy.

THE EDGE OF EXPERIENCE

The most satisfied customers, people who have found themselves happily married for a number of years, are those who went **looking for love the second time with a greater sense of self-awareness, maturity, and an understanding of the defects that marred their first marriages.** Undoubtedly, these couples were better equipped to select a new partner and to make their second attempt at marriage a lifetime relationship.

The Compatibility Factor

Living together as husband and wife is the only surefire endurance test of a marriage relationship. I hesitate to say it, but picking a mate can be a stab in the dark. Look diligently until you find the "marrying kind." Quizzes, counselors, and tests can help you figure out how compatible you are. The experiences of the remarried duos recounted below might tell you a few things as well.

MARRYING TOO YOUNG

During the course of my research, talking about marriage to everyone and anyone anywhere, I discovered an interesting consensus.

MOST MEN AND WOMEN WHO EXPERIENCED FAILURE AT MARRIAGE PUT THE FINGER ON MARRYING TOO YOUNG AS THE BIGGEST CULPRIT.

Although both women and men are marrying at a later age than did previous generations, couples are still relatively young when they tie the knot. In 1986, the median age for women marrying for the first time was twenty-three and for men, twenty-five.

"It is a miracle any of these marriages last when you look at the young ages at which people get married," says a second-timer whose first bride was nineteen. How true! They were too young to make a critical life decision, too inexperienced to grasp what is needed for a good marriage, too immature to comprehend the qualities of a good mate, and too vulnerable to good looks, lust, the promise of riches, and the urgency to wed.

This opens the door to too many surprises. And, unlike Penny and Herb, our example in the previous chapter, some couples are not able to handle the troubles of early marriage.

Cassie married the first time for sexual attraction. Twenty years later, her ex is still on the beach frolicking with young things in bikinis. Yvette had no idea her man was a Peter Pan type. "He didn't want to grow up. He thought it meant growing old," she explains. Emily thought Richie was the family type just because he said he wanted children. But actually he was untrainable and incorrigible when it came to being a husband and a father.

STAND STRONG AND TALL

No one is putting all the blame on the spouse, for sure.

WOMEN CITED THEIR OWN INABILITY TO STAND STRAIGHT AND TALL AS THE SECOND MOST SIGNIFICANT FACTOR THAT FIGURED IN THEIR FAILED MARRIAGES.

In our vernacular, they had no hint that marriage requires a worthy captain with the maximum amount of self-esteem and assertiveness.

"Marcie looked great, but she had no self-confidence." This is the first thing on Phil's list that clearly separated his first from his second wife. "She never spoke her mind. I had no clue anything was even bothering her until she reached the breaking point. I surely don't have to worry about Claire letting me know what she is thinking. She is about as straightforward as you can get. I wanted a woman who would let me know what I needed to do in a marriage."

There are a lot of Marcies out there who have learned their lessons and have changed tremendously since they waved goodbye to their first spouse. They attribute their newly found happiness the second time around to personal adjustments that enable them to act as captains.

"I didn't know how to assert myself in my first marriage," says Meg. "I didn't ask for things I wanted. I didn't communicate well or tell Steve how I was feeling. My husband was very controlling. Maybe if I had spoken my mind he would have backed down more. After some therapy and with a more mature outlook, I am no longer trying to make everyone happy but me. My current husband and I make each other happy."

Kathy had much the same problem. "I tried to be what my husband wanted me to be instead of who I was. I was practically a puppet." Too bad she didn't know that puppetry was not the way to a man's heart!

What You Ought to Know Before the Second Round

You have to discover your own likes and dislikes, needs and desires before you settle on a new partner or even get rid of the old one. A woman, married for the second time who found she was less than satisfied wrote me, "If I had to do things all over again, I would still be married to my first husband. I was married for twenty-four years. My first marriage was much better than my current one."

Here are some useful observations voiced by divorced women as they approached matrimony for the second time. You might find their opinions beneficial in getting you to start thinking about your own marriage.

FRIEDA decided, "Most people are pretty phony. I found someone who was honest and I could be honest with. There is love every day. Adult love. I wanted someone capable of sharing my life. I was more realistic in my choice and chose with my eyes open. I didn't go for an illusion. I wanted to be able to say, 'I like this person.'"

POLLY learned a lesson. "I am more practical now," she says. I'm not perfect, and neither is he. I think for the most part you have to be practical to achieve happiness in marriage."

JANIE says, "You have a better idea what is really important and what isn't after you get kicked in the teeth from a first marriage. I wanted someone who was gentle and whom I could trust."

Many women said they were looking for men who were sensitive, compassionate, and fun, traits missing in their first spouse. They wanted men who they could count on and call a friend.

Smart ladies that they were, they weren't looking for perfection.

Men thinking of going around for the second time also had some thoughts on the subject.

BURTON says, "I was looking for someone who likes to do the same things I do. I wanted that feeling you read so much about, like there is no one else for you, someone who is concerned about what happens to you."

Not quite as romantic, but very realistic, BRUCE describes what he went looking for and found the third time. "I wanted a woman who would not provide extra stress for me. I eliminated from my list women who got manicures at home and weekly massages. I didn't want anyone so spoiled. I went out with a lot of neurotic, spoiled women."

MEAGAN knew what she needed. Do you? She found him, too. "I needed a man who could understand me. Tommy knows me so well. It is shocking how well he understands what I'm feeling by a look on my face or the way I answer. He is much more appreciative and concerned about me than my first husband."

Can you guess Step Two for those who reported newfound

matrimonial success? Once they found their desirable new spouse, these men and women knew what to do with them!

THE SECRET VOWS FOR HAVING A LIFETIME LOVE AFFAIR WITH YOUR SPOUSE

The big secret of success is to accept the message in the vows listed below and to employ a special blend of secrets. For a surprisingly large number of rematches, these secrets have become an automatic code of behavior that has made the work of marriage seem almost effortless.

—I pledge to love, understand, and respect my mate.

—I am willing to compromise and am ready to meet his or her needs.

—I appreciate my partner and the loving, caring way he or she treats me.

—I am grateful for the sacrifices he or she makes to enhance our relationship.

—I will remain loyal to the trust we have placed in each other.

A PEEK AT MARRIAGE SECRETS BREWED BY EXPERIENCE

Here are some secrets to add to your list for the first or second time around.

MERCEDES: "There are still some old ghosts that are hard to bury from the first marriage. I have learned you don't have to tell everything. I don't think it is necessary to burden a new relationship with some of the bad baggage. He doesn't need or want to hear all those things that were bad from my first marriage or my romances. It hurts. It may be a side of my life he doesn't like. It's not going to add to our relationship."

ADAM: "My first marriage is so far behind me. You have to let it pass. It is history. There is no reason to dwell on it unless you can pick out what mistakes you made. We discuss our previous mates once in a while if it has something to do with the children. Otherwise, we don't dwell on them at all."

TAMMY: "I make a point of sitting down even if we are yelling at each other and say, 'Let's get this in check here.'"

KIM: "You don't just pump somebody up by saying something nonsensical like 'Gee, you are the greatest person in the world.' I make Tim feel good about himself by telling him he has a good or bright idea or that he did something I couldn't do. I use real situations to pump up his ego."

STACEY: "I think it is important to have fun, sexy evenings, because no matter how crazy you are about your husband the second time, there isn't the same spontaneity and urgency as when you were dating and before you lived with four kids and two dogs. You need to re-create a new environment."

MARTHA: "I learned it is easier to give if it is appreciated. I see him doing these things for me so I want to give back more."

MORTON: "You have to be capable of compromise. You can't be totally selfish. You have to give everybody their due, otherwise, forget it. It won't work."

HERBERT about GLORIA: "My third wife is dedicated to everything, to me, to her work. It is easier living with a woman like that. The lines are defined. You know what to expect. She is stable and supportive and helps me through my highs and lows. My business is demanding. There are times I have to fly off without notice. It's good to get a 'Have a good time, good luck and hurry back,' instead of 'Jesus Christ, again?' There is a lot of sharing."

RALPH about DARCIE: "This marriage works because she treats me like she really cares. It shows and makes me feel important."

SPENCER about HEIDI: "Heidi is more understanding. I begged and pleaded to play golf in my first marriage. Here it is the opposite. Heidi will say, 'Why don't you take some time off and play golf? Relax and take it easy.' There is more compassion and understanding."

A Trio of Rematches

It is always simpler to learn a lesson by example. Despite the fact that each couple's relationship is unique, the three rematches examined here offer impressive clues to achieving a high level of marital satisfaction. They will also turn up those thumbs pointing downward at the mere mention of giving matrimony another try.

Faith and Edward, a Refreshing Look at Marriage

Faith was married at nineteen. Edward's first wife was also nineteen at the time of their marriage. Faith thought she would have a good marriage. "At least the best I could expect," she says, explaining that she grew up as a witness to her parents' poor relationship and consequently was not aware of what comprised a really good marriage. Edward grew up in a home with devotion, love, and respect. He married expecting to emulate this example. Both were dismally disappointed living with partners who had minimal regard for their feelings. Both agreed they should have divorced their partners early on, before children, before bonds that are not so easily broken.

Despite a tumultuous union and her husband's philandering and gambling, Faith put up with eighteen years of marriage in exchange for financial security for herself and her children. Edward was unequivocally loyal in every sense of the word for over twenty years, hoping year after year that his wife—miserably unhappy and angry within herself—would find a measure of peace and finally bring harmony to the home he hoped to keep intact.

"Marriage was and is important to me," Edward says. "Even if I knew what was missing then, I was caught up with what you have to do to get from point A to point B with our children."

When Faith had finally had enough and called it quits, she was not soured on marriage but was determined to be cautious in seeking out another permanent relationship. **Edward, set free after it was clear that his wife's attitude and their relationship would never improve, had lost all vision of how wonderful a loving partnership could be.** But a self-avowed "marrying kind," Edward still preferred marriage and settling down to the limbo of being single.

Here were two handsome, bright, successful, well-educated, sensitive, caring, very eligible people who had what it takes to make a love match. Fortunately, fate and the help of friends brought them together.

"I was so fearful of being taken in that when I started dating a very rich man with his own plane—but an emotional zero—I kept notes to remind me of the things that were missing," reveals Faith in total honesty, very much her own person when she was age thirty-eight. "The night I met Edward, I can't say I fell madly in love with him at first sight." But after a few months of dating, Faith valued the man she had found and became aggressive. "I couldn't be too strong with this man. He was just coming out of a relationship. Certainly he was feeling scared." But that didn't stop her from asking what his intentions were.

Edward laughs when acknowledging that Faith brought the relationship along quickly, adding, however, that he had no desire to date anyone else after they met. His intentions and hers must have been clear enough. The time lapse from the first date to the altar was less than nine months. What was it they found so attractive in one another, and what made them feel optimistic as they were about to take a fresh plunge?

"I did think *Edward was the nicest person I had ever met,*" begins Faith, describing the kind and gentle man who attracted her. "And I guess if you want a good foundation for a relationship, that would certainly be one of the keys. **I wanted a partner I could be equal with.**"

"There is no question that there is an element of luck," agrees Edward. "I just started dating people who were recommended to me. My relationship with Faith just grew. We were very compatible. We had similar interests. We were already adults, and it was easier to figure out, when we were dating, what that person was going to be about."

It doesn't matter that bells didn't ring and birds failed to sing at their first meeting. Married ten years now, Faith and Edward have a Cupid firmly implanted in their home. Totally missing in their first matches, commitment, respect, and consideration pervade this second marriage. These qualities characterize their relationship and provide fertile ground for a rich and deeply appreciated love affair that continues to grow.

"I wonder if the best way to become humble about a relationship is to have a devastating marriage," Faith says, questioning the behavior of other couples. "I find myself annoyed with friends when we are out and see them doing dumb, selfish things just to stick it to one another. One person will suggest something they could do together the next day and the partner will reply, 'Why should I do that? I'm not interested in that!' Things like that outrage me.

"I don't understand why everyone doesn't want to be as happy as they possibly could be. *It is just a matter of giving pleasure to someone else you love. Call it manipulation. Call it savvy.* I know sometimes I am being manipulated with a present or an extra phone call during the day and an invitation to lunch. It is the little things that count, and I like doing things for Edward. He loves to see me when he walks in the door. He likes a big show of affection. He can tell I am thrilled to see him. *Interestingly, my first husband said I never looked happy to see him,"* finishes Faith.

Happy, however, is exactly what Edward makes her and she him. "The love and affection I have from Faith is something I never even came close to in my first marriage. It never ceases to amaze me. A day doesn't pass that she doesn't say, 'I love you,' or just walk up and kiss me. It is a great experience. I think she is keyed into my needs. I want to tell you something," Edward says sincerely. "To this day, I just don't believe that someone could show this kind of love and affection toward me. It is like a fairy tale. This is the most remarkable thing about our relationship. My first relationship could never come close to this. *Faith makes me feel like I am the center of her life, but she can make anyone feel that way. She makes her children feel that way, too. That is one of her great talents."*

What Faith Does for the Sake of Harmony

Okay, you say, this all sounds lovely. But how do they handle the ups and downs? Just the same way, with care, respect, commitment, and compassion. That's what it took to get through ten years of dealing with his and her kids, family illnesses, and business setbacks.

I spoke with Faith in her downtown apartment, which re-created the cosmopolitan, sophisticated atmosphere that characterized her life before a major disruptive move a few years ago. It was clear she had had to summon all of her experience to keep love and harmony in her marriage during that personally trying period. Starting all over in her mid-forties proved to be a harsh lesson in reality, one Faith mastered with Edward at her side.

"Moving out of Chicago was extremely difficult for Faith," explains Edward about the change necessitated by conditions in his business. "She had never lived anywhere else. She had friends and a successful business. After a month she had made a few friends. But the biggest flaw was still her business, which had taken fifteen years to establish. I felt terribly guilty. I still do. She has never made me feel guilty. Every now and then tears well up in her eyes when she thinks about it. But I am very lucky. She is very resilient. I asked her if she wanted to commute and said we could set up an apartment for her. I thought it was important to give her that space, because I knew how much the business meant to her. She turned it down. She absolutely refused. She said she wanted to be with me."

Faith has this marriage thing in the bag. She must have listened to those old lyrics and taken them seriously, *"Once you have found him, never let him go."*

Faith, however, will concede, "There were times I wanted to scream and yell at him, 'God damn it, how could you do this to me?'" Instead, she started a new business. And she says, "I talked to myself. He didn't do this to be cruel but for survival and for hopes of good things. I tried not to place my anger on him, but I did need to express what I was feeling. We would sit down and I would tell him I just don't know what to do. We talked. It was comforting. It wasn't like confronting the other person. What I needed was more therapeutic. **I would have devastated him if I had approached him in a more accusatory manner. I don't need to spit out everything that is making me angry or unhappy. I don't give him information that he has to carry around and worry about and that I will get over quickly."**

Are they an unusually happy pair? Maybe, but what they have is not beyond the realm of possibility for any one of you who is willing to act a little older and wiser.

Abide by give and take, add a measure of genuine appreciation, and practice the formula that requires "giving 99 percent on both sides." Then see if other success stories become your own.

Faith may have thought this type of pleasure was impossible to obtain from marriage, that is, until she hooked up with Edward. "The demands and expectations I have in my second marriage are absolutely normal," explains Faith. "My first husband thought they were beyond fulfilling." What is it she expects? Just the respect and understanding that is due any worthy mate. And she gets even more from this ideal man.

When I said to Edward at the end of our interview, "Lucky Faith," he promptly and earnestly replied, "Lucky me!"

Gloria and Ken, Forsaking and Then Retrieving Love

It is time for a love story, a true story of heavenly proportion, but one not without its hitches.

Poor timing and a questionable set of values created a rift between two lovers that cost them eighteen years of happiness and the opportunity to have a child together, something Ken deeply regrets. Once he and Gloria reclaimed their love, what better reason could there be for a rematch?

"We met when I was eighteen. Ken was a few months younger. I was a college freshman, and he was a senior in high school. I went to the drug store on a rainy Tuesday. He was there because his track practice was canceled due to rain. My roommate introduced us," Gloria begins.

"I knew there was something special," Ken says, vividly recalling every detail of that day in the mid-sixties. "I was in heat for the most part and saw those tight plaid pants she had on. She looked so cute with those big blue eyes. I said, 'There's something special about this girl.'"

"He asked me to go to the movies that night," continues Gloria. "We saw *Bird Man of Alcatraz*. We hit it off real well. He would come over every Friday night and take my roommate and me out for a drive, and then Ken and I would go alone to the quarry and neck. We dated a lot that spring, and then I went back east for the summer."

Not in any financial position to pursue his college education immediately after high school, Ken went into the service and was shipped off to Vietnam. Gloria and he wrote back and forth and became engaged in 1966. When he returned to the States in '67 to start college with his eye on a degree in dentistry, Gloria was showing signs of ambivalence, switching her engagement ring from one hand to another. Ken's mother approved of the match and announced the engagement. Gloria's did not.

"In November, she was supposed to come and visit, but she didn't," Ken remembers. "I got a 'Dear John' letter that said she had other plans. I was absolutely crushed. It was her mother's fault. She wanted Gloria to have coming out parties and marry a doctor or a lawyer. Her mother still doesn't like me. She tolerates me. They had to keep me away from open windows and high places. Two days later the ring showed up. I tried to call right away and sent flowers. I should have gone to Boston, but I didn't have any money. I should have hitchhiked. A week later, I was feeling defensive and said, 'The heck with her.' I couldn't forget her and a year later I called her up. She was married—to a lawyer."

Gloria was married for eighteen years, and happily, she thought. It wasn't until she and her first husband grew apart and divorced and she then married Ken that she realized how empty her marriage had been. "What I had before was a facade, a surface kind of thing," she evaluates.

Ken meanwhile had married and divorced. "I thought about Gloria all the time, constantly. One thing or another set it off, a thought or a smell. My wife knew I was thinking about this other woman. I never thought I would be unfaithful, but I guess I went searching for that one special thing that was missing. My first marriage probably had no chance of working out. It was sort of set up on the rebound."

Not years or miles seemed able to dissolve the passion Gloria and Ken had felt for each other in their young romance.

"It was time for my twentieth high-school reunion, and Ken wanted to inform me about his divorce. He contacted my high school to find out my address. The chairman of the reunion wouldn't give it to him but agreed to forward a letter to me," explains Gloria.

"After I wrote Gloria, I waited on pins and needles for a letter to show up. It was my fantasy she would want to get together again. But she didn't even write back. Then in 1986—eight years after I was divorced and getting ready to settle down again with a really nice woman—this Christmas card came with no return address, just a postmark. It was two weeks before Christmas and I went out to the mailbox and pulled out this letter. It had all of these address corrections on it. I recognized the handwriting immediately. I said, 'Oh no, it can't be. What in the world is going on?' I was almost afraid to open it. My heart was beating. My life was beginning to fall into place, and boom! Just like that, another big bolt of lightning. It said, 'I have been thinking about you. Hope you have a nice Christmas.' I called my mother and told her if she ever got another letter to just keep it. I didn't want to take a chance on losing it. My birthday was in a few weeks, and I got another card. I had an instant transformation. My girlfriend was climbing the walls because of me. My attitudes changed. I was still madly in love with Gloria, but there was no way to reach her."

"When I was legally separated from my husband, I decided I wanted to call and talk to Ken," explains Gloria. "That's when I got in touch with his parents. His mom told me he still talked about me. I asked her if she thought it was okay if I got in touch with him and she said yes."

"It was snowing outside and I was folding clothes and the phone rings. I had my arms full of pillowcases. I pushed the speaker button. Her voice was just as magical as the letters," Ken tells me, still breathless when he repeats this critical moment from a love story. "I dropped everything and thought, 'Oh, God. Don't push the wrong button and disconnect her.' I said, 'Gosh, where are you? I'll just go get a plane.' She wouldn't tell me. Several calls later she told me she was in Florida and gave me the telephone number at the school where she was teaching." But Gloria still wasn't ready to meet Ken face to face.

"The first time I heard his voice, I cried," says Gloria. "It was so easy to open up to him. It was the most amazing thing. We spoke back and forth, but one day he called and said he didn't feel comfortable keeping this up because he was going with someone. I was crushed. Three months later, he sent me a Mother's Day card. I knew I needed to get back in touch with him. We saw each other three weeks later."

"There was no denying her, no matter what the situation was," confesses Ken. "Even if I had gotten remarried, I would have been working on my second divorce. I was nuts about her. There is no doubt about it. Gloria's values were different. After all those years, she realized there was more to life than the things she was trying to get at twenty-one or twenty-two."

"I hadn't seen him for eighteen years. It was like no time had lapsed," Gloria explains. "It was great. I got him at the airport, and it was very comfortable. We went right back to the way it had been. The feeling would have been there if we didn't meet up until we were in our sixties or seventies. I don't know why, but it is. We had a wonderful warm embrace. We didn't even go out to dinner but slept with each other. It was like we were completing unfinished business. It was absolutely wonderful. It still is.

"Our marriage is very different than what I had known before," Gloria reveals about their four-year union. "It is a lot more intimate. I don't think we could have stayed away from each other if we had met up before. We have a strong attraction to each other. We still think of each other as being eighteen. It's nice having that background together. Ken and

I care deeply for each other. We are just together. This is a real kinship. We joke about how we met up in heaven on a baby-conveyor line.

"I am very happy and grateful that I will not have to go to my grave without this experience, without knowing that I could be so open with someone else. Now it is like, okay, this is the way it is supposed to be. Love is a combination of a lot of things, being concerned about his welfare, wanting to build something together. Lust is part of it, too. Love is having that kind of feeling, deep feeling that is hard to describe. I just know that I didn't have it in my old marriage. There is something very unique about this relationship," Gloria explains.

Ken describes his love. "It is a good feeling of security. Our love is unconditional, exciting, sexual, stimulating, fun, satisfying, and gratifying. There is a great feeling of devotion. I appreciate knowing that we both feel this way. No one else could make me love them as I love Gloria. We feel we were supposed to find each other because the chances of us meeting were so slim. Talking about this still puts a lump in my throat and makes my lower lip quiver."

The Meaning of L-O-V-E

Not many couples experience this kind of timeless love and passion. **Shere Hite notes in her book, *Woman and Love*, that only thirteen percent of her respondents married more than two years professed to be "in love" with their spouses.** This is characterized by an inexplicable intense, passionate feeling. **Eighty-three percent preferred to say they loved their husbands, inferring a love built on companionship and caring.**

The few couples I found who describe not only loving their spouse, but being "in love," are the ones who believe they were made for each other, that no one else could take the other's place. "I would have found her if she were half way around the world," declares one of these kind of lovers, even after twenty-five years of matrimony.

Having a loving relationship can be just as powerful for husbands who experience feelings similar to these expressions of love: "My loving relationship gives me a feeling of complete unity in mind and body with that one special person who gives more than she expects to receive." The love he has for his wife, explains another husband, encompasses "the highest level of respect, concern, caring, and admiration that can be given another person."

Either way you take it, it is no secret that *LOVE is the lifelong magic in a relationship. Don't forget to tend it regularly!*

Margaret and Bryan Determine to Implement a New Set of Rules

When Margaret and Bryan divorced their respective partners, neither was in any hurry to remarry. But once they fell in love and set their sights on trying again, they began with an improved set of rules and expectations.

It doesn't take long to see what was falling apart in Margaret's marriage and why she looked in the opposite direction when choosing a man. "Everything that could go wrong did from the beginning of our marriage. I was still in college and got pregnant. I felt I had to finish, and couldn't live with myself if I didn't. Then I was going to settle down to be a traditional wife and things would be wonderful. But something was missing. I was bored. When my husband's job looked shaky, I didn't mind going to work. I took a job in investment banking, got some career clothes, and became successful right away. **I felt like I was doing everything, taking care of the household responsibilities and working. We weren't a team.**

"The turning point in our marriage came after I became seriously ill and spent several months on my back. My husband showed no compassion. I came out of it knowing I couldn't stay married to this person."

Bryan went through what he calls an "awakening" that, among other things, made him realize he was unhappy with his loveless marriage. It was impossible for him to deny who he felt he had become and that he and his wife had absolutely nothing in common. To stay in his marriage was too painful to contemplate.

Margaret and Bryan met casually through business. Their friendship and romance evolved over two years of business lunches before turning into a more intimate affair, which lasted several more years before they finally opted to marry.

When Bryan asked Maragaret to marry him, she was careful from the start to nurture their marriage and help it along by following a new set of rules and expectations. For instance Margaret did not like the tenor of Bryan's proposal. "Bryan told me we would *have* to get married because he wanted to have a relationship. I was consumed by a job day and night at the time, trying to make money. I said, 'You didn't say the right words.' The next night I had to work, but a few nights later he wanted to take me out to a nice dinner. This time he said, 'I want to *share* my life with you.' I told him, 'That's closer.'

Both had to overcome the problem of blending their respective families, which produced a brood of incorrigibly destructive boys. It took a real partnership, love, and a serious commitment. "If we hadn't loved each other so much, we wouldn't have gotten through it," says Margaret, referring to the enormous difficulties they had contending with one another's children, all of whom lived with them.

Margaret and Bryan are both aware of the practical considerations that pulled this marriage off. **Margaret takes full advantage of the fact Bryan will do anything for her, and divides up the household responsibilities.** Bryan uses new insights to keep things running smoothly at home. **"I am**

more gentle than in my first marriage, and even more so than at the beginning of this one. If I am troubled or angry, I am more inclined to count to ten before I verbalize it. Part of getting along is exercising sufficient self-control to know when not to say something if you want to do the opposite. When Margaret becomes too explosive, she recognizes it and tells me she is wrong and makes it better. She will hug me and kiss me and make up with smiles. It is nice being pampered."

Margaret, competent and authoritative at work, is just as much the orchestrator of love to keep marriage on track at home. She is the planner of mystery trips, the sender of flowers, the initiator of compliments, and the instigator in adding excitement to sex. What does Bryan think of these little obvious touches? "Without them, the marriage wouldn't be as good. They make me feel appreciated."

For Margaret they are labors, but labors of love. "I wouldn't be married for the sake of being married," she says. "It is much more work than the first time." To make sure Bryan stays in love, Margaret has another batch of secrets. "I watch my figure, style my hair to please him, and I work hard at trying to remain the mistress in bed. I feed his ego when he is all dressed up. I will tell him, 'Boy, am I glad I'm going out with such a handsome guy tonight.' And he blushes. It's cute. Or I'll say, 'Everybody is so jealous because I have such a good-looking husband.' He isn't really all that demonstrative so I'll take his hand and tell him I need his hand right now."

And that is just how they proceed, hand in hand. The friendship, companionship, and support they give and receive is well worth the trouble.

"Everybody likes strokes," Bryan explains. "We are complimentary to each other in public and supportive of each other not just when we are alone. I am proud of Margaret's success. To be with someone less accomplished wouldn't be

as much fun," he says, an attitude that makes Margaret
happy, especially considering her first husband's total denial
of her talents.

"We get along pretty darn well as friends too," acknowledges Bryan, who is high on sharing and trying anything
new. There is no lack of common interests in this rematch.
"Margaret is curious and interested in things. We travel a
great deal to unusual places; we are now into scuba diving."

I hear the reader shouting, *"Who wouldn't like to share these
things?"*

Well, this couple takes sharing seriously, and it doesn't
have to be sailing the Caribbean. "Marriage means sharing
life together, sharing each day, making goals and having a
relationship with a friend and companion," concludes
Margaret.

Are You Getting the Picture?

Marriage the second time around as seen through these
well-adjusted, contented couples is just a glimpse into how
good a marriage can be. If you still need more convincing
that marriage secrets and working toward the best marriage
possible are worth the effort, wait until you read in "You've
Got Me, Babe" about all of the joys that accrue to the most
happily married among us. Before you reach these testimonials, however, turn the page and acquaint yourself with
a different kind of secret—secrets that can sound a note of
alarm and sabotage any effort to sail peacefully into port.

12

Lock Up Those Secrets and Throw Away the Key

"Do you have a secret that you keep from your wife?" I asked a man in his early forties. My question caught him completely by surprise.

"We have a great marriage," he replied, too quickly and too defensively. "I really don't hide anything from her."

I was used to his kind of response. Many people think having a secret implies wrongdoing. Nonetheless, I gave him an envelope and told him to send me a note if he thought of anything. Two days later a lengthy letter arrived on yellow legal-sized paper. He described how he finds himself admiring other women close to his wife's age who do a better job of maintaining their looks than she. He preferred to call his observations about these women who caught his eye "personal opinions" rather than secrets or fantasies. I won't argue over semantics.

Women with similar observations and notions don't just blurt out their fantasies and lustful daydreams to their husbands, either. Like this happy husband of twenty-plus years, they keep their "personal opinions" to themselves, they say. That sounds reasonable to me.

IN MANY INSTANCES, THERE IS NOTHING WRONG WITH HAVING SECRETS FROM YOUR PARTNER.

Certainly Marriage Secrets fit that bill and are probably what one man, hitched forty-one years, means when he says, "I hope my wife keeps some secrets from me. I never want to understand her completely. It would be all over." There are a number of women to oblige him.

As I concluded many an interview, turning off my tape recorder, and walking out the door, the wife asked me not to reveal the contents of our conversation if and when I spoke to her spouse.

In other cases, secrets signal fatal flaws that are not nearly so easily dismissed.

SOME SECRETS ARE COVER-UPS FOR PROBLEMS AND DEFECTS IN RELATIONSHIPS THAT NEED ATTENTION.

I repeatedly asked husbands and wives directly or in questionnaires what special secrets they kept from their spouses. Quite a number of mates replied they had nothing to hide. A smaller number of men and women said they had secrets but had no intention of sharing them with me or you! After a bit of persuasion, some gentle prying, and persistent coaxing, numerous spouses relented and entrusted their secrets to me.

There were secrets hidden from mates to save relationships, secrets kept in the name of love, secrets to keep them out of trouble, and secrets harbored to maintain peace and harmony. These were confidences that fit into neat little categories. There were Ho-Hummers, Eyebrow-Raisers, and Toxic Tales. How these affect marriage relationships is the *SECRET* of this chapter.

The purpose of shedding light on other people's secrets is not to satisfy our need for juicy tidbits or to experience a little voyeurism. **This exploration is geared to enable you to make better judgments about the secrets in your own relationship.**

HO-HUMMERS: BENIGN SECRETS

The more benign secrets, which I call "Ho-Hummers," most often belonged to the happiest, most successfully married pairs. Significantly, this group had the fewest secrets as well.

PRUDENT SECRETS

The frequent replies in this category had to do with a less-than-genuine orgasm now and then, a fictitious body weight, and MONEY—how much of it he or she spends where, when, and on what. Numerous women in second marriages reported with some regularity that they kept closed books on the purchases made for their children. It got a little stickier in the life of a man with two previous marriages, who finally settled happily into one homestead and wrote that he had no plans to inform his present wife of the terms of his will. It seems he sensed her probable disapproval of the preference given to his children's state of affairs over her own.

SECRETS FROM BEFORE YOU WERE MARRIED

Another group of prudent secrets applies, as one woman put it, to prior "love interests." **Spouses of both genders and of all ages kept their premarital love affairs to themselves, whether the flames were totally extinguished or they still lived on in vivid memories.** This was a good choice for the

women, and there were more than a few, who said their
husbands were not the best lovers they'd ever had. I found
secrecy especially wise in the case of a young woman
married less than three years who claimed to have had more
than thirty lovers before climbing under the exclusive bed
covers of her hubby.

Second-timers were on target not telling they slept with
their previous spouses while dating the new partner. How
bright of them not to voice their opinions when the new
mate did not do X, Y, or Z as well as the old one. I applaud
the second Mrs. Sam Kling for not telling her man that she
saw his first wife out and about town with a number of
dudes before he had any notion a divorce was pending.

A woman of twenty-five, married for only five years, feels
she should keep hidden a secret that might cause a needless
rift, even if a minor one at that: "Before we married but were
engaged, my ex-boyfriend was coming around. He asked me
to marry him. Of course, I said no. But it was a tough
decision. I have never revealed this to my husband. I think it
would bother him quite a bit, knowing that someone else
had asked to marry me." Who knows, in time, she might
find that this is a good secret to drop on her mate if he slips
up and takes her for granted one of these days.

It is probably comfortable for the forty-eight-year-old man,
married anew for six weeks, to fail to tell his bride about the
affair he had during his first marital go-round. But this is
pertinent information she might want to know. It could alert
her that she might need to keep her eyes open in order to
keep him in line in the future. Another man, hitched for
only ten months, sounds like he could eventually get into
trouble without his wife's watchful eye. He confessed to
removing his wedding band when out and about. A young
woman who slept with an old beau after she became
engaged better not tell; and she better stick to the straight
and narrow if she wants to maintain that marital satisfaction
index of eight she assigns to her relationship after four years.

If these men and women stay straight, then I suppose no harm is done. All the rest of the Ho-Hummers harbor rather harmless secrets, which appear to be prudently kept. Revealing them would be of no value, no benefit to the marriage relationship.

EYEBROW-RAISERS: INTERMEDIATE SECRETS

Eyebrow-raising secrets are a little more complicated and could have an adverse effect on the marriage relationship if they were to slip out. On the other hand, keeping these secrets may mean shying away from an issue that ought to be confronted.

BEDROOM SECRETS

Women and men who kept secret their spouse's less-than-thrilling or even inadequate performance in bed may be closeting an issue that should be addressed. Very carefully, that is! I especially felt for the lady married almost two decades who wrote: "I masturbate to fulfill my sexual desires." She was obviously getting shortchanged. That would be a hard one to keep quiet about. My eyebrows went way up when an attached guy rated the importance of a good sex life as a ten and a half, but rated his own sex life as poor. He went on to characterize his current level of marital satisfaction after three years as tops, and revealed the need to visit call girls because of his wife's prudish behavior. Whew!

Cautionary flags are waving at the following several escapades kept secret from partners. In the wrong hands, they could easily cause a temporary or even permanent disaster. But to all intents and purposes, evidence seems to point out that these husbands and wives stopped short of creating "Toxic Tales." They have things in order, report good marks on marital satisfaction, and don't have any horrible skeletons to hide. If those who rate their marriages satisfying are the teachers of this course, we had best gather some warnings from their Eyebrow-raising secrets, but keep them under lock and key.

WOULD-BE AFFAIRS

Men, it seems, are intolerant of their wives' male friends. At least, that's why most women who have them told me they are relatively secretive about these relationships. It was not out of the ordinary to come across a wife who neglects to tell her spouse about a friendly lunch date or some telephone chatter with a male friend: "We are in touch once or twice a year. Part of the reason I keep this secret is that it is my relationship, and I just want to keep it to myself. Also, I don't want to start something that isn't important right now. I recognize it for what it is, and it isn't necessary to talk about it."

Hardly anyone disclosed a would-be affair or tempting indiscretion to an unsuspecting mate.

"I was on a plane and got stranded in the air," says Liz. "There was a tornado, and we had to land in another city. We were in the air a long time waiting, and this guy next to me, who was probably eight years younger than me, tries to hustle me. He was very complimentary, and we were getting ripped on this plane. I told my husband that this guy was putting some pretty heavy moves on me, but I wouldn't want him to know the extent of this. I responded to him. I enjoyed his flirtation. We went out to dinner when we landed. I was feeling no pain. He did propose that we sleep together. I did not sleep with him, but we spent the night together in the airport. My husband would not like that. It was kind of fun to have someone think I was kind of neat even though I was older. I was flattered."

Why Ella Kissed and Didn't Tell—Her Husband

When Ella was married but a few years she picked up a secret that has been with her for a dozen years now. Going through a marital and personal slump, obsessed with getting pregnant, and being particularly vulnerable, she almost stepped into an affair that could have blown her honeymoon bungalow into smithereens. "I had the opportunity to have an affair. It was at a time I could have said forget Harley (her husband). All I wanted was a baby, and he wasn't ready. We talked a lot about it, argued about it, and I cried a lot about it. I met a tall, handsome, married man through work. He acted like he cared about me by sending flowers and buying wine and fancy dinners. It lasted six weeks, but we never slept together. It was really kind of romantic, kind of had the spark the marriage had lost. It was nice to have someone think I was really attractive again. I even called this man while I was on vacation with my husband and my parents."

What happened that prevented this tale from slipping into a more serious category? Luck had a lot to do with it. Ella became pregnant, sensibly reaffirmed her commitment to Harley, got her life in order, and three kids later is thankful she didn't go any further. "In some ways I regret that I didn't have the maturity to tell this man, 'Look, we are both married. Forget it!'" She has that maturity now.

But Ella, I want you to know here and now, that maturity isn't always the safeguard you assume it to be. Kathleen can tell you that. In fact, it is too much maturity that gets many middle-aged eyes roaming. Kathleen was looking for some youthful elixir and excitement, so she carried on a flirtation with a younger man. Her thoughts were not as pure as the afternoon date that ended more innocently than she anticipated. That's probably why she elected not to tell her husband about it when he asked what she did all day.

For Fred Once Was More Than Enough

Women aren't the only ones holding back this kind of information from their husbands. Fred admits a would-be affair, not an actual affair. "I had a fling with someone, but it didn't go past mutual affection," qualifies Fred. "I was attracted to someone at work. She evidently had the same feelings for me. We went to the movies, held hands, and became semi-intimate later. This happened three or four times. I didn't feel that guilty at the moment. I felt I needed it, but I didn't want to risk shaking up my marriage. I felt it would be too selfish to continue. Pat and I have too good a marriage. I just needed some fun, but it wasn't the kind of fun I want to have. It would have hurt my wife. It was wrong. I admit I was dying to experiment once. It was enough."

Let's hope so, lest his chest of secrets gets too full.

TOXIC TALES: DANGEROUS SECRETS

Without a doubt the biggest and most potentially damaging secrets men and women withhold from each other have to do with extramarital sex.

This is true whether it is a full-blown bona fide passionate affair or a one-night fling. Whatever the reason—and there are many—these secrets can be the toxic event that bring down a marriage, old or new.

Extramarital Affairs and Marriage

Whether we want to accept it or not, a majority of married men and women have sex outside of marriage at one time or another and most want to keep this a secret! Whether these indiscretions should or shouldn't be kept under wraps is an age-old question. Haven't you ever debated if you should tell your best friend that his or her wife or husband is having an affair? For the purpose of our mission, which is to create the best permanent love relationship within a marriage, there are several things to keep in perspective when looking at the Toxic Tales of philandering.

A REALLY COMMITTED RELATIONSHIP MAKES AN EXCLUSIVE SEXUAL ARRANGEMENT POSSIBLE.

Not everyone is so blasé about extramarital affairs or so lacking in commitment that an exclusive sexual arrangement is impossible to maintain. Couples who adhere to this standard of behavior may not be in the majority, but they are not a tiny insignificant minority either. I went searching for the faithful after listening to a married man in his late fifties tell me that women will never understand it, "But men, all men, engage in extramarital sex. That's just the way it is. Do you want to eat chicken every night?" he asks, equating his gastronomical preference for variety with his choice of partner.

He will never believe what I found, but you should. There are men—and women—out there with good intentions and lofty values. The results of my informal survey revealed that two-thirds of the men I asked believed it was possible to be monogamous in marriage.

"Yes, I know men who are loyal." "Yes, I am loyal myself," a few offered without being asked. "Yes, I have every intention of remaining faithful," volunteered several relatively newlyweds. "Yes. Hell, yes! You can be loyal," barked more than one husband, obviously indignant at my question, which had been taken in the form of an accusation.

So who are the loyal, faithful minority, and why do they hold out while so many men don't? Most of the men who replied "No, it is not possible to be monogamous," in this less-than-scientific study, were employed in blue-collar jobs. Conversely, the largest expectation for male infidelity, reported by a sociologist just a few years back from a study she deemed to be highly pertinent, fingered men earning over $70,000 a year. In this group, approximately 70 percent were unfaithful. For men who abstained or felt that others do and can, it was a matter of conscience, conviction, respect, self-control, love, morality, trust, and commitment. Now, those are admirable values in any spouse, husband or wife.

The women I encountered who engage in extramarital affairs come in all ages and from a wide variety of backgrounds. They are out for excitement, attention, affection, experimentation, sexual fulfillment, love, and revenge. Surveys show a large discrepancy in their findings and report anywhere from 10 to 70 percent of married women have an affair. Nonetheless, only 6 percent of the women who believe they have good emotional foundations in their marriages have affairs. And 89 percent of the women in Shere Hite's report kept their indiscretions a secret.

Why on earth then did so many confess these toxic secrets to me, saying they had never revealed so much of themselves to anyone before? It was a welcome relief for them to find a stranger to confide in without fear of recrimination. A young woman married for three years put it succinctly at the end of her anonymous note to me: "I could never tell anyone. I sort of feel relieved, this survey was my shoulder." Signed, "Phantom."

Some of the confessions, especially face-to-face over coffee, made me skeptical of all the verbose locker-room bragging from both males and females that contributes so heavily to the perception that extramarital sex is the norm. "I didn't know if I should meet you today," confessed Paulette. "I have never had an extramarital affair." So where did her wild and crazy reputation come from? It began accidentally during an argument with her husband over his affair. "Dear, I can play the game as well as you can," she told him, implying that she was experienced in this area. "I never denied it or confirmed it. I just kept him in limbo. When it gets to that point, I can't. I have kissed and petted but going to bed, no. I can't."

Paulette has extended the charade of her affair at work. It keeps men from making annoying passes and placates her female coworkers, who think her husband is getting just what he deserves. Her secret is a little twisted for sure, but count her in as one among the vigilant minority who think extramarital sex is wrong.

A good many of the men and women who fooled around did not have at the time of their indiscretions, the kind of mature and fulfilling marital relationship that is the goal and subject of *Marriage Secrets*. We have seen that over and over again in examples throughout the preceding chapters. Undoubtedly, you have gotten the picture that marriage is a dynamic and ever-changing relationship between two people. It is rarely perfect and most certainly never perfect for long. Often it requires a significantly greater degree of maturity, respect, and willingness to sacrifice to accept the type of commitment mandated by an exclusive relationship. Not all marriage relationships incorporate these qualities immediately but many develop them over time. That may be why some surveys report such a large number of married men and women engaging in extramarital sex earlier in their marriages.

Most people who value their marriage and who openly and honestly discussed their sexual indiscretions with me admitted something was missing in their relationship at the time, whether it was sex, compassion, understanding, or companionship. It was particularly true of the women I spoke with who talked about current and past indiscretions and described having real problems with their marriage and often had divorce in the back of their minds, tucked away for after the children left home.

A more *laissez-faire* attitude accompanied with little or no guilt or remorse was generally characteristic of those men and women with less regard for their marriage or the feelings of their spouses. Their own individual satisfaction was the primary motivation for sexual variety and experimentation. In most instances, these men and women were talking in the past tense about marriages that ended over their excessive sexual exploits or which used the idea of secrecy as a magnanimous gesture for sparing their partners the pain of discovery.

It takes a few secrets to protect you and your spouse from the temptation of an extramarital affair. For the ladies and gentlemen who want the lifetime partnership this book is all about, there is no room for naïveté. You must be prudent in steering yourself and your spouse away from potential liaisons. And, don't keep it a secret that you not only expect, but demand, absolute loyalty.

☞ SECRET NO. 1.

Everyone and anyone is considered fair game. *No one is immune to the advances and dangers of an admiring eye.* Ladies— particularly the 60 percent who wrote that you do not believe other women see your husbands as "fair game"—take your head out of the sand now! Married men will tell you constantly they are being "hit on." "If a woman is attracted to a man she couldn't care less if he is married," says one experienced husband.

The escapades of a telephone repairman ought to tell you a thing or two. "I came to this lady's door and she asked me to wait a moment. She came back wearing a negligee and said the problem was in the bedroom. She lay down on the bed, threw back her clothes, and said, 'Do you want to work on this?'" A woman at another service call shouted that her door was open and to come into the bathroom, where she was soaking in a tub full of bubbles. Another woman reported that she had a bad jack in the bedroom. When the repairman bent over to take a look, he found a pile of sexual paraphernalia. The lady of the house said, "My husband can't please me. Do you want to try?"

Gentlemen, pay attention too. Men are not put off by your wife's wedding band. I can tell you that firsthand. A young man attending the same convention as my husband asked me on an elevator if I was married. Arriving at the fifth floor, where I was getting off, the elevator stopped but he didn't. "Are you available?" he asked.

☞ SECRET NO. 2.

Neither of you should press your luck or dangle your spouse like bait the way one Good Samaritan did. It is hard to imagine what was going through the wife's head who encouraged her "house-husband" to befriend a new lonely lady neighbor while she herself was off at work. Showing this new woman on the block the grocery store and sharing car-pools turned into permanent playtime. Giving your spouse away is not included in the Welcome Neighbor Handbook.

There just isn't any sense acting foolishly. I was personally relieved when a friend decided against purchasing a big city condo to accommodate her husband and his female assistant on frequent business trips. Enough damage can be done with separate hotel suites, not to mention social situations with those who supposedly call themselves friends.

☞ SECRET NO. 3.

Assess your social set and be fully aware of what lurks in the shadows. Even innocent bystanders get sucked into the messy business of affairs, which pervade a number of social scenes. "My husband and I had developed a really nice social life," starts this female storyteller. "There were lots of parties. I always felt it was a very dangerous time of life. Every Saturday night we got dressed up and went to a party.

It was like dating again, dancing, drinking, and flirting. Before I knew it, I started developing a relationship with another man. I danced with him for a year and then all of a sudden we wanted more than Saturday nights. We have been together several times a week for nine and a half years."

Jessica, on the other hand, wouldn't allow herself or her man to get caught in that web. "A woman James had grown up with and dated in high school and college called after twenty-seven years," begins Jessica. It seems her husband had just died, and she wanted to renew old acquaintances and have lunch while she was in town visiting. Jessica understood the meaning behind her first invitation and the second phone call a day later asking James to join her for a round of golf at the country club with her brother and his wife.

"James came home and asked me if I thought that was a funny invitation. I told him to call her back and say that we would get a fourth player and that all of us could meet for lunch and golf. She said she would think about it but never called back."

The Veil of Secrecy

If you do find yourself embroiled in a Toxic Tale, be advised that **the rationale behind the veil of secrecy is to protect the perpetrator as well as the victim.** It is obvious that men and women feel that bringing their affairs out in the open will not help their marital relationship and fear reprisal. A few are embarrassed to show their weakness in succumbing to the temptations. And some, now showing greater compassion for their mates, do not want to inflict the pain of betrayal. The people I am about to introduce you to have experience with Toxic Tales and adhere to the principal of secrecy. They claim to have a high level of marital satisfaction. However, in spinning their tales, there is evidence of flaws in their relationships that do not appear among the more lustrous marriages and are not part of the ideal marital partnership that *Marriage Secrets* seeks to help create.

Toxic Tale No. 1: A Healthy Affair?

Norma unfortunately reports having a bad sex life in her first marriage and now in her second marriage. "My first husband and I were both virgins. After my divorce, I was curious about sex and felt a need to experience more sexual partners. I still have problems and am uncomfortable expressing my sexual desires and telling my husband what would feel good. We are so affectionate and loving. That seems more important than being sexually active and compatible. Yet sometimes I feel this incompatibility reduces the total quality of our marriage. We both feel badly about it, and we have discussed it quite a bit. We have gone for counseling, and some things have come up that have helped. We are committed and nurturing to each other, and we care and support one another as much as one can hope to. Sex seems to be caught up in all of my taboos. Sometimes it becomes a major issue. I feel as if we could be doing more, but that would take some major work and seems minor when compared to our whole relationship. We are not very sexually active together."

Norma tries to put her finger on the reasons she seeks these outside sexual experiences and why she might be able to achieve more satisfying sex with a stranger. "I think it is a question of having sex with people I really care about and struggling to make a passionate sexual relationship fit into a friendship. I even thought about writing about my affairs and what makes them different than sex with my spouse, but I though that was dangerous. My husband might find it. Making love at the end of a long day in your own bed is very different, I think, than setting aside a period for that and being in a hotel room where you don't have to change your sheets and the phone doesn't ring. I think there is something about familiarity. I think the newness of someone else serves as an aphrodisiac. I am not turned on by my husband. Seeing him nude is not enough to get my juices flowing. I do get turned on by a man who is not familiar, becoming naked with me. I think I never satisfied my need to know that I could be desirable to other people. I am the one who travels a lot to professional conferences. I get involved—almost a zipless fuck kind of thing—no strings attached. I enjoy myself sexually. That is it, a quick one-or-two-night thing.

"My husband has told me on occasion that it would be all right if I had affairs. He just doesn't want to know about it. What he was saying was, 'I trust you not to let an affair get in the way of our relationship.' I think he suspects my affairs, but we don't talk about it. Affairs create this secret area, this thing that you can't touch together. I wonder, if he knew about my affairs, would it shake this very strong base we have. I suspect it wouldn't, but it feels like a real risk. I justify the affairs by saying they have no impact on our marriage. But I also recognize that what it does is enlarge this secret area that we can't talk about."

While researching an article on extramarital affairs, I met a psychologist who, while not advocating extramarital affairs, did believe there was such a thing as a healthy affair. A healthy affair provides a secondary relationship that satisfies needs unmet by the primary relationship without blaming one's partner for the inadequacy or threatening the marriage. The description fits Norma's dilemma. However, there are hints that this is riskier business than this psychologist suggested to me.

"There has been some negative residue from these affairs," remarks Norma. "It makes me feel sad. I don't have as much desire or opportunity for them as I used to. I feel like I should find ways to build excitement into my sexual relationship with my husband. I just haven't. I thought of proposing ways of doing things to excite us, but it would feel artificial. I don't know how to make it happen. I think we could work through this if we focused on it. We don't make it a high enough priority. I wonder if I had worked harder on our sexual compatibility whether I wouldn't have had these other experiences."

I left Norma aware of her ambivalent resolve to attempt once more to rectify her sexual dilemma: would she encourage her unromantic husband to take more action and seek ways to arouse their passions? Unquestionably, this was a painful thorn in Norma's marital relationship. Spending several hours telling me about her affairs while professing her love for her husband brought the problem to the surface and enabled her to expose the toxic substance of secrets she has tried to hide.

Toxic Tale No. 2: Pain or Deception?

I met Cynthia quite by chance at a restaurant. She openly acknowledged that her husband used to run around when he was younger. Cynthia made a case for secrecy when it comes to Toxic Tales: She prefers to avoid the pain of discovery. She has already suffered deep wounds from a wandering and emotionally abusive first husband who cost her the custody of her three small children, and from her second and present husband's own up-front admission of sex on the side. Cynthia has been willing to go along with this as long as it does not interfere with their marriage.

"I would never tell a woman if her husband was having an affair," Cynthia states, explaining her preference for secrecy. "It is just a man's makeup. Why upset somebody's life? What you don't know won't hurt you. I wish that I had never known. I felt like a fool and that everyone must be laughing at me."

Unfortunately, Cynthia was to suffer another painful deception, which has made her even more adamantly in favor of silence. Everything was fine until Marshall disobeyed the rules and started a romantic affair with a neighbor. Suspecting the liaison, Cynthia came right out and asked Marshall if he was having an affair with Ellen. He did not deny it.

"When I found out, it hurt," she says. "How can I describe it? It is like a knife in your stomach that is just there and doesn't come out. There is no way to describe it. I just hurt very badly. I had to make myself feel better and understand. I had to talk about it and get it out. Yes, I thought about leaving him, for about a minute. I had already been through all the difficult years with him; nobody else was going to get him for the good years. About seventy-five to eighty percent of the women who divorce their husbands turn around five years later and wish they hadn't. They are miserable single. I don't want to end up seventy and alone. I said at work I needed a few days off. I went out of town with Marshall for a few days. We did nothing but talk about it. I said, 'Let's get it out in the open and not talk about it again.' We had a closeness that we had never had before. The affair ended."

Secrecy is an obvious means of self-defense and perhaps even a worthwhile accommodation. But is it indicative of the type of marriage we are after? Let's ask Cynthia how she really feels about fidelity. "Oh, I think it would be wonderful. Why do I think it would be? I just think it would. There is no question that this is not the best possible marriage. I think my daughter and her fiancé will have that. They are very lucky. I wish I could have had a marriage like I think theirs will be. But I think that kind of man is very rare.One out of every ten thousand might have that kind of marriage, so why wait around forever trying to find that man?

"I love Marshall, and I think he loves me. I like having him here, but I am independent. I want to know somebody is there if I need him. I am happy with myself, my life, my job. I think being happy is a way of life. If you took my kids away and my job and just put me with Marshall, I might be miserable. Happiness is a total package."

It's not the package, though, that happy marriages and lifetime love affairs are made of.

To Tell or Not to Tell, That Is the Question

If you are hiding a Toxic Tale, only you and you alone can decide whether it is best to lock up the secret and throw away the key. *There are some important questions to ask yourself before you allow your relationship to rely on too much secrecy which could cause just as much damage as the Toxic Tales themselves.*

• **If I tell my partner, am I ready for the consequences?** They can be plentiful and not necessarily productive in terms of maintaining the marriage relationship.

Women are more forgiving than men and much more likely to look for underlying causes. Men are hard-nosed when it comes to their wives' affairs and find it much more difficult to forgive and forget. Disclosure may lead down the path to a total dissolution of the marriage.

• **Will I permanently damage my marriage relationship if I tell?** Discovering an affair drains the trust right out of a marriage and almost always replaces it with a lifetime supply of cynicism about love. Once you have lost that initial faith in one another, new roots have a hard time taking a firm hold. There are couples who manage to do this.

• **Would revealing my Toxic Tale help my marriage?** Some partners have said that they need to know in order to strengthen the partnership. The variables are too individual for anyone to make the call but you. Brandon says he would resort to a shabby cover-up knowing the havoc an affair would wreck on his marriage. "If my wife came in and caught me naked on the couch with you right now, I would deny anything was going on. I would convince her it was an illusion."

• **Is opting for secrecy a cop-out?** This is a tough one for
the transgressor and the transgressee. Secrecy can throw a
shroud over issues that can be resolved and that would
enable a marriage to move forward to greater heights.
Secrecy may be a way of washing one's hands of the hard
work, sacrifice, and commitment that a truly loving marriage relationship takes. Perhaps secrecy offers a sanctuary
of protection and prevents the expressions of anguish and
pain that both men and women suffer when they discover a
partner's affair.

• **Is choosing secrecy a green light?** Expecting your mate
to close his or her eyes to your indiscretions can be interpreted as giving a silent sanction for fooling around.

• **Can my secret be a plus?** Is there a way that I can keep it
but use my past experience to benefit my marriage relationship without inflicting pain on my spouse?

Not all indiscretions result from a total lack of conscience
or commitment. Renewed, genuine efforts toward respect
for a spouse and a partnership is a good place to begin to
keep love on track.

THERE IS NO NEED FOR SECRECY IF YOU ANSWER THIS ONE THE RIGHT WAY

Marriage Secrets are one thing. Ho-Hummers and Eyebrow-Raisers, well, they pass, too. Toxic Tales, however,
signal trouble. If there are too many of them, it is likely that
your answer to the following question should be kept a
secret, too.

Question: What does my marriage relationship really
mean to me? Answer: EVERYTHING.

13

"You've Got Me, Babe"

The lyrics "You got me, and baby, and I got you, BABE" come from one of Sonny and Cher's most popular songs of the sixties. More successful in matrimony, however, than this famous duo singing of the power of their love and optimism for a future together, are happy couples who take the meaning of the song seriously.

Commitment to being one another's lifetime Babe through the joys and tears, trials and tribulations, and stages and phases that life has to offer enhances the quality of these partners' lives.

The following testimonials give a clear view of the best that marriage has to offer. This ideal *should* shape the expectations that you hope to have met through your rigorous regimen of secrets.

WHAT THE BEST MARRIAGES SOUND LIKE

There is no doubt about it, a majority of men and women find it lonely to be without a partner. They want to be

married. They want to find one special Babe and settle into a
permanent love nest. What *few people understand, especially
those who haven't experienced it in their own marriages, is just
how meaningful, lasting, and fulfilling a genuinely good marriage
relationship can be.*
I will let the most satisfied among us tell you what
marriage is and what it should and can be. Just remember,
all of these relationships took nurturing and hard work.

How Women See Marriage

STUDENT, AFTER TWO YEARS: "It is calming. It is a wonderful
feeling. I grab each moment with great appreciation knowing that life is short and you never know what is around the
corner."
NURSE, AFTER TEN YEARS: "A good marriage makes me
happy."
SALES ADMINISTRATOR, AFTER EIGHTEEN YEARS: "A good
marriage has meant living with a man I can feel comfortable
with, someone I can trust and confide in, someone I can be
myself with."
HOMEMAKER, AFTER NINETEEN YEARS: "Marriage is two people struggling together on the journey of life, helping each
other to leave a positive mark on the world."
JOURNALIST, AFTER TWENTY-FOUR YEARS: "My marriage is
the happiest and most gratifying part of my life. Each year
we have been together it has gotten better and taken on a
more significant meaning. Without this relationship,
nothing that I have experienced or achieved would be as
important. We are partners for life and ever after. I am a
lucky woman and never let myself forget it."
ASSISTANT PRINCIPAL, AFTER TWENTY-FIVE YEARS: "Being
together and enjoying it so much, I wonder how I ever
managed before I met him."
PSYCHOLOGIST, AFTER TWENTY-NINE YEARS: "Marriage has
given me a certain amount of self-confidence. I get love from

another person, which makes me feel good about myself. I get feedback that says I am special. There is something very pure about having had a long-term relationship as compared to having five broken hearts. There are fewer scars from life."

NURSE, AFTER THIRTY YEARS: "Marriage means a sharing, loving, and trusting relationship. It means to take mutual pride in one another and give mutual respect."

SECRETARY, AFTER THIRTY YEARS: "Marriage is everything in the world to me."

COMMUNITY VOLUNTEER, AFTER FORTY-THREE YEARS: "Being married to Joe gives me the feeling that there is always someone there for me. I feel safe and loved. I know I must be okay, even if there are those days I don't like myself very much, because Joe is there to tell me I am."

HOMEMAKER, AFTER FORTY-FIVE YEARS: "My marriage has given me a whole way of life that is preferable to any other for me."

HOMEMAKER, AFTER FIFTY YEARS: "The biggest reward of my marriage is always having someone there for me to share the good and bad times, the joys and the sorrows. There has always been the feeling that we are a team. My husband is my best friend. We have been fortunate that as the years mount up, we have become closer and more intimate in our relationship."

HOMEMAKER, AFTER FIFTY-TWO YEARS: "I have enjoyed companionship and a sense of security in marriage. We have developed a real friendship throughout the years. His sense of understanding has lead to a peaceful existence."

COMMUNITY VOLUNTEER, AFTER FIFTY-SEVEN YEARS: "The rewards of our marriage have been the genuine respect and caring we have had for each other and the satisfaction we get from the devotion and admiration of our children and grandchildren. I know that their high regard for their families and for us is the result of the example that our love has given them."

These romantically gushy, yet realistic endorsements aren't just the work of women. NO WAY! Men had no problem coming up with pluses too.

How Men See It

SALESMAN, AFTER TEN YEARS: "Marriage means giving to my wife when her needs call for it, and her giving to me when my needs call for it."

MARKETING, AFTER TWELVE YEARS: "A relationship has meant to me not only having a sexual partner but a best friend as well. My partner and I share everything—joy, sadness, success and failure. We not only give something to the relationship, we depend on each other to be able to take as well."

BUSINESSMAN, AFTER TWELVE YEARS: "My marriage is a relationship full of love and understanding between two people with common interests able to share and enjoy each other. It is a relationship that has good communication and provides us with the ability to resolve problems when they exist."

BUSINESS OWNER, AFTER TWELVE YEARS: "My wife has helped me to go far beyond my expectations of myself."

ATTORNEY, AFTER THIRTEEN YEARS: "It is a real anchor for me and affects every aspect of my life and gives meaning to the things that I do. It would be hard to come to work if I didn't have a purpose. I couldn't even think about having it without a wife and children. It is stability. I think it affects your health and all aspects of your well-being."

DETECTIVE, AFTER FIFTEEN YEARS: "Marriage is two people living their lives together and reaching their goals and dreams together."

BUSINESSMAN, MARRIAGE NO. 3, AFTER SIXTEEN YEARS: "Marriage is the most important ingredient for happiness. I should know!"

BUSINESSMAN, AFTER EIGHTEEN YEARS: "A good partnership has meant love, sex, children, memories, and a strong commitment to each other."

CORPORATE PRESIDENT, AFTER TWENTY-FIVE YEARS: "Marriage has made my life complete. My partner makes everything I do more enjoyable, including going to a football game or fishing. Marriage has given me children and made me more responsible. It has offered me the opportunity to continue being educated by pursuing new avenues of interest my wife has introduced me to. There are things I never would have done if I weren't married. It has given me a whole life."

CORPORATE VICE-PRESIDENT, AFTER THIRTY YEARS: "My marriage means everything to me. It is number one. Without it I am not sure I could survive. I wouldn't have had the benefit of children and all the joys that meant to me. I found contentment, purpose, and fulfillment. I just can't imagine not being married and enjoying life as a result of that. As I look around at all of our acquaintances, there isn't another woman I would rather be married to."

FOREIGN SERVICE, AFTER THIRTY-EIGHT YEARS: "My marriage has given me a sense of fulfillment. My wife and I have each contributed to the growth and development of the other."

CEO, AFTER FORTY-FIVE YEARS: "My marriage has been the most important thing in my life."

INTERNATIONAL BUSINESSMAN, AFTER FIFTY YEARS: "My achievements along the way during the past fifty years would have been meaningless and also unlikely without my wife."

Keeping Your Expectations Great

Plant these precedents in your mind and set some high expectations for yourself, your partner, and your marital relationship. This is not fantasy. This is not fiction. **This is marriage at its lustrous, shining best. If you don't aim for the top and insist that your marriage assume its rightful prominent place in your life, there is no chance of reaping all of its rewards.**

Keep a bookmark on this page and your book in a handy spot. When you are ready to explode, on the verge of becoming a nonbeliever, or are questioning why you are trying so hard to make your marriage work, read this section again!

Remember: **Expect the best and you will get the most out of your marriage.** Keep these key words in mind to remind you what a good marriage has to offer!

Comfort
Happiness
Partnership
Companionship
Love
Purpose
Family Life
Fulfillment
Devotion

ABOUT GIVING AND GETTING

If you view your participation in your marriage as a series of significant sacrifices, you are probably a martyr in the wrong cause.

Surprisingly, women of all ages, partners in successful marriages going on from five to fifty years, did not report feeling that they had given up anything to make their marriages work. This does not imply that they fail to put the necessary energy into their partnerships. On the contrary, it signifies they had the best secret in town: **knowing how to**

give and take. This surely enables them to cope and compromise effectively and willingly in order to be there under all circumstances for their BABES.

In order to add your own testimonial someday alongside those of the couples in this chapter, you'd best get this secret down pat. This is true for both partners.

How Marian and Albert Cared for Each Other Through Hard Times

"If you want to interview a couple with a really great marriage, call Marian and Albert Harris. They've been married almost fifty years," a number of people in their age group told me. Sitting and talking to this couple in the living room of their home proved to be one of the highlights of my research for this book.

Childhood sweethearts, this attractive twosome fell in love, married, and embarked on a traditional life together—one fraught with pain and illness as well as pleasures and joys. Through it all, they had each other. The tone they set and the attitude they adopted from the very beginning has made their partnership successful. "I would do anything in the world for Albert, and I think he would do the same for me," Marian says.

"We had some tough moments. You take what you're dealt and cope with it," says Albert. **"It is a question of whether or not you choose to handle the low sides or not. It is the way you cope, the way you handle the bad times that counts."**

The Harrises coped by giving—giving to each other in the form of love, support, and protection. I suppose one could call it a steadily flowing stream of Responsible Love Talk. To think of any of this devotion as a sacrifice of personal time or aspirations draws only a laugh from this dedicated couple. "Sacrifice what?" Albert asks.

Giving of themselves from every angle was and is no

sacrifice. Rather, it is an expression of the value they place on one another and their desire to show this by making each other's lives easier. "I protected him, and he protected me," Marian explains.

When they first married, money was tight and desirable jobs were at a premium. Albert worked nights managing bars well into their life together. His significant financial success didn't come until after nearly twenty years. Marian didn't care at all, she confesses, as long as she had "her" Albert. "Why should I have thrown guilt on him and make him feel bad? I was thrilled he could support us. I couldn't wait to see him at night, and I waited up for him."

Unassuming, gentle, contented people that they are, Marian decides to be risqué and share a story illustrating how they had fun and added romance despite an economic situation that might provoke the contempt of young couples today. "Albert called me one morning and said he would have access to a great hotel suite for the afternoon after he set up for a cocktail party. He asked if I wanted to meet him. I told him I would be there at two. I asked my mother to pick up the children after school, and I took the streetcar downtown. I got off in front of the hotel and imagined everyone knew what I was doing. I felt so whorey. We had the best afternoon I ever had in my life. Those are the romantic things that don't cost a penny."

"I feel sorry for younger couples today," Albert says. "They are so concerned over their material gains and place such great demands on each other that it creates problems which fester. Then they walk away from it."

Walking away from hard times or problems is definitely not the Harrises' style of doing things. Marian explains, emphasizing the importance of traditional family values: "Albert's father lived with us for almost seventeen years. He wasn't easy, but I never let Albert know it. I would never do anything to make him feel bad. We both have feelings, and we cared about each other."

Shortly after Albert's father died, Marian's father joined their household. "We didn't need to thank each other for taking care of our parents," Albert explains. "That was understood, maybe with just a touch."

It would seem that by the midpoint of their marriage this couple was due for some fun. But, like Albert says, you deal with what you are handed, and for them it was Marian's devastating eight-year battle with cancer. "When I was very sick, he brought me through it," she says simply. "He never allowed me to think I wouldn't make it. We gained strength from one another. I think we have the same heartbeat to tell you the truth. When his heart beats, so does mine. When one of us hurts, so does the other."

It was not difficult for me to sense the delight they must have felt in being able to hold onto each other the first New Year's Eve after Marian's surgery. "I couldn't make it off the couch to go out with our friends," Marian recalls. "But at midnight we got up and danced, alone in our living room."

"She tried to make things better, and I hid my fears. I wanted to keep her spirits up," Albert adds.

Not long ago, Marian was able to give back all of Albert's encouragement when he underwent open-heart surgery. While it may seem there is sacrifice involved in caring for one another, Marian says she is still nourished by their marriage. "When I lay my head on my pillow, I am content. If I feel his body next to mine and he is breathing smoothly, I say Thank you, God. I am so content with my life. We went through the crummiest times, but I have had the best. I couldn't have a better life or a better guy."

Nor Albert a better woman.

Taking Turns Meeting Each Other's Needs

Some issues have become a little stickier these days as noted in our discussion of space and priorities in Chapter 8.

TAKING TURNS MEETING EACH OTHER'S NEEDS AND SIDE-STEPPING ONE'S OWN AGENDA FOR YOUR BABE IS A SIGNIFICANT FORM OF GIVING AND TAKING.

It is a secret used more and more by contemporary couples and one that a couple married twenty-three years explained to me in depth.

Her Turn

"My wife and I did a lot of talking in the mid-seventies," starts Jake. "I was unhappy living where I was. I hated the Midwest and I wanted to move to the Rockies. My wife had a rough time leaving the family. It took a lot of support and time together to make it work. It was hard for her, but we did it together. She learned a lot about herself and wanted to go back to teaching. I supported her. She came close to giving up, but I knew all she wanted was to teach. I did my best to encourage her to stay with it. She had to sub first. It was hard to get assignments, so I went so far as to have business cards made up for her and told her to tack them up on school bulletin boards. It worked.

"When I made some serious business mistakes in Colorado, it was never, 'I told you so.' It was always, 'What can we do to solve the problem?' I couldn't have asked for better.

"We moved again, and *this time* it was to further my wife's career. We investigated the market for the best place for her to get a job and then moved to Florida. Today I do as much as I can for her. I help around the house and tell her I love her every day. Since she has been working, she has a lot to talk about. I try hard to share that with her. I am not an uninterested listener. I see it as her turn now," he concludes.

His Turn

I met Delores, a female fan of the taking turns idea, who says the concept is working quite well in her household. "Tally has always required a great deal of attention," she explains. "He has never been afraid to show me how much he needs me, and I have always tried to arrange my graduate work and my professional life in a way that would allow me the freedom to be by his side at home or on business and pleasure trips. There was a time when my children were young that I was criticized by other women for not taking a more aggressive approach to my work. It would have necessitated giving up my availability for Tally. I felt our marriage relationship benefited by me being just where I was. I may be a little behind the other women in my age group who have high powered positions, but I am catching up now with Tally's undivided support. He thoroughly likes the idea that it is my turn to make my mark."

CAN YOU GET AWAY WITH LESS?

Without qualification, **no!** Marriage requires you to give enormously of yourself. That's why it just doesn't work for the selfish Johns and Joans. There is no getting without it. If there are no returns for your earnest efforts, however, it may be time to test to see if you have a worthy mate.

THE PHASES AND STAGES OF MARRIAGE

Your level of marital satisfaction is never constant. You grow in stages and you go through phases. So do your children, your husband, your parents, and even your pets. To assume that your relationship with your spouse is any different is foolish indeed. Think of marriage in terms of stages and exercise patience. Steer your way clear of undesirable phases and keep moving!

Setting Goals and Dreams

I like the agenda set by one wise young wife to ensure passage to safe and secure marital stages. After the couple's second child arrived with severe health problems, she knew their relationship would be strained. Instead of focusing on getting by day by day, she set her sights on making it to their tenth anniversary. "That was going to be our first milestone," explains this charming young lady sitting next to me on an airplane. With that kind of foresight and determination, no wonder she made it!

This couple has made a habit out of dreaming, which keeps them moving in a forward motion. Their dreams, however, aren't about castles in Spain. "We have little goals and large goals and work toward them. They are endless but not unattainable, and they are sincere goals. We dream that someday we will live on the water and achieve a certain life-style together. We can't split up and also fulfill our dreams."

A bit more philosophical, yet still instructive, is the case of an educator, married twenty-nine years, who has enjoyed the progress of a relationship in a long-term marriage. "Marriage has afforded me the opportunity to have a long-standing relationship and see the evolution of commitment between two people. It's a rare opportunity, and one I would have taken for granted. Now I see it is very precious," she declares thoughtfully.

Predicting Marital Ups and Downs

Is there any way to predict when your marital ups and downs will start tugging at that grip you and your partner have on each other? Experts say they really aren't sure. There are too many contingent factors, and the evolution of each couple's relationship is unique. While statistics indicate that marital satisfaction declines during the middle years, Letha Dawson Scanzoni and John Scanzoni, the authors of *Men, Women, and Change* point out that these data are derived generally from couples seeking therapy. If they were so contented, so blissfully happy in their married lives, why would they have sought marriage counseling anyway? A good point!

The authors of this widely read volume on family sociology note that **marital satisfaction increases over time when measured by the interaction of mates in communicating with each other.**

Popular studies talk of the "U-shaped curve" that reveals a low ebb in marital satisfaction during childbearing years. This is probably what my friend's husband is experiencing. Heidi, a mother of three ranging in age from two to eight and a part-time career woman, mentions that Adam has been complaining lately that they are drifting apart and don't seem to have any time for each other. "What does he expect?" she asks. "We took a vacation several months ago, but it was with the kids. We can't afford the time or money to go again."

Adam is not, as they say, a happy camper at this juncture. Children can be stressful for both mothers and fathers. I remember staying alert when a dentist, working on my teeth while I was seven months pregnant with my second daughter, went so far as to tell me that having children broke up his marriage. Even the mom least obsessed with her troop has trouble juggling demands and making sure dad gets his required allotment of attention.

I confide to Heidi what I used to do in her situation. It is obvious to me that Adam was saying, "I'm not getting my fair share. I'm neglected."

"If you have a key to your office building, you will be able to use this one if you like. Help yourself," I offer Heidi. "It cost very little and gave Mark and me the same benefits as a quick vacation. Get a Sunday afternoon sitter. If you want to add an element of surprise, tell Adam you need him to hang some pictures at the office. Have a picnic lunch, a blanket spread on the floor, wine on ice, soft music, and be ready and waiting."

And then I told her, "Tell Adam to exercise some patience. The best is yet to come."

How I Gave My Marriage a Boost
When It Most Needed It

I have a story for you. While I may be the author and the characters are Mark and myself, the cast is really anyone who makes it through the child-rearing stage and lives to tell about it. I think you may enjoy this little tale, which I call "A Marriage Fix." It came just in the nick of time to help prepare me for what were to be some of our best years.

It was meant to be a family excursion and, to the extent that both of our daughters accompanied us, it fit that definition. In retrospect, however, the effects of this vacation were more akin to those of a premeditated sexy weekend escape or preplanned romantic interlude.

Our Los Angeles destination was chosen simply on the basis of greed. A flight to the West Coast took the greatest advantage of accumulated frequent-flyer points and two freebie tickets anywhere in the continental U.S.A. The thought that we were returning to the city where we had lived as newlyweds was not even a secondary motive. My apathy partially dissolved in exchange for a brief romantic blush during the four-hour travel time as I began to give some thought to our first love nest. Buckled in my seat, I felt a guarded excitement at the prospect of returning.

Traipsing around L.A. did not immediately bring back memories. When we pulled up in front of the apartment building that we had called home in 1967, it no longer resembled the place we remembered. The green fields in Century City, where we had protested the Vietnam War, had succumbed to the push for an exclusive condo development. We were too lost on the tangled freeways to even find Griffith Park, where we had attended love-ins.

It was not until we met John and Myra, the couple who

shared our first few years, that I felt that same giddy
excitement of being the new Mrs. Rosen. Walking along
Venice Beach, with its street singers, jugglers, dogs sporting
visors, and men with snakes draped around their necks,
produced a flood of memories peculiar to this time in our
lives. I could vividly see the four of us digging into the sand
with our feet and covering our bodies with blankets as we
awaited Fourth of July fireworks to explode overhead.

I almost laughed out loud, remembering John asking why
we were late one night for dinner. He correctly answered his
own question with the statement that as newlyweds we
probably couldn't resist the chance to make love.

We were just beginning then to find our way, ourselves,
and each other. At times we were lonely so far from home. At
times we were depressed about school or work. But we had
each other, and there was an excitement, a challenge to
being on our own together.

After a full day with John and Myra, the years had peeled
away so convincingly that it was incongruous to think that
our children were those rowdy young adults who sat a table
away. I slid a little closer to Mark, rubbed against his
shoulder, and patted his leg under the table.

Later that night, and for the remainder of our stay, I would
rewind and replay that day and evening in my mind. The
descent back into that period of life with Mark in L.A.
reminded me of our spontaneous trips into the mountains,
uninterrupted lovemaking day or night, weekends that
existed for the sole purpose of being in one another's
company, and the thrill over meeting each other at the end of
a day in our apartment. It was just the two of us, pure and
simple.

Habit, routine, accommodation, car pools, swim meets,
school plays, hockey games, chicken pox, birthday parties,
parent–teacher meetings, community commitments, litters
of puppies, family crises, and work had been the more
recent reality. Our relationship was and is typical to the

extent that frequently it got sandwiched in between all of the above and had lost some of the delicious flavor of our more uncomplicated youth.

And secretly I was looking forward to that fall, when both my girls would be headed out the door and off to college, and I would be greeted by liberation. I was looking forward to concentrating on *me*. Statistically, this would have placed me smack dab in the middle of a large category of women who see empty nests as a time reserved to center on their personal needs.

But after L.A., I was keenly aware of the pleasures inherent in those early years, and my goals changed along with my attitudes. What we would and could have together in our empty nest was so much more inviting than my plan to think just about me, myself, and I instead of Mark and me. We have always had a marriage filled with love. We have always been one another's Babes. And I have always used *SECRETS*; but now there was time to reclaim some of that youthful spirit.

Trite but true, we did become honeymooners, not empty nesters, two years ago. We still are. A teasing playful passion allows us to stop in our tracks and make love on the floor; it is the same passion with which we greet each other daily. It has been worth the havoc of a slight U-shaped curve, a few rocky seas, and the inevitable phases and stages that "Babes" in a lifetime marriage confront together.

I am one of those who believes that marriage keeps getting better and better. Committed to Mark, committed to secrets, I will continue my trek. I even have a growing admiration for those little old couples people chuckle over when they walk down the street stealing kisses and patting each other on the derriere.

Not bad role models.

WE'VE GOT EACH OTHER, BABE

By now, you should understand what it means and what it requires to be each other's Babe. This side of marriage has been downplayed so much that some out there have lost sight of how satisfying and fulfilling it can be. I sincerely hope that you are motivated now to go after the best marriage can offer you. The prescription for keeping love on track is almost complete. Let's add it all up, offer a few more prudent and artful secrets, and then I'll wish you good luck and send you off to captain your own ship.

14

Adding It All Up

Marriage Secrets: How to Have a Lifetime Love Affair provides you with a total package that can empower you to achieve a permanent love relationship and wisely manage your marriage and your mate. There are just a few small, though significant, items of unfinished business yet to cover to complete the agenda.

IT STILL TAKES TWO TO TANGO, BUT SOMEONE HAS TO LEAD

It is absolutely amazing how the topic of marriage has generated conversations wherever I happened to be over the last year. I almost always learned something from these informal encounters. A husband in his late thirties, seemingly astute about the dynamics of relationships, asked me a pertinent question after hearing the theme of my book.

"Are you giving the message that if the marriage fails it is all the woman's fault?" he asked.

"Absolutely not," I replied. "Of course, it takes two to

tango, but someone has to lead. And more often than not, the couples I interviewed confirmed that women were it."

The goal of secrets and the assignments to captains is prudently and artfully to rally their spouses to participate fully in the marriage, ensuring a mutually satisfying lifetime partnership.

To Expose or Not to Expose Secrets, That Is the Question

The answer is not a simple one. It is both yes and no.

On the "yes" side, there is something to be gained by disclosing your efforts to keep interest, passion, friendship, communication, and fun at an all-time high. Doing this successfully is, in fact, another artful secret. Allowing your spouse to get a feel for the lengths you are willing to go to create a healthy, happy marriage and permanent love match by conjuring up your own brand of secrets shows how much you care.

On the other hand, it is a prudent secret to keep mum on the ways in which you generally appease your mate. Try not to go as far as I have in disclosing my creativity to Mark. It took even more secrets to get me out of a few of the precarious situations that resulted. Yes, Mark was supportive of my endeavors, but when he read in black and white about my marital maneuverings, he became touchy, to say the least. A few misunderstandings ensued.

Finding myself in slightly rocky waters over my tactics, I wriggled out from under the dilemma with another secret. "Okay," I told my husband. "No more secrets for you. Let's try married life without them." I knew that it wouldn't take long for him to catch on that life could be bland and that I could be more than bitchy without my arsenal of secrets. For several days, I paid little attention to his needs and concentrated solely on my own. I took a vacation, shall we say, from administering my normal dosage of secrets. Shortly thereafter, he acquiesced and agreed that secrets were productive. In a little while, you will see how he has become entirely converted to my way of thinking.

WHERE AND HOW TO BEGIN

Start at the beginning, assess your self-esteem and your marriage, be willing to take a good look at your relationship, and accept the challenge of Marriage Secrets. You won't succeed if you take the negative attitude of one competent female business administrator who told me, "I never mailed your questionnaire back. Once I started looking it over, there were things I just didn't want to get into, things I didn't want to think about."

To begin charting your own course, here is a composite of my questions that appeared on a variety of surveys for men and women. The topics covered in individual interviews were in greater depth and variety. These questions should help direct a probing but constructive evaluation of the state of your marriage.

1. **What is your level of marital satisfaction on a scale of 1 to 10?** _____
2. **What is your secret plan for getting along better with your spouse?** _____
3. **Give the two qualities you like most and two you like least about your spouse.** _____
4. **List two things it takes to have a happy marriage.** _____
5. **Give at least two ways you add romance to your marriage.** _____
6. **Give two ways you encourage your spouse to add romance to your marriage.** _____
7. **How do you persuade your spouse to do things he or she is reluctant to do?** _____

8. Give one good tip for communicating with your spouse. _____

9. How good or bad is your sex life? Is there anything you disagree on sexually? Describe one way in which you make your sex life more interesting. _____

10. Give two ways you feed your husband's ego. _____

11. Do you think other women/men see your husband/wife as fair game? What do you do about this? _____

12. Are you in love with your spouse? Has there ever been a time you weren't? When? _____

13. What do you do to make sure your husband/wife stays in love with you? _____

14. What are four obligations or expectations you believe your spouse should fulfill? _____

15. Are there any activities you have learned to participate in to maximize your time with your spouse? _____

16. How and why do you put up with your spouse's most aggravating habits? _____

17. Give at least one secret you would never divulge to your spouse. _____

18. What does a good marriage mean to you? __

19. Prioritize the following: children _____, spouse _____, job _____, friends _____, private time _____, social life _____, other family members _____

20. Finish these sentences:
    a) I wish my husband/wife would _____
    b) I would be a better mate if I _____
    c) I would be a better lover if I _____
    d) I would never tell my spouse he or she is _____

21. Several things I have given up to make my marriage work are _____

22. Is marriage worth the obvious time and effort it requires to make it work? _____

23. What is the most romantic thing you ever did for your spouse? Did he or she show appreciation? _____

24. List one insecurity your spouse exhibits and how you handle it. _____

25. How do you encourage your spouse to be your friend? _____

26. How important to you is a good sex life? ___

27. How important is it to feel you have satisfied your spouse in bed? _____

28. What is love? _____

29. Does your spouse give you enough space? ___

30. Complete the following sentences:
    a) I would never tell my wife/husband that she/he _____
    b) My wife/husband makes me feel _____
    c) I wish my wife/husband would _____
    d) I am happy that my wife/husband is _____

31. What were the best and worst times of your marriage? _____

32. What are you looking forward to in the future with your spouse? _____

THE SECRET GREETING CARD

If you are shy about getting into the secrets mode, start simply. Try a card. The problem is you may not find one that expresses what you need to convey after reading *Marriage Secrets*. You might have to make up your own. Here are a few suggestions which you are welcome to use.

```
Cover: I want to be your Best Buddy
Inside: Let's go
             fishing ........................
             golfing  ........................
             bowling ........................
             hiking  ........................
             other  .........................
```

```
Cover: I love you
Inside: But I would love you more if  ...
```

```
Cover: We need to talk
Inside: I want to tell you I love you.
```

```
Cover: Something is on my mind
Inside: Meet me
             for lunch  ....................
             at the office ..................
             for a walk ....................
             in the tub ....................
             other  ........................
```

```
Cover: I need you
Inside: To be my friend
```

```
Cover: Thank you
Inside: For being there when I needed
             you
```

Cover: Because I love you
Inside: Because I appreciate you
         Because you're mine
         Because you're special
         Here is a little gift

Cover: Thank you for ..... (making the
bed, just being you, loving me)
Inside: Your reward is
         an afternoon or evening out
         with your friends
         dinner for two
         other ....

Cover: Let's Make Up
         Inside: (giant red lips)

Cover: Ever get the feeling there is a
gulf between us?
Inside: I want to get closer

Cover: You are the man (woman) of my
dreams
Inside: This position is reserved
         exclusively for you

Cover: I'm so glad our relationship is
built on LOVE, TRUST, and LOYALTY
Inside: Don't screw it up!

> Cover: Someone is throwing too much
> weight around here
> Inside: Let's get things in balance

> Cover: Guess What
> Inside: You were the number one man
> at the party!
> Aren't you lucky you were with
> the number one woman!

JUST A FEW MORE SECRETS

This is one final, motivational section to encourage you to begin being creative in getting your secrets ready. Here are a few odds and ends that we haven't covered.

Loving You More

After interviewing one woman in her late forties with a thriving business and a thriving marriage, I was just about ready to put my tape recorder in my tote bag when she began talking again. "Okay, do you want to know what is really important?" she asked me.

I nodded and held up the recorder to catch her words as we left the restaurant together. "If it is going to work, one person should love the other one more," she said, shamelessly adding, "it should be the man."

I have never gone this far. I do believe that secrets keep your man in love with you, and because of this love, he will go to greater lengths to please you. Then I suppose if you take it one step further, she is right. The ultimate would be to have your spouse love you the most in order to make him the most compromising partner. This is her secret, though not necessarily mine.

I must suggest to the bearer of this secret that it would be prudent to keep her observation a secret from her husband. Disclosure of this one could be hard to handle.

Love makes us all more pliable. Would anyone doubt that? One hundred percent of the men and women who rated their marriages eight or above said they were in love. The goal of Marriage Secrets in securing that lifelong relationship for you must be to keep love on track. Give your mate reason to be crazy about you and evidence that he or she can't live without you. Show your spouse that success in business and personal happiness are a result of your partnership, not just individual talents. You are better as a team, as a couple, than either one could ever be alone.

A Potpourri of Secrets

That message was complicated, these are not.

A SEXY THANK YOU

Angela's husband bought a family car she had been dying to own. He was not enthusiastic about it; he did it strictly for Angela. It was a handsome foreign convertible that she had thought about buying on her own but decided was too impractical for her job, which required her to carry large, bulky portfolios. I asked her how she was going to thank her husband for giving her the car.

She smiled. She had it all planned and was waiting for a warm summer night when she would invite him to take a ride with the top down, stop in a secluded spot, and make love in the open air. "I would have told you no if you had asked me if I used sex as a reward. I guess I do, though," she says, laughing at herself and suggesting her friend tell me about the time she met her husband at the airport wearing a trench coat and nothing underneath.

WHEN TO DROP EVERYTHING

It doesn't sound like these women have time to find their husbands boring, a trap Charlene says is very dangerous to fall into. "I think women who don't think their husbands would appeal to anyone else are bored with them. It is a mistake to think others see him the same way you do."

I had a feeling I would have gotten the same type of advice from an attractive, sexy female doctor in her mid-forties. I was a little disappointed I could never seem to catch her at just the right moment. We made several plans to meet but timing was always a problem. She gave me a pretty good glimpse of the success of her marriage, however, when she asked me to forgive her for canceling an interview so that she could be with her husband, who traveled a great deal for business. "My friends accuse me of dropping everything when Bill comes home; I have to cancel this weekend," she explained.

How could I be mad at a set of priorities like this?

DO UNTO EACH OTHER

One couple continually tries to improve the working order of their marriage by making New Year's resolutions that pertain to how they should treat one another. The top secret for the list was no secret to many women.

TREAT YOUR HUSBAND THE WAY YOU WISH TO BE TREATED.

Penny would have made a resolution that year to become the new banker in her household. After she and Kent realized most of their fights were over her excessive spending, they decided she should be responsible and shoulder the worries.

AN ARTFUL CURE

Gwen couldn't wait for the New Year to use her playful secret to give Alfred a lesson. "Alfred is a perfectionist," she says. "He likes everything his way. That's okay at his office, but our home is my territory. I was collecting recyclables in the garage for an organization I am active in; I was waiting until I had a large bundle to deliver. They were there for about two months and weren't in anyone's way but Alfred's. He took it upon himself to throw them out. I was really proud of myself. I didn't fight. A week later, I went over to his office during lunch. He had several people in town for a meeting. I rearranged his desk, drawers and all, to suit me. I left a note with my initials. He evidently came back and started fumbling around looking for things. He got my message! He hasn't pulled this one again."

BEDROOM INSTRUCTION

Sophie instructs in her own style. She would never accuse Hal of being a bad lover, but she makes an effort to bring him up to a more satisfactory level. "I think women can teach their husbands how to be the way they should be in bed," she begins. "Rather than accuse or attack Hal personally, I asked why he thought most men were so hung up on the number of times they screw a woman rather than on the quality of the loving they give her. He was very quiet and thought about it. Actually, I was trying to get him to see that I preferred quality. He responded, 'Quality is more important to me.' After that, things improved drastically. I often teach him by asking questions this way."

Lesson number two for Sophie is one used by many others. "I read passages from romantic or erotic novels out loud to Hal to get us both turned on." (A tad more kinky than Sophie's secrets are those I heard of from couples who act out sections of erotic novels.) "If I see an article in the newspaper or a magazine about sex that would help make it better, I make sure I read it to him," she reveals. "He enjoys my reading to him and then I ask for his opinion. He will come up with what he likes, and I will come up with something I like."

READING THE HIDDEN MESSAGES

Alicia would approve of that tactic. **"People don't come with owner manuals. You have to tell each other how you feel to keep things in working order."**
Sometimes spouses use obvious hints that are almost as direct as words. Listen for them! "Martin always tells me how lucky he is that I don't look like Jill, my friend who is twenty pounds overweight, or Deborah, who doesn't care that she is aging quickly. If he notices these things and comments on them, I think they are pretty darn important. It's his signal to me that he likes the fact I keep myself attractive. I work like hell at it, but it makes me feel good that he is so turned on to me. I feel it is as good as any present that I can give him."
Are these giving you any ideas of your own yet?

Some Secrets of My Own

I was having lunch with a local editor when I divulged my plans for the remainder of the day. Laughing at my elaborate arrangements, she said, *"You really live it (secrets), don't you?"*

FUN AND GAMES

Proudly, knowing the fun that was in store for Mark and me, I replied, "Certainly. Yes!"
It was a week before Mark's fiftieth birthday and to get

him over the blues and into the spirit of a week of festivities, I devised a pre–birthday treasure hunt. I was the treasure. The most important item for this plan was a car phone— although notes could be strategically placed instead. Several weeks before, I had asked my husband to scratch off a few hours on his calendar. On the morning of the hunt, I told him to be in his car at noon. I would call with instructions. After a half an hour series of stops, calls, and clues, he arrived at a local hotel that we had never been to before. We'll close the door on this one after I tell you that he walked into the suite to find me, a bottle of wine, and a carefully selected lunch.

I haven't passed this hotel with my husband for the last six months without seeing a smile on his face.

Not all of my secrets are so enjoyable. Some clearly teach Mark a well-deserved lesson.

LEARNING HIS LESSON

While on vacation he called the office to get his messages and failed to relay one for me. It seems he had decided on his own that it wasn't very important. When I found out two days later, I was livid and vowed this would never happen again. I did not holler or lecture. Such tactics rarely help. Dishing up the same medicine does.

For two weeks I used this sugarcoated strategy, teasing him about his error in judgment. If he asked me a question, I replied good-naturedly that I would tell him the answer in two days. If he needed me to do him a favor, I laughed and told him I would do it, but in two days. When he wanted to have sex, you guessed it. I apologetically suggested he hold his urges for two days.

I think we have this problem under control.

BE READY TO ACT

The finesse in using secrets that I have wanted to illustrate is evident in the next episode.

I am one of those women who thinks she has a real catch. So I never fall short of protecting my interests by failing to seize the moment to interject a (secret) twinge of guilt, deserved or otherwise. Once while I was keeping a previously planned dinner date one evening, Mark went to a sociable meeting attended by a large number of women. As usual, we kissed when we met at home, and I accidentally got lipstick on his collar. I walked away and surreptitiously wiped off the remainder of the red color on my lips. Then I asked him who had come up and kissed him that night. Without any hesitation, he rattled off a number of our friends.

"So who got the lipstick on your collar?" I asked with a slightly accusatory and angry inflection in my voice. He didn't figure it out and protested his innocence for days.

A WORTHWHILE LIFETIME CAMPAIGN

I adopted this tactic years ago and plan to keep it in action indefinitely. One day when I was in a particularly appreciative mood, noting my husband's good qualities and good looks, I turned to him and told him not only did I love him, I absolutely adored him. He grinned like never before and said, "I like that!"

Well, right there and then I began my "I Adore You" campaign. I tell him this frequently to make sure he knows how special he is to me, to make him feel happy and content, and to take out a little extra insurance that he will not have to go elsewhere for any ego nourishment.

SURPRISING RESULTS

Secrets never outlast their usefulness and even the best love matches around can use them in steady company. The results of these gems can even be surprising to veteran users like me.

I hoped my explorations for this book would give me a batch of new secrets to try out on Mark. In part, that is certainly what happened, creating some memorable times, loads of laughter, a surge of fun, a renewed intensity of feelings, and tricky approaches to old problems.

But the surprise is that this flood of secrets inspired my nearly perfect spouse to use his own secrets. He developed his own "I love you" campaign and brings me coffee in bed each morning. I don't care that it is 6:00 A.M. and his ulterior motive is to get me up and working. He comes home at night interested in every word I write and insists on reading my drafts. This is the same guy who read the introduction to my master's thesis several years ago and stopped abruptly to ask, "Do you mind if I never read this?"

My secret performances of late have been exaggerated for sure, but they have been rewarding and pleasurable in every sense. That's what comes from concentrating day in and day out on Marriage Secrets and keeping my promise to test new ones.

Mark asked me what would happen once I finished this book.

"Don't worry, I will keep the book by my bedside to remind me how exceptional the last year has been and how terrific the next year will be," I assured him and myself.

In closing, let me offer you my sincere wishes for the best of luck in using secrets to help create years of happiness and a lifetime love affair for you and your spouse in the glorious state of matrimony.